GILBERT AND SULLIVAN'S LONDON

GILBERT AND SULLIVAN'S LONDON

Andrew Goodman

Edited and presented by
Robert Hardcastle

SPELLMOUNT LIMITED
Tunbridge Wells

HIPPOCRENE BOOKS
New York

In preparation in this same illustrated London Guide series:
LAWYERS' LONDON

First published in U.K. in 1988 by
SPELLMOUNT LIMITED
12 Dene Way, Speldhurst
Tunbridge Wells, Kent TN3 0NX

ISBN 0-946771-31-6

First published in U.S.A. in 1988 by
HIPPOCRENE BOOKS INC.
171 Madison Avenue
New York, NY 10016

ISBN 0-87052-441-0

British Library Cataloguing in Publication Data
Goodman, Andrew 1956–
    Gilbert & Sullivan's London
    1. Sullivan, Arthur – homes and haunts –
    England – England 2. Gilbert, W. S. –
    Homes and Haunts – England – London
    3. London (England) – Description – 1981
    – Guide-books
    I. Title
    914.21 ML410.S93

Printed in Great Britain by Adlard & Son Ltd, Dorking, Surrey

To Adam, my son

AUTHOR'S NOTE AND ACKNOWLEDGEMENTS

This book represents for me a voyage of discovery. As one long interested in the lives of the Savoyards, I have often sought to colour in the story by finding those places where the action occurred. With this great city changing so rapidly the need becomes pressing, and the task difficult. However, I hope and intend that the reader may discover for himself the paths I have trodden to reveal some 226 places of relevant interest. Some, of course, are more relevant, and more worthy, than others. I feel sure that there are yet more discoveries to be made, and I wish all those who use this book as a guide a very pleasant and serendipitious journey.

In its research and writing I am indebted to a great many people, but may I first thank Sir Charles Mackerras CBE for his kindness in writing a most valued foreword. I am also particularly grateful to my editor Robert Hardcastle who, despite the many problems, has given coherence and shape to my rough manuscript.

I am obliged to the following for their very kind assistance, their time and, indeed, their interest both with the basic research and in the choice of illustrations: Ralph MacPhail Jnr., Clare Lambert, Peter Joslin, John Cannon, the late Albert Truelove, Lillian Carter, Philip Plumb, Brian Jones, Jesse Shereff, David Eden, F.W.Wilson, Julian Waldon, J.R. Choisette and, not least, Spike Milligan.

For so courteously dealing with my more specific demands I thank the Press Office of the Survey of London, the ever-helpful Victoria and Albert Museum, the local history librarians of the London Borough of Harrow, the Royal Borough of Kensington and Chelsea, and the Guildhall Library; Colin Crook, Group Librarian at Gravesham, Kent; Messrs. A.C. Frost and Co., and David MacLean-Watt of Struttons; Linda Soultanian of Pickfords; Albert Batteson of Ede and Ravenscroft; Alastair Wynne, General Manager of the Mansion House at Grim's Dyke; Miss S.W.Evans, Army and Navy Stores; Richard Stewart-Liberty of Liberty & Co.; Betty Beesley, the Garrick Club; David Beida of the Seven Dials Monument Committee; the Crystal Palace Foundation.

And to the many others who have offered their help and encouragement along the way I give my grateful thanks. If this book brings half the pleasure to the reader that it brought me in its undertaking I shall be very satisfied. And if it finds a place on the bookshelves of those who love London and those who love Gilbert and Sullivan I shall not only be very satisfied, but amply rewarded as well.

November 1987

Andrew Goodman
Cloisters, Temple

CONTENTS

FOREWORD

What a brilliantly original idea of Andrew Goodman's to present us with a veritable goldmine of information and fascinating detail not only on theatres and concert halls with Gilbert and Sullivan connections, but really on every facet of Victorian London life. What would I not have given for such a Gilbert and Sullivan-slanted reference book when, as a young Australian arriving in London and knowing the Savoy Operas fully by heart, I first came across Swears and Wells, Somerset House, Camberwell and Peckham, Madame Tussaud's, Belgrave Square and Seven Dials (I couldn't see why the air of this last was so 'lowly').

Everything you wanted to know about Victorian London and its people, not to mention earlier historical details about the city and personal facts about Gilbert, Sullivan and D'Oyly Carte, is all packed into this fascinating book, written in the form of a travelogue but actually a cornucopia of biography, social history, musical and literary comment.

The really committed Gilbert and Sullivan freak probably knows every phrase of the Savoy Operas, but I'll warrant that he will learn many things he didn't know about those references which jostle one another with such amazing rapidity in the patter songs of the Major-General or of Colonel Calverley.

As we walk through London and its suburbs with Andrew Goodman, starting our journey – appropriately enough – at the Savoy, he doesn't allow us to pass any building, statue or house of interest without a fascinating and succinct history. Who would have thought that the famous shop, Liberty's, was bound up with the creation of *Patience* and, later, *The Mikado*, or that One Tree Hill was so topical when *The Sorcerer* was being written?

Furthermore, you don't have to be a Gilbert and Sullivan fan to enjoy this book, so rich is it in surprising historical detail. However, if you are interested in the operas or in other facets of Victorian musical and theatrical life, Mr.Goodman can fascinate you still more with strange facts about the theatres in which Gilbert worked before the dawn of the Savoy era. Also – and especially interesting to me – are the details about Sullivan's activities in 'serious' music, such as the site of the makers of the huge bells which begin *The Golden Legend* and his premiere performances of Schubert's *Rosamunde*, and the overture to *Tannhäuser*.

The amount of research that must have gone into this book is almost beyond imagination. I believe it will be of immense value to all readers, not only those who want to take the trouble to walk with Mr. Goodman through the great city, but as a valuable reference book of everything associated with London, whether musical, theatrical, architectural or historical.

November 1987

Charles Mackerras
London

INTRODUCTION

London is still a Victorian city. Glass, steel and concrete may now encase its heart, but within a radius of ten miles from Charing Cross there are many houses, schools, churches and other public buildings that reveal their mid-19th century origin. Some would say that they are not the only survivals and that many of London's institutions, notably the Bar, the Church, the Civil Service and central government itself, remain essentially Victorian in outlook.

Such considerations are beyond the scope of this book, the main purpose of which is to provide the general reader and the Gilbert and Sullivan enthusiast with a travelling companion, a volume which the Victorians themselves, being much better classicists than we are, would undoubtedly have called a *vade mecum*, to be dipped into and consulted before setting out on a Savoyard quest. By moving from place to place, and backwards and forwards in time, it is hoped to unfold the story of the greatest partnership in the history of British musical theatre in its proper setting, against an authentic background of the period in which it flourished and came so thoroughly to represent.

It is also part of our purpose to celebrate Gilbert and Sullivan's London; its lost grandeur and forgotten theatres; the great centres of popular entertainment such as Crystal Palace, the Royal Aquarium and Rosherville Gardens; its swirling fog and spluttering gas lamps; its horses and four-wheelers with their irascible cabbies. The London of the high-born, the nobility and the *nouveaux riches*, the clubmen and the courtiers. The London of contrasts, from the languid elegance of Regent Street to the shoeless squalor of Seven Dials.

The lives of Gilbert and Sullivan span the astonishing transformation of London from a small, albeit commercially important, centre to the largest and most important city in the world, heart of the greatest empire the world had ever seen. 1836, the year before the young Princess Victoria came to the throne, was the year of Gilbert's birth. At that time, the capital consisted of little more than the square mile of the ancient city of London and its attendant satellite, the city of Westminster, the royal palaces between the two, with their mews and yards and barracks, together with a few elegant Georgian squares and some handsome Nash terraces. Across the river lay the historic boroughs of Southwark and Lambeth. Beyond, deep in the surrounding countryside, were a number of villages with strange-sounding names, such as Peckham and Tooting.

By 1862, when Stanford published his *Library Map of London and its Suburbs*, without doubt the most useful and detailed commercial map of Victorian London, the basic shape of the nation's capital had remained unchanged despite the rapid growth of the railway system and the construction of large termini in or near the city centre. There were, of course, major projects afoot. From Thomas Helmore's house at 6 Cheyne Walk, Sullivan in his teens would have watched the building of Chelsea Bridge, along with the Prince Albert's great project to drain the Battersea marshes and turn them into London's first formal landscape gardens. But also across the river he would have seen fields stretching towards Battersea Rise and Lavender Hill. Chelsea itself was still a rural market garden from which fresh supplies of fruit and vegetables were sent to Mayfair and Belgravia. And in those newly-fashionable areas gipsy girls sold lavender during the season, freshly gathered from the fields of Mitcham. Kensington and Knightsbridge, Hampstead and Highgate, Homerton and Bow, Clapham and Wandsworth were small villages, each with its own character, detached from the city by open countryside.

Then the housing explosion occurred, and within a few years all was changed. In 1875 Gilbert got a rueful laugh from his audience in *Trial by Jury* when he described Camberwell as a 'bower', and Peckham as that 'Arcadian vale'. By 1888 London had achieved the population and the status of a separate county. Between the 1841 census and that taken 50 years later in 1891 the population had gone up from just under 2 million to just over 4 million in inner London, and to nearly 6 million in outer London, which included districts such as Acton, Finchley and Walthamstow to the north of the Thames, and Dulwich to the south. It is not at all surprising that the huge demand for new housing created by this increase in population resulted in a land grab by mid-Victorian developers and builders on an unprecedented scale. The miracle is that in those days of unbridled free enterprise the open commons of Streatham, Wandsworth, Tooting Bec, Clapham and the like, remained intact.

At the peak of all this development Gilbert wrote a short story in 1869 entitled *Foggerty's Fairy*, which he dramatised for the Criterion Theatre in December 1881. Foggerty was a confectioner in the Borough Road whose surname clearly fascinated Gilbert, for we find him mentioned also in the *Bab Ballad, Bishop of Rum-ti-Foo*. In *Foggerty's Fairy* he is a young surgeon, much in need of a practice, who in Act III tries desperately to escape the unwanted attentions of one Miss Malvina de Vere. He leads her on a merry dance throughout London and in doing so gives us a very clear idea of the boundaries of the metropolitan area at that time:

'I have given her the slip at last. When I left the house I bolted up Harley Street. Malvina followed. I got into a cab; she got into another. I said "drive anywhere." He drove everywhere. I told him to drive like the devil. He drove like the devil. So did Malvina. Regent's Park, Primrose Hill, Kentish Town, Holloway, Ball's Pond, Dalston, Hackney, Old Ford, Bow, Whitechapel, London Bridge, Southwark. At Southwark my horse fainted; so did Malvina's. I jumped out – got another cab. So did Malvina. Off again, Old Kent Road, Peckham, Camberwell, Walworth, Kennington, Brixton, Clapham, Battersea, Wandsworth. At Wandsworth my horse fainted. So did Malvina's. Jumped out, but no cab to be found. Bolted, on foot, followed by Malvina; ran through Putney, Barnes, Mortlake, Kew, Chiswick, Turnham Green, Shepherd's Bush, Kensal Green, Malvina after me. At Kensal Green I fainted; so did Malvina. Off again, through Westbourne Park. At Westbourne Park I found a cab; so did Malvina. Off again; Maida Hill, Edgware Road, St. John's Wood, New Road, Harley Street. As I passed the door, jumped out unobserved, and left my empty cab tearing on ten miles an hour, and Malvina after it.'

With the development of London on so massive a scale it was inevitable that social change would quickly follow. Not revolutionary upheaval as Marx had predicted, but a series of much smaller changes in the pattern of the lives of ordinary people which, taken together, were no less significant. The place and the nature of their employment, for example. The standard of housing and of basic amenities such as running water and mains drainage. The spread of elementary education and the development of social and welfare services. The

The cartoon of Sir Arthur Sullivan by 'Ape' (Carlo Pellegrini) published in 'Vanity Fair', March 1894. The Faustin caricature of Richard D'Oyly Carte appeared in the 'Figaro in London' cartoon series, c. 1890

rapid growth of cheap public transport and the greater mobility which resulted. The fundamental change in the distribution and sale of goods and services. And changes, too, in the patterns of worship and in the use of leisure time.

Within that final entry in the long catalogue of change comes popular entertainment, with which so much of this book is concerned and in which music played so prominent a part. In the shops there was a very wide choice of musical instruments to be had, some manufactured in the north of England, others imported from abroad. But it was the upright piano which dominated the domestic scene: no Victorian household was complete without one. Behind the net lace curtains and the carefully-tended aspidistras a piano occupied pride of place in the parlours of all but the most impoverished families. They gathered round to hear the daughter of the house pick her way through arrangements of the popular classics, or to hear Uncle Bertie, recently-returned from India, sing *O Fair Dove, O Fond Dove*, before moving on to the latest narrative ballad, or a rousing, patriotic song more appropriate to his military calling. It is easy to poke fun at the Victorians at their leisure – much too easy, in fact. What will our grandchildren have to say of us, each shut away in a private world, lost before a flickering, inanimate screen in the corner of the room?

15

Music in the home formed part of the very fabric of Victorian life, and one of the consequences was an enormous sale of sheet music of all kinds, the publication of which became very big business and provided a major source of income to successful composers such as Arthur Sullivan.

Profound changes were also taking place in public entertainment in theatres and in concert halls, once the preserve of the idle rich and their hangers-on. Now the rising middle classes had money to spend, and they demanded entertainment which conformed to their ideas of what was, and what was not, proper for their families to see and to hear. Even the lower orders of society could afford the occasional 'night out' if they so chose, and shrewd managers offered a wide range of seats at prices most people could afford. During the latter part of the 19th century social legislation was introduced to ensure some leisure time for the new working classes. By today's standards the provisions were meagre in the extreme, but the creation of bank holidays and some guarantee of free time at weekends made their impact on the entertainment industry, as did the expansion of public transport and the growth in the number of restaurants and eating houses of all kinds. And so, theatre outings became for many people living in London and other major cities part of the regular pattern of family life.

Theatres and concert halls were becoming safer, pleasanter places. Electric lights were replacing the old gas lamps and flares; queues for the pit and the gallery were being encouraged so that it was no longer necessary to scramble and fight for the cheaper tickets; new and more comfortable seating was being installed, and strict rules were being enforced to keep gangways clear and to reduce the fire hazard in all places of public entertainment.

Spectacular as it was, the success of Richard D'Oyly Carte and his Savoy operas did not burst upon the London scene entirely without precedent. To a limited extent the ground had already been prepared to take the seed. By the early 1850s Thomas German Reed and his wife, at their Gallery of Illustration, had successfully steered a middle course between insipid, churchified drawing-room entertainments on the one hand and coarse, vulgar burlesques on the other hand, later to be perpetuated by the music halls. The new audiences flocked to see the German Reed productions, and it was their style of entertainment the Savoy triumvirate followed and developed beyond recognition. They created a new theatrical *genre* which became enormously popular, yet which still held its appeal for people of fashion; a form which was entirely musical, but not at the expense of the witty, topical libretti; plots which were most amusing, without being in any way indelicate, and all produced to a new, dazzling standard, the like of which had not been seen before on the British stage or, indeed, anywhere else in the world.

By the turn of the century, as Queen Victoria's reign neared its end, London had become the centre of an empire which ruled one quarter of the world's land mass and one-third of its population. By a judicious blend of enterprise and ingenuity, high courage and low cunning, determination and good fortune, dedication and opportunism, administrative skills and political bluff, one small nation on the edge of Europe contrived to dominate the conduct of the world's affairs and its trade. The value of the legacy left behind including, as it does, the English language, is beyond calculation.

But what of the legacy left by Gilbert and Sullivan themselves? Many of the theatres Gilbert knew have been swept away. The Opera Comique and its rickety twin, the Globe: the Gaiety, the Olympic and the Royal Strand – all fell victim to the development of Aldwych and Kingsway from 1900 to 1905. Memorials to the great men are to be found by Hungerford Bridge, in the Embankment Gardens, St. Paul's Cathedral, the Savoy Chapel and in a number of houses and churches at various places in the suburbs. Their portraits hang in the National Portrait Gallery, the Garrick Club and elsewhere. There is a bust of Sir Arthur Sullivan in the entrance hall of the Royal Academy of Music. But surely none of these will prove as enduring as their own unique compositions?

In the early days before the Savoy Theatre was built, D'Oyly Carte mounted the original productions wherever he could find a theatre in central London and from the 1880s onwards he sent out touring companies to take the repertoire to the widest possible audience. Their tours make fascinating reading today: Kennington, Wood Green, Camden Town, Bishopsgate and Richmond. The Brixton Theatre, the Coronet at Notting Hill Gate, the Chiswick Empire, the Croydon Empire, the Croydon Grand, the Lewisham Hippodrome, the Royal Artillery Theatre at Woolwich, the Borough Theatre at Stratford, the Streatham Hill Theatre and the Wimbledon Theatre. After the main circuit closed down in 1949, Rupert D'Oyly Carte kept his father's tradition alive right up to the 1950s and '60s by taking the touring company to such well-known venues as the People's Palace in Mile End Road, the King's Theatre at Hammersmith and the Golders Green Hippodrome.

During the past 100 years the principal company has mounted many revivals of the Savoy operas at many different venues in central London. From the Savoy Theatre the company moved to the Prince's Theatre (now the Shaftesbury) in 1929, and thereafter was based at the Sadler's Wells Theatre, apart from occasional seasons at the Scala Theatre. For many years the expiry of copyright in the published operas in January 1962 hung as a threat over the D'Oyly Carte Company. It was forecast that a large number of new and 'unauthentic' productions would invade the London stage. But in the event, this threat proved to be greatly exaggerated and it was not until the closure of the company some twenty years later that new productions, as well as the original, classical versions, appeared side by side. A rejuvenated *Pirates of Penzance* from America, and a *Mikado* from Canada have been staged with great success at the Theatre Royal, Drury Lane and at the Old Vic respectively. Parodies of *Iolanthe* and of *The Mikado* were presented during the campaign against the abolition of the Greater London Council. The English National Opera have taken both *Patience* and *The Mikado* into their repertoire at the Coliseum. And many other pieces written by Gilbert and Sullivan independently, outside their partnership, have been revived by professional and amateur companies in recent years. Despite a long struggle and considerable financial sponsorship, the D'Oyly Carte Company eventually collapsed under the commercial burdens involved in producing Gilbert and Sullivan operas in repertory on the professional stage. However, there are many amateur groups all over the country – indeed, all over the English-speaking world – very well placed to sustain and enhance an honourable tradition which began on 30 April 1879. For it was on that date, in a drill hall at Kingston-upon-Thames in Surrey, that the Harmonists Choral Society presented the very first amateur production of a Savoy opera – *H.M.S.Pinafore*.

Wherever the English language is spoken, wherever English music is played and wherever the English sense of humour is understood and enjoyed, Gilbert and Sullivan operas will continue to be performed. That is their true legacy to us, and the delight and applause of audiences over the years is our true tribute to them. It is one which both these men of genius would have been more than happy to accept.

W.S. Gilbert. Cartoon by 'Spy' (Leslie Ward). Published in 'Vanity Fair', May 1881

*The Victoria Embankment
from Charing Cross pier
c.1908. The Savoy Hotel
is the second building
from the left*

Chapter 1

VICTORIA EMBANKMENT
AND THE SAVOY

**Circular walk from
Embankment Underground:
allow 4 hours**

The area of London most closely associated with the triumphs of Gilbert, Sullivan and D'Oyly Carte is the Strand, extending to Charing Cross in in the west and to the site of Temple Bar in the east. Here are situated Gilbert's birthplace, D'Oyly Carte's London home, his offices and the the two theatres in which the partnership grew and prospered – the Opera Comique, long since gone, and the Savoy, happily still with us. And where the land falls steeply down towards the Thames, memorials of a very different kind have been placed to honour the author and composer.

Gilbert's memorial takes the form of a medallion set into the south wall of the Victoria Embankment in the shadow of Hungerford Bridge, directly across the road from the riverside exit of the Embankment Underground station. It was put there in 1915 quietly and without great ceremony by a group of his friends. The designer was Sir George Frampton RA, among whose other works in London are the statues of Edith Cavell near St.Martin-in-the-Fields, and of Peter Pan in Kensington Gardens. The medallion shows Gilbert's left profile flanked by two figures which represent Comedy and Tragedy.

*The Gilbert memorial
in the shadow of
Hungerford Bridge*

At Gilbert's left shoulder, Comedy holds a puppet of the Mikado in one hand, while from the other dangle more puppet characters from the operas including Jack Point, Despard Murgatroyd with Mad Margaret, a dragoon and King Paramount. Facing Gilbert is the figure of Tragedy with an open book on her knees, offering him a palm in her outstretched hand. Further down there is a coat-of-arms surmounted by the following inscription suggested by his friend Anthony Hope, author of *The Prisoner of Zenda* and *Rupert of Hentzau*:

> His foe was folly, and his weapon wit.

No reference is made to Gilbert's knighthood which he often dismissed as a 'tin-pot, twopenny-halfpenny sort of a distinction'. If such a view is one which might not be expected from a Victorian gentleman, it is well to remember that it is very characteristic of the English to affect to belittle those things in which they take most pride and to which they attach the greatest value. Perhaps it is their way of appeasing jealous gods.

**From the memorial cross
Victoria Embankment, turn
left and walk to the
Embankment Gardens**

The Victoria Embankment is an 8ft-thick granite wall with foundations of up to 30ft below low water level. It was built between 1862 and 1870 to reclaim an area of land regularly covered by the tide, and to create a broad, pleasant roadway joining the City of Westminster and the City of London. Hitherto, the Strand itself had been the only road link, flanked on the southern side by the houses of the gentry, each with its own access to the river with a private dock or landing stage. Some of the turnings off the Strand leading down to the river were extended to join the new embankment. One such was Savoy Street, which previously finished in a dead end in front of Duchy Wharf. The reclaimed land, although well below the height of the Strand itself, provided many important new building plots. These were developed during the 1870s with plenty of valuable open space retained for the Embankment Gardens.

Skirt the bandstand and make for the end of Buckingham Street

The old line of the river bank can be determined by standing at the Water Gate of the former York House at the foot of Buckingham Street. Looking east towards the City of London, everything to the right-hand side was built during the lifetimes of Gilbert and Sullivan. This highly ambitious Victorian engineering project left intact an earlier development of the Thames riverside by the Adam brothers, James and Robert, who left so indelible a mark on English taste and interior design. They had the idea of building a series of immense arches, with wharfs and cellars underneath, to carry terraces of elegant town houses. The most important and desirable of these faced the river, and the whole scheme covering more than three acres of land involved creating two new streets to provide the necessary access.

Keep in the Gardens: walk towards the City until you reach Savoy Place on your left

The outstanding feature of this development was the Royal Terrace which stood above the present Savoy Place. This later became known as the Adelphi Terrace in a graceful classical tribute to the brothers. It comprised eleven houses, each four storeys high, built over double basements, with ends extended to reach the new streets. Underneath were servants' cottages, each with its own access at a lower level. In the main public rooms of the houses above, ceilings were painted by leading artists of the day and every aspect of the design, from the magnificent facade to the smallest interior detail, carried the stamp of the Adam brothers' work at its very best.

However, as so often happened with their ventures, vision outstripped resources, and they soon found themselves in difficulties. Matters were not helped by the intractable Thames mud, which made the sinking of the foundations to support the great arches more difficult an undertaking than they had bargained for. One of their many friends, the actor David Garrick, tried to help by taking out a lease in 1772 well before any of the houses were ready for occupation. Complete financial collapse was averted only by the desperate expedient of putting up another of the houses for sale by lottery, with tickets at £50 apiece.

David Garrick lived at No.5 Adelphi Terrace until his death in 1779. He had been even more generous than he knew, because his residence in the area helped to give it an early reputation for high fashion and exclusivity. Later comments by the novelist Thomas Hardy, who studied architecture at No.8 Adelphi Terrace under Sir Arthur Blomfeld between 1863 and 1867, were less helpful in fostering a proper image for the neighbourhood. He complained that the stench of Thames mud and of drains at low water was injurious to his health, and after four years he fled back to his native Dorset. Another distinguished resident was George Bernard Shaw, who brought his new wife to No.10 in 1896 and lived there until 1927. At No.6, from 1890 onwards, the Savage Club met regularly at a time when both Arthur Sullivan and the Prince of Wales, later King Edward VII, were active members. On an upper floor of the same house rented rooms were occupied by the 'Guv'nor', George Edwardes. By the time Richard D'Oyly Carte with his newly-wed second wife Helen Cowper-Black, otherwise Lenoir, moved into No.4 Adelphi Terrace in April 1888, much of the external elegance had been destroyed as a result of 'improvements' made in 1872. These involved, among other things, ripping out the delicate wrought-iron balconies and covering the whole facade in concrete. But the attentions of the Victorians are as nothing compared with the destruction of the area achieved by a later generation in the 1930s, when many of the original Adam houses were destroyed to make room for the solid, square blocks we see there today. Public awareness and concern over

The handsome façade of Adelphi Terrace in 1913. Richard D'Oyly Carte lived at No. 4

George Edwardes, D'Oyly Carte's protégé

such matters were less developed than they are now, but many voices were raised in protest against the loss of houses of such great architectural value and against the brutal, intrusive buildings that replaced them. By a curious irony, the wheel appears to have turned full circle because pressure is now being exerted to protect virtually every structure more than thirty years old, which means that Shell-Mex House and the others will in all probability be spared the fate handed out to their predecessors on the site.

But to return to the more gentle days of D'Oyly Carte. As soon as he took possession of the house he started to redecorate it in a style of considerable flamboyance to match his own highly theatrical taste. He lost no time in enlisting the help of his friend James McNeill Whistler who soon found himself not only producing designs, but also mixing paint for the Yellow Room, soon to become famous all over London. D'Oyly Carte added French windows to reveal the superb view across the Thames, and fitted out the splendid room to accommodate his library. Entering into the spirit of things, Whistler had the billiard room painted a rich green to match the colour of the beize, and every carving and moulding in the house was either brightly-coloured or gilded. A remarkable innovation was an electric lift, the first installation of its kind in any private house in England. Great care was taken not to damage the many fine features in the house during the building and decorating work. These included Angelica Kauffman medallions on many of the walls and ceilings, which survived until the demolition gangs moved on to the site in 1936.

It was in this house that D'Oyly Carte entertained in private, away from the

21

Part of the ceiling decoration of the Yellow Room on the 1st floor

Sullivan's memorial in Embankment Gardens, funded by public subscription. Not long after it was unveiled the following bit of doggerel appeared:

> Why O nymph,
>   O why display
> Your beauty in
>   such disarray?
> Is it decent,
>   is it just
> To so conventional
>   a bust!

Early in 1988 the statue was voted the most erotic in London.

public gaze, although he often used chefs from the Savoy hotel kitchens to prepare food for his dinner parties. Sullivan was a frequent guest, but Gilbert only called at the house on two occasions. The first of these visits was in 1890 when the three men met quietly in the house rather than at the theatre to discuss accounts. It was this encounter that ultimately led to the notorious Great Carpet Quarrel. The second visit made by Gilbert, on 16 August 1895, was to agree terms for the production of *The Grand Duke* at the Savoy Theatre. This was altogether a happier occasion for it paved the way for a more far-reaching agreement by which Gilbert restored to D'Oyly Carte the right to present all the operas which he and Sullivan had written to date.

One final scene at No.4 Adelphi Terrace. When D'Oyly Carte married Helen Lenoir, Arthur Sullivan presented the couple with a handsome sofa which occupied pride of place in the Yellow Room. Many years later, it was from this sofa, so soon to become his own death-bed, that the old man struggled to his feet and made his way to the window to watch a funeral cortège passing slowly along the Embankment. He knew, without having to be told, who was being carried in the hearse.

Sir Arthur Sullivan had become such a renowned public figure that his funeral on 27 November 1900 was almost a state occasion. He had no wish to be buried in state and splendour. On the contrary, he had asked for a simple, family affair with minimum fuss. But it was not to be. It was as if the nation had made up its mind to hold a dress rehearsal for an even more important funeral it knew must soon follow, that of the aged Queen Victoria herself.

Within a matter of days a Sullivan Memorial Fund was set up under the patronage of HRH Princess Louise, Duchess of Argyll, who was a personal

The decoration of Carte's famous library, the Yellow Room, was supervised by Whistler

Turn from the Adelphi, carry on through the Gardens, passing the statue of Robert Raikes. To the right of the path stands the memorial to Sir Arthur Sullivan

friend of the composer. The design of the memorial was entrusted to Sir William Goscombe John. It takes the form of a bust of Sullivan mounted on Portland stone with a weeping Muse of Song and Harmony draped across the pedestal. On the west face appears this inscription, which Gilbert chose from *The Yeomen of the Guard*:

> Is Life a boon?
> If so, it must befall
> That Death, whene'er he call,
> Must call too soon.

The monument was unveiled on 10 July 1903 by Princess Louise before a large and distinguished gathering. A programme consisting entirely of Sullivan's music was played, including a transcription for cornet solo of *The Lost Chord*. Speeches were delivered by Lord James of Hereford and by Lord Monkswell for the County Council. Gilbert proposed the vote of thanks to the Committee and to its royal patron, whose husband spoke in reply. It was a very formal affair, in sharp contrast to the ceremony which was to pass almost unnoticed more than a decade later under the shadow of Hungerford Bridge.

Wreaths used to be laid at the foot of the memorial every year on the anniversary of the composer's death, and visitors in their thousands still come to pay their tribute. The bust of Sir Arthur seems to have been positioned, by accident or design, in such a way that his gaze is directed at the river entrance of the Savoy Hotel some 30 yards away. It was in 1884, with the success of the Savoy Theatre and the operas assured, that Richard D'Oyly Carte felt able to turn his attention to to the site he had earlier purchased to link the theatre with the new embankment. Even by his high standards it turned out to be a remarkably shrewd investment.

During a number of visits made to the USA to deal with complex legal and copyright problems arising from the many pirated productions in that country, the great impresario had been much impressed by the comfort and luxury of the hotels, especially those in San Francisco. There was nothing in Europe quite like them, and he came to the conclusion that the growing number of Americans crossing the Atlantic each year would flock to a hotel offering a level of service and standard of accommodation they were used to back home. The wealthy and fashionable audiences who came to see the operas at the Savoy Theatre might well feel inclined to stay in town afterwards, particularly if a comfortable and well-appointed hotel were near at hand. And so, the idea of building his own luxury hotel behind his own successful theatre took root in Carte's imagination. It took seven years to come to fruition.

Make for the riverside entrance of the Savoy Hotel

The Savoy Hotel, with its seven floors resting on a steel frame, was the first hotel in London to be built mainly of concrete, a brand new construction material at that time. The building also had its own power generator, while in the basement an artesian well was sunk to guarantee an independent water supply. Helen D'Oyly Carte played a great part in choosing the décor, the fittings and other amenities, and the fact that the hotel was as innovative and as imaginative as any of her husband's theatres is due in large part to her taste and foresight. A courtyard with its own fountain formed the original hotel entrance in Savoy Hill, while above were suites of rooms, each with its own terraced balcony commanding a view of the Thames. The rooms were sound-proofed, another novel feature, and each had its own bathroom, an unheard-of luxury in those days. An opening publicity announcement had this to say:

> The perfection of luxury and comfort. Artistic furniture throughout. Shaded electric lights everywhere at all hours of the night and day. No gas or artificial light used. The Hotel is arranged chiefly in suites of rooms, consisting of one or more bedrooms, with sitting-room, private bathroom, lavatory, etc. Large and luxurious ascending room running all night. Top floor rooms equal to the lowest. All corridors warmed night and day. There are no less than 67 bathrooms altogether in the building. The Hotel enjoys the finest river and garden view in London; it has wide balconies running all along the front, commanding a panorama of the Thames with its many features of interest from Battersea to London Bridge and embracing St.Paul's Cathedral, the Monument, the Tower of London, the Surrey Hills, the Crystal Palace, the Houses of Parliament, Westminster Abbey and the various bridges.[1]

On the fascinating topic of bathrooms en suite, so much taken for granted these days, some idea of just how far the Savoy Hotel was ahead of its time, in Europe at any rate, may be had from the fact that the new Hotel Victoria in Northumberland Avenue, which offered 'first-class accommodation' for 500 guests, provided no more than four bathrooms. Guests had to make do with a free-standing bath brought to their own room and filled with hot water by a succession of chamber-maids armed with cans and jugs. At the Savoy, on the other hand, it was possible to enjoy the luxury of running hot water and *service de luxe* for just 7/6d a night.

Each suite had a speaking tube to room service which guests were much encouraged to use. The choice on offer was extremely wide and when that genius of creative chefs, Auguste Escoffier, was brought to the kitchens the gastronomic standards of the Savoy rose higher than those of any other hotel in Britain. Not only was Escoffier recruited. Another prize catch was the famous Swiss hotelier César Ritz. After months of cajolery D'Oyly Carte persuaded him to take up the managership, but only after he had tested all the facilities as a staying guest. The new marvels of the hotel won him over, as they did royalty and the cream of society – those we would today describe as the international jet set. Among the guests in those early days were the Shah of Persia, the Kaiser, the King of Greece, Dame Nellie Melba, Sarah Bernhardt, Puccini, Lehar, Leoncavallo, Mascagni, Joseph and Austen Chamberlain, Lillie Langtry and Diamond Jim Brady. The

[1]*The Times* 2 August 1889

24

view from the rooftop attracted many artists: both Whistler and Monet painted sunrise over London Bridge from that vantage point.

The Savoy Hotel was officially opened on 6 August 1889. Sullivan was invited to become a director together with Michael Gunn, manager of the Gaiety Theatre in Dublin, the Earl of Lathom, the Lord Chamberlain, and Hwfa Williams, a prominent member of the circle surrounding the Prince of Wales who was, himself, a regular visitor to the Savoy. By the end of 1895 Sullivan had invested quite a lot of his own money in the hotel: £17,810 to be precise. He was a member of the confidential 'Committee of Taste' which was set up by the D'Oyly Cartes to advise the management on on such matters as recipes, menus and wines. His diary records that he went to the Savoy on 6 September 1896 to discuss 'kitchen affairs' with sous-chefs François and Charpentier. It was in this advisory capacity that he often dined in the opulent Grill Room overlooking the river. Here many other famous men including Carte's erstwhile protégé George Edwardes had places permanently reserved for them.

Sullivan was also frequently invited to join private dinner parties or after-theatre suppers. These were held in the small, discreet rooms set aside for such purposes and which were later named after the operas, as we can see today. Six members of the original cast of *The Gondoliers* had their first read-through of the text in one of these rooms rather than in the theatre. On 13 May 1900 Sullivan's last birthday party was given in the hotel: among the thirteen guests present were the D'Oyly Cartes, Sullivan's nephew Herbert, Wilfred Bendall, Lady Catherine Cooke, Lionel Monckton and other close friends.

Thirty years later, on 21 October 1930, David Lloyd George chaired a celebratory testimonial dinner for Henry Lytton on the occasion of his knighthood. By then a new entrance and substantial extension fronting the Strand had been built, which later housed the offices of the opera company. Ballroom dancing had become all the rage, and in the art deco setting the Savoy Orpheans under their conductors Debroy Somers, Carroll Gibbons and Geraldo became world-famous as a result of weekly broadcasts by the BBC. Guest bands such as Fred Elizalde with the singer Al Bowlly appeared regularly, and on one memorable night Gershwin gave the first British performance of his *Rhapsody in Blue*.

Turn into Savoy Hill, to the right of the hotel

Savoy: the word is inescapable in this tiny area. Savoy Hill, where the first regular broadcasting service in the world was inaugurated by the British Broadcasting Company, as it then was, under its call sign 2LO. Savoy Street, Savoy Court, Savoy Place, Savoy Steps, Savoy Chapel and Savoy Buildings. The name goes back to the 13th century and to Henry III, who built the Savoy Palace and who, in 1246, granted it to his wife's uncle Peter, Count of Savoy. It passed down to Edmund, brother of Edward I, who was created first Earl of Leicester in 1267, and in due course to John of Gaunt, Duke of Lancaster. Under his protection it is known that John Wyclif preached at the Savoy Palace and it is believed that Geoffrey Chaucer was married here in 1366 or thereabouts. In 1399 John of Gaunt's son, Henry IV, annexed to the crown all Lancastrian estates including the manor of Savoy. During Wat Tyler's Peasants Rising the palace was burned down in 1381. It remained derelict for a long time, until Henry VII granted funds for it to be rebuilt as a hospital. He died before the project was completed in about 1515: it was in that year that one of the three chapels attached to the hospital, the Chapel of St.John, was consecrated.

Turn left out of Savoy Hill into Savoy Place

Formerly known as the Chapel Royal of the Savoy, it is more correctly described as the Queen's Chapel of the Savoy. It is the private chapel of the ruling monarch as Duke of Lancaster. Much in use until the end of the 18th century, it then suffered a series of disastrous fires. After one of these, the chapel was visited in July 1843 by the Prince Consort, who took an active interest in its restoration. Twenty-one years later, on 7 July 1864, the good work was undone by another fire. Restoration work was put in hand once more, the fruits of which can be seen today. By the latter part of the 19th century the chapel had become well-known under its chaplain Henry White for good choral music and for fashionable weddings. Richard D'Oyly Carte and Helen Lenoir were married here on 12 April 1888 at 11.30 a.m., according to the records, with Arthur Sullivan as best man. Two years later it became the first church in England to be illuminated by electricity: another example of the pioneering spirit of D'Oyly Carte at work? Whether or not this is so, he has a memorial in the chapel in the form of a stained-glass window (the second from the west, on the south side) which was unveiled by Sir Henry Irving in 1902. This was designed by E.J.Priest, and depicts a procession of angelic musicians. Many of the other windows were destroyed during the heavy German air raids on London in World War II, and some structural damage was also caused. Contributions towards the repair of the

A stained glass window in the Queen's Chapel of the Savoy is dedicated to the memory of the D'Oyly Cartes, father and son

26

chapel took the form of a memorial to D'Oyly Carte's son, Rupert, whose name also now appears on the window. In the Honours List at the time of his coronation in May 1937, King George VI decreed that the Chapel Royal should be put at the disposal of the sovereign's Royal Victorian Order which, among other things, had the effect of placing its finances on a much sounder footing.

Regular services are held at the chapel and visitors are welcome, but photography is not allowed. Once a year, shortly after mid-July, the ancient ceremony of beating the bounds of the Liberty of the Savoy takes place.

Make for Savoy Way

Just beyond the Chapel the Savoy Hotel bridges Savoy Way, where the service and goods entrances are situated. Near at hand is the original Embankment entrance to the Savoy Theatre, giving a view which would have been very familiar to both Sullivan and to D'Oyly Carte. Gilbert lived to see the construction of the Strand entrance, but its predecessor is now in a very sorry state. Only the elegant mouldings which can still be seen over the bricked-up balcony windows give any indication that this was once the threshold of the most imaginatively-designed, comfortable, safe and modern theatre in the kingdom. Every luxury had been introduced by D'Oyly Carte in his determination to do justice to the revival of English light opera. It was a unique feature of the partnerships he created that he was content to concentrate on front-of-house matters – looking after his audiences, in other words – leaving his writers and musicians completely free to deal with casting, costume, scenery and stage design, acting and singing direction.

In an era of heavy dark velvets, satins and flock wall coverings so beloved by the Victorians, the Savoy Theatre opened on 10 October 1881 in a blaze of white, pale yellow and gold. It was this light and airy scheme which was chosen by Collison and Lock for the costumes and sets of *Patience*, a production which was transferred from the Opera Comique in just eight hours. The opening performance at the new theatre was conducted by Sullivan in the presence of the Prince of Wales. Many descriptions have come down to us of this great gala occasion, truly a landmark in the history of British theatre. The opening address by Richard D'Oyly Carte has twice been published in full.[2]

The original entrance to the Savoy Theatre

The exterior of the Savoy Theatre was dressed in new red brick and white Portland stone. One of the blocks bears the inscription of C.J. Phipps, who also designed the Queen's Hall, 12 other London theatres and no fewer than 40 in the provinces. He supervised every stage of the construction, which was completed in a remarkably short space of time, and incorporated many revolutionary ideas in theatre design. For example, he built a cantilevered circle which did away with supporting pillars and gave a clear view of the stage from every seat in the house. It also made possible a larger seating capacity – just under 1300, including 18 private boxes. He used the natural steep slope of the site to place the stage well below street level. The circular vestibule was paved in black and white marble: no expense was spared to create an auditorium of the greatest elegance and style.

The greatest single innovation was undoubtedly electric lighting. The Savoy was the first theatre – indeed, the first public building in Great Britain – to be lit in this way. On the opening night only the front-of-house areas were so illuminated: the performers and backstage staff had to rely on old-fashioned gas lighting. But by the matinée performance on 28 December 1881 the entire building had gone over to the new system, with power supplied by its own

[2]Fitzgerald, P. *The Gilbert and Sullivan Operas* Philadelphia: Lippincott, 1894
Dark and Grey *W.S. Gilbert – His Life and Letters* London: Methuen, 1923

27

The interior of the
Savoy Theatre, c. 1883

'Mikado' programme from
the 1932 season at the
Savoy Theatre

generator. To reassure his audience there was no danger, D'Oyly Carte staged his famous demonstration. He held a muslin-covered electric light bulb in his hand, smashed it with a hammer and then brandished the cloth to show that there were no burns or scorch marks. The history of the Savoy Theatre from that time on is well documented. The first new opera to be produced there was *Iolanthe* which opened on 25 November 1882. The peers in their splendid robes and the fairies with electric lights in their hair and at the tips of their wands caused a great sensation. During the run D'Oyly Carte introduced a queue system for pit and gallery tickets to avoid unseemly scrimmages in front of the box office. In subsequent years there followed *Princess Ida* [1884], *The Mikado* [1885], *Ruddigore* [1887], *The Yeomen of the Guard* [1888], *The Gondoliers* [1889] and revivals of other Gilbert and Sullivan operas. This run of successful productions came to an abrupt end in April 1890 when the financial dispute erupted, leaving Gilbert and D'Oyly Carte facing each other in the High Court. During the breach, an attempt was made to find Sullivan other collaborators: *Haddon Hall* [1892], *The Chieftain* [1894], *The Beauty Stone* [1898] and *The Rose of Persia* [1899] all resulted, but without lasting success. Even after the reconciliation with Gilbert it seemed that the magic could not be recreated, for neither *Utopia Limited* [1893] nor *The Grand Duke* [1896] enjoyed the success of earlier works. The posthumous *Emerald Isle*, to a libretto by Basil Hood and additional music by Edward German, received its premiere on 27 April 1901, and Gilbert's last comic opera *Fallen Fairies* appeared on 15 December 1909. Although there were a number of successful revivals in the seasons from 1906 to 1909, the Savoy Theatre had ceased to be the true home of Gilbert and Sullivan. Even as early as 1896, after the failure of *The Grand Duke*, D'Oyly Carte tried his hand with a piece by Offenbach. The tradition weakened from that time on, and appeared to be lost irretrievably.

The next major episode in the history of the Savoy Theatre took place in 1929, when large-scale conversions were carried out to produce the building of today. The exterior was redesigned by Frank Tugwell to match the art deco facade of the Savoy Hotel, while interior works were handed over to Basil Ionides. Dr. (later

28

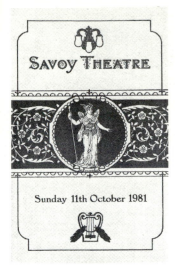

An early cover design featuring the electric lighting, was used for the gala evening to celebrate the centenary of the Savoy Theatre

Turn right into Carting Lane, and right again into Savoy Court

The 1930s entrance to the Savoy Hotel

Sir) Malcolm Sargent was called in to design a new orchestra pit. The D'Oyly Carte determination to secure the best talent for the job clearly remained very much alive. For the grand re-opening on 29 October 1929 it was decided to revive *The Gondoliers*, the first Gilbert and Sullivan work to be staged at the Savoy for twenty years. Since then the D'Oyly Carte Opera Company has presented a number of seasons at the theatre, including Henry Lytton's farewell season in in 1932-3, a remarkable wartime season in 1941, another for the Festival of Britain in 1951, and others following in 1954 and 1961-2. This last season, in fact, saw the end of the remaining copyrights: the last opera to be performed under copyright protection was *Princess Ida*. In 1975, from 29 March, a complete cycle was staged to celebrate the centenary, with *The Gondoliers* given before Her Majesty the Queen and the Duke of Edinburgh.

Following the west wall of the theatre northwards, Carting Lane ends at a flight of steps by the Coal Hole pub, a very familiar landmark. On the immediate right is a passage leading to the stage door of the Savoy Theatre and then, up a few steps, to Savoy Court. Here, until the site was cleared for the theatre, stood 11 Beaufort Buildings, which housed D'Oyly Carte's concert agency offices from 1880 onwards. His ambitious plan to develop the site went back as far as 1878 at a time when he was managing director of the Comedy Opera Company, and when *H.M.S.Pinafore* was starting to build a reputation at the Opera Comique. Even at that early stage D'Oyly Carte had his eyes firmly fixed on the future. An entry in Gilbert's diary for 23 September 1878 notes an appointment for the three men to meet at the Royal Opera House where Sullivan was conducting a promenade concert, after which they were 'to visit the site of a proposed theatre at Beaufort Buildings'. It was even suggested at the time that the theatre should be called the Beaufort. Plans went ahead, and early in 1880 Carte acquired the plot, next to Rimmel's perfumery, for £11,000 plus a contribution towards the cost of a new roadway to be built on the southern flank.

Savoy Court is now the main entrance to the hotel and to the theatre. The gilded figure of Peter, Count of Savoy, stands on the canopy, lance in hand, with his coat-of-arms bearing three barbed arrows symbolising the token rent he had to pay for the land. He also had to provide 100 retainers 'to put down riot within the precinct'. Panels on the pillars of the hotel extension set out the fascinating history of the courtyard, which is all that remains of the top end of Beaufort Street, and which has the distinction of being the only place in London where driving on the right-hand side of the road is permitted. This is another tradition for which we have to thank Richard D'Oyly Carte. He realised that it would be more convenient for his patrons to alight from their carriages if they entered the courtyard in an anti-clockwise direction – and so it remains to this day.

The Strand, looking east,
at the turn of the
century. On the left
can be seen the canopy
over the entrance to
the Gaiety Theatre

Chapter 2

THE STRAND AND CHARING CROSS

To continue the tour enter the Strand from Savoy Court

Augustus Hare[1] described the Strand as 'the most interesting approach to the City of London .. a vast thoroughfare crowded with traffic ... down which the tide of labour flows daily to the City'. There has been a road along this route for a thousand years or more, but the area itself was not intensely developed until after the Great Fire of London in 1666. Before then the land was was given over to palaces and the great houses of the aristocracy. As well as the Savoy Palace, there were fine London mansions belonging to the Protector, the Duke of Somerset, the Dukes of Northumberland, York, Ormond, and Monmouth, and the Earls of Leicester, Bedford, Salisbury, Arundel and Essex, as well as the Archbishop of York and the Bishops of Norwich, Carlisle and Durham. Many of these resonant titles are remembered in the street names of today.

After the Great Fire the ordinary people started to move westwards out of the City of London and to build their houses on the fields between Drury Lane and the convent garden of Westminster Abbey. By the mid-19th century this area north of the Strand, which Disraeli described in his novel *Tancred* as 'perhaps the finest street in Europe', had become one of the most pleasant residential districts in the whole of London.

Two chance meetings occurred in the Strand which have their place in the story of Gilbert and Sullivan. The first was on 2 January 1878 when Gilbert met D'Oyly Carte fuming after an argument with the directors of the Comedy Opera Company about the guarantees both Gilbert and Sullivan had called for before going ahead with *H.M.S.Pinafore*. Some seventeen months later, D'Oyly Carte ran into Michael Gunn quite by chance, and asked him to manage the Company during his visit to the United States.

Turn right and walk towards the City until reaching the entrance to Somerset House

Where the Strand meets the approach road to Waterloo Bridge the facade of Somerset House, added in 1854, comes into view. The main entrance is further along the Strand, and from this point the courtyard can be seen. The present building is actually the second to bear the name of Somerset which dates back to Edward Seymour, Duke of Somerset, who, on this site, built the first vast palace between 1549 and 1554. He was the brother of Jane Seymour, and uncle and Protector of the young Edward VI. He did not survive to see his great project completed, for he was beheaded on Tower Hill in 1552.

There is far more historical interest in the original building than in its successor. Elizabeth I lived in it before she became Queen. So did Anne of Denmark, Queen to James I and, later, Henrietta Maria, wife of Charles I. During the Commonwealth the palace was occupied by General Fairfax, who used it as the headquarters of the New Model Army. Oliver Cromwell lay in state here for eleven weeks before his funeral. After the Restoration, and upon the death of Charles II, Somerset House became the residence of his widow, Catherine of Braganza.

[1] Blanchard Jerrold

31

The present building was designed by Sir William Chambers and took 15 years to build, from 1775 to 1790. Even by that date a lot of decorative work, by such artists and craftsmen as Wilton, Carlini, Cerrachi and Cipriani, remained to be done. From 1780 to 1838 the new building housed the Royal Academy whose first annual exhibitions, now a well-established tradition in London's art and social calendar, were held in the upper rooms. On his death in 1792, Sir Joshua Reynolds, much-revered founder of the Academy lay in state here.

By Gilbert's time, much of the building was occupied by Government departments. Both the Navy Pay Office, where Dickens's father had been employed, and the Navy Office (or Commissioners of Internal Navigation, as Trollope would have known it) were to be found here. Also the Board of Inland Revenue, and the Registry of Births, Deaths and Marriages. Of these, only the first remains, although the Registry was moved to St. Katherine's House in Aldwych as recently as 1976. The south wing is now occupied by the Principal Probate Registry and by the Divorce Registry of the High Court. Between Somerset House and the river Thames is a broad terrace which provided access to a naval museum, which was later moved to Greenwich. In the 1870s it was open to the public on Sundays and soon became one of the most popular promenades in London. Now we have to be content with merely a view of the frontage of double Corinthian columns, stretching along 200 yards of the river bank. From the opposite bank or from Waterloo Bridge it is a magnificent prospect, especially when floodlit at night.

From Somerset House to King's College

Just beyond Somerset House is King's College, part of the University of London. Beyond the modern main entrance, the building on the right, abutting on to the east wing of Somerset House itself, looks much as it did in Gilbert's day. In 1853 he joined the General Literature & Science faculty with every intention of going on to Oxford afterwards. His time passed uneventfully save in one regard. In 1857 he became a member of the Engineering and Scientific Society and within a short space of time – either by cajolery or by bullying, for which he earned an unenviable reputation during his time at school – he got himself elected Secretary. He then proceeded to persuade the membership to amend the constitution in order to become the King's College Dramatic and Shakespearian

The magnificent frontage of Somerset House

Reading Society. College records show that as soon as Gilbert had left King's, after getting his B.A.degree in Law, the Society reverted to its former status except, for reasons which are not at all clear, for a brief time in 1866. The manipulations of their former Secretary may have left the members with their aims and objectives confused and in disarray.

Pass St Mary-le-Strand for Aldwych Underground station

Where the Aldwych Underground station now stands at 168-9 Strand, on a site bounded by Surrey Street and Strand Lane, formerly Surrey Steps, there was once a theatre – the Royal Strand. This opened in 1803 as the Panorama, but in 1832 it became the New Strand Subscription Theatre. The star of the time was the comedy actress Fanny Kelly, who eventually left to found her own drama school and theatre in Dean Street, Soho, which later became known as the Royalty.

Yet another change took place in April 1858 when the theatre reopened as a home for burlesque and extravaganza. The new management took the opportunity of shortening the title to the Royal Strand Theatre. It was here on 2 October 1876 after an encouraging trial run at the Theatre Royal, Nottingham, that Gilbert produced his three-act opera, with music by Fred Clay, entitled *Princess Toto*. It was a success with the critics. Punch declared that 'it was unsurpassed in London at the present time'. At the end of the run, *Trial by Jury* was transferred to the theatre and ran for 200 performances.

During 1882 the structure was pulled down and then enlarged within the remarkably short space of five months, July to November. It soon became very fashionable, and was especially popular with the Prince of Wales. But this heyday was short-lived, for in May 1905 after the completion of major roadworks along the Strand the theatre was sold to the Underground Railway Company and demolished soon afterwards. An underground station, originally called 'Strand' and not 'Aldwych', was built in its place. As if to preserve continuity, within nine days of the old theatre closing another Strand theatre was opened on the northern side, almost opposite the Savoy, by the Shubert Brothers of New York. Unlike its predecessor it has survived until the present day: long may it continue so to do.

Cross to the northern side of the Strand and make for Melbourne Place

From Aldwych station the block which comprises India House, Australia House and Bush House can be seen. Indeed, they can hardly be missed, for here we have imperial architecture on a grand scale, the sort of thing you expect to find in Rome, not London. This is all part of the Aldwych/Kingsway development of 1900-05 which the recently-formed London County Council designated without intentional irony the 'Strand Improvements Scheme'. Fourteen streets, dozens of rookery courts and several hundred properties of various kinds were swept away, and in the process five theatres were lost as well. Almost overnight the Strand ceased to be the hub of London's theatreland: the centre of gravity became Shaftesbury Avenue, and with the theatregoers went many of the fashionable cafés and restaurants. The Strand has never recaptured the glitter and glamour it enjoyed during its late Victorian heyday.

More or less where the pedestrian island facing Aldwych Underground station now stands there was a large block of properties on the Strand with Holywell Street, which no longer exists, at the rear. Holywell Street ran from the site now occupied by the BBC World Service shop to St. Clement Danes, a distance of about 500 yards. At one point along the frontage of this block, opposite Surrey Street, there was a doorway that gave access to a tunnel leading under the properties, under Holywell Street, and eventually to the Royal Opera Comique Theatre, which was actually situated in Wych Street. A more complicated or unsavoury way of entering a theatre can scarcely have been devised.

33

*The hidden entrance
to the Opera Comique*

The Opera Comique opened at 299 Strand on 29 October 1870 with the first appearance in Britain of the Comédie Française and their famous leading actress, Mlle Dejazet. Among the distinguished audience was that enthusiastic theatre-goer, the Prince of Wales. The location and curious access had already attracted a good deal of attention, as may be seen from this report in *The Era*, after the opening night:

> Without being a large area such admirable art has been employed in the architectural plan, and in the elaborate decorations, that the spectator is impressed with a feeling of space and airiness, which has hitherto been associated with our largest Opera Houses and similar establishments. The combination of really high art with the convenience, comfort and luxuries necessary for a cultivated audience is so completely carried out in every detail, that we may without flattery, unhesitatingly pronounce the New Opera Comique perfection .. .
> The position of the theatre will puzzle many readers when we write of the principal entrance being from the Strand (exactly opposite the Royal Strand Theatre). In fact, by means of a clever contrivance on the part of the architect and builder, a subterranean passage under the south side of Holywell Street has been made, and forms the communication with the main thoroughfare.

Opinions varied considerably. Walbrook[2] described the Opera Comique as:

> ... a charming little theatre ... It had no pit, but excellent seats at 2/6d in a large and very comfortable circle. Its walls and ceilings were decorated with graceful, classic paintings ... altogether one of the most elegant playhouses in London.

John Hollingshead was not so easily impressed:[3]

> Probably the worst designed theatre in London. It has four different entrances from four different streets, and to get to the auditorium audiences have to make their way through a series of dismal underground tunnels.

During that sweltering summer of 1876, Jessie Bond had no doubts at all:[4]

> ... a mean theatre in a slummy area where audiences perspired and gasped, and was not quite the place for decent and respectable people.

Goldberg[5] described it as 'a cavern of a playhouse', while Cellier and Bridgeman[6] were equally damning, but in rather more detail:

> .. a subterranean theatre that lay hidden between and beneath Holywell and Wych Streets, narrow, emaciated, grubby thoroughfares devoted for 100 years to bookworms. Access to the stage was through a narrow, dingy door-way in Wych Street, and directly by a straight, very steep, flight of stone steps.

Perhaps the new breed of planners at the fledgling County Hall had a point after all. Conditions backstage at the Opera Comique appear to have been no less unsatisfactory. Many dressing rooms were in neighbouring houses, while the rear of the stage backed on to that of the Globe Theatre next door, and was of such flimsy construction that the performers could actually hear each other through the common wall.

Such, then, was the setting for the entry of Richard D'Oyly Carte on to the scene in 1874. Not that he was any stranger to the Opera Comique, for three years earlier, on 22 August 1871, he had staged *Marie* at the theatre, the first of two of his own operettas. This was later followed by *The Doctor in Spite of Himself*,

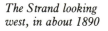

*The Strand looking
west, in about 1890*

[2] H.M.Walbrook *Gilbert and Sullivan Opera* London: F.V.White 1922, (p.41)
[3] Hollingshead, John *Good Old Gaiety* London: Constable, 1903 (p.24)
[4] Baily, Leslie *The Gilbert and Sullivan Book* London: Cassell, 1952 (p.52)
[5] Goldberg, Isaac *The Story of Gilbert and Sullivan* New York: Crown, 1935 (p.188)
[6] Cellier and Bridgeman *Gilbert, Sullivan and D'Oyly Carte* London: Isaac Pitman & Sons, 1914 (p.33)

adapted from Molière's *Le Médecin Malgré Lui*. It was the usual practice for the Opera Comique to remain closed for long periods outside the touring season because it had built a reputation for presenting visiting companies from abroad. As soon as he took over as manager D'Oyly Carte determined to change all this, and he launched a season intended to put English comic opera firmly on the map. It flopped. His short-lived management came to an end, and it was doubtless with some relief that he accepted the managership of Selina Dolaro's following season at the Royalty Theatre.

D'Oyly Carte played no part in the March 1876 production of *Trial by Jury* at the Opera Comique, which was followed by a successful burlesque season given by Burnand, of *Cox and Box* fame. By this time the management of the theatre had been taken over by Charles Morton, who recognised the potential of *Trial by Jury* and asked Gilbert and Sullivan to write for his theatre. They had already agreed to write for Carte, but he was unable to raise the 100 guineas advance fee each of the two men, not unreasonably, had asked for. The uncertainty was resolved only when certain music publishing houses interested in Sullivan agreed to finance D'Oyly Carte's new Comedy Opera Company. The outcome was *The Sorcerer*.

The next hurdle to overcome was finding a suitable theatre. Carte was not at all anxious to book the Opera Comique in view of his previous failure there, but in the event it turned out to be the only available venue. He took out a personal lease from Lord Kilmorey, the Earl of Dunraven, who held the licences for the theatre and its neighbour, the Globe. Michael Gunn put in a strong recommendation that his cousin, George Edwardes, should be offered the management of the box office: a recommendation which Carte was only too willing to act upon.

The Sorcerer opened on 17 November 1877 and enjoyed a moderately successful run of 178 performances. No overture had been written for this first production, but for the 1884 revival Sullivan used some of his incidental music to *Henry VIII*. By the end of the run, the next full-length opera *H.M.S.Pinafore* was ready for the stage, and it followed on immediately to be greeted by rapturous notices and extremely enthusiastic audiences at the outset. Later, the extremely hot summer had an adverse effect on bookings and over Christmas the theatre had to be shut down completely to enable long-overdue drain repairs to be carried out. Nothing daunted, Sullivan mounted his well-judged rescue operation by including an arrangement of all the popular *H.M.S.Pinafore* tunes in a promenade concert programme, and the production went on to complete a successful run of no fewer than 571 performances. Gilbert and Sullivan had arrived, but not without considerable drama. For during the run a bitter dispute arose between Carte and his composer and librettist on the one hand, and the directors of the Comedy Opera Company on the other as to who actually owned the rights in *H.M.S. Pinafore*. Litigation followed, and then the famous riot on the evening of 31 July 1879 when some of the directors hired a group of ruffians to remove by force properties and costumes on the eve of their own lapse of rights in the theatre.

It was a desperate bid that failed, because the following day the rights were held by D'Oyly Carte in his own name. Thus began the unique partnership between Gilbert, Sullivan and D'Oyly Carte which lasted eleven years until their own bitter quarrel over a carpet. *H.M.S.Pinafore* continued her triumphant voyage, despite rival productions mounted by the Comedy Opera Company first at the Aquarium Theatre and then at the Olympic Theatre only a few yards away.

Even greater successes were to follow. *The Pirates of Penzance* opened on 3 April 1880 and continued for 363 performances. Then came the first night of

Martyn Green as Sir Joseph Porter in the D'Oyly Carte Opera Company's 1939 production of 'H.M.S. Pinafore'

Turn left out of Melbourne Place into Aldwych

Patience just over a year later, on 23 April 1881, which was transferred to the new Savoy Theatre on 10 October. Although D'Oyly Carte's interest in the Opera Comique ceased at that point his stage manager, Richard Barker, stayed on and was joined by John Hollingshead. Their first production after the departure of *Patience* was a revival of Gilbert's *Princess Toto*. In May 1882 a send-up, *The Wreck of the Pianfore*, by Horace Lingard and Luscombe Searelle was staged, using the characters of Porter, Rackstraw, Corcoran and Buttercup, but made only a very brief appearance. A succession of managers failed to bring audiences to the Opera Comique and by 1884 it stood empty. After a complete overhaul the theatre reopened its doors a year later, and Marie Tempest made her debut here in November 1885. But the days of long and profitable runs had gone for good: the curtain came down for the last time on 28 April 1899 and the theatre was demolished shortly afterwards. Both the Opera Comique and its neighbour the Globe Theatre were built by Sefton Perry as part of a speculative development. Without putting too fine a point on it they were jerry-built, so much so that they were known as the Rickety Twins. The main feature of interest in the Globe was its glass roof which meant that the auditorium had natural light day and night and could be ventilated at all times. In an age of gas lighting and other more natural hazards this was by no means a small advantage.

The Globe opened in November 1868 with *Cyril's Success*, a play written by Gilbert's friend Henry Byron. Two years later the theatre was taken over, redecorated and partly rebuilt, which says much for the quality of the original workmanship. On 21 January 1874 Gilbert's *Committed for Trial* was presented, and during the 1880s there were a number of quite successful seasons. The longest run started in January 1893 with a new farce by Brandon Thomas, *Charley's Aunt*. Charles Hawtry was then actor-manager, and he cast W.S.Penley, Gilbert's original foreman in *Trial by Jury*, in the outrageous title role. The piece ran for no fewer than 1466 performances, eclipsing the runs both of *The Mikado* and *Dorothy*. But it was the last great triumph: a few years later the theatre was pulled down to make way for the formidable Bush House.

Some 100 yards west along Aldwych, over the now forgotten junction of Houghton Street, Stanhope Street and Newcastle Street, is a narrow alley marked Craven Buildings, in which was to be found the rear entrance to yet another theatre, the Olympic, which also fronted Wych Street. The original theatre on the site, built in 1806, was named after its manager Mr.Astley. It burned down in 1849, but was rebuilt with such speed that on Boxing Day of that same year it reopened, proudly bearing its new name, Olympic. Phoenix might have been a more fitting choice, or even Nemesis, for within three months the lessee, Walter Watts, was arrested for fraud and committed to Newgate Gaol, whereupon he hanged himself.

As far as can be judged from contemporary accounts the Olympic was not an unattractive building, with its arabesque interior and a horseshoe-shaped auditorium capable of seating no fewer than 1850 people. Gilbert came to know the theatre well during the 1870s for on 8 January 1870 his blank verse parody on Tennyson's *The Princess* opened what was to prove a long run. Never one to waste a good idea, he drew upon this work almost in its entirety for *Princess Ida* at the Savoy some 14 years later. In 1876 he wrote *Dan'l Druce* with Edward Southern in mind for the leading role, but this popular actor had too many American commitments at that time and was therefore unable to accept the part. A year later he asked Gilbert to write another piece, and paid him the large fee of £2,000 for the exclusive acting rights over a ten year period. Gilbert duly obliged with *The Vagabond*, but when Southern read the script he promptly rejected it.

Gilbert returned half the fee, and went on to produce the play independently after changing the title to *The Ne'er-do-Well*. It opened at the Olympic on 25 February 1878, failed completely and was withdrawn. Southern thus appeared to be fully vindicated, but nothing daunted, Gilbert re-wrote the third act and presented the play again, one month later, under its original title *The Vagabond*. It ran tolerably well from that point on. We know from Gilbert's diary that he attended a performance on 13 April 1878, after spending the day in Portsmouth with Arthur Sullivan and Lord Charles Beresford to inspect ships and ships' rigging, with *H.M.S.Pinafore* very much in mind. Gilbert's last venture at the Olympic, a blank verse version of the Faust story, *Gretchen*, which opened on 24 March 1879, was not a success.

Other notable productions at the Olympic during the 1870s included stage adaptations of *The Woman in White* (1871) and *The Moonstone* (1877) by Wilkie Collins, and in 1879 the rival production of *H.M.S. Pinafore* staged by the directors of the Comedy Opera Company in an attempt to spike D'Oyly Carte's guns. As we know, this ended in failure and the ill-fated production crawled away and died in a much cheaper venue at Shoreditch in London's East End.

Continue along Aldwych to Drury Lane

Surprisingly enough, Drury Lane used to be known as the Via de Aldwych and it was not until the 1690s, when Sir William Drury built his house there, that the present name came into common use. A cluster of narrow streets, passages and courtyards developed over the years, but as with others in the neighbourhood most of them were destroyed at the beginning of this century to make room for the broad sweep of Aldwych and the approach road to Waterloo Bridge. Probably the most well-known and best-loved casualty of them all was the old Gaiety Theatre, which occupied the site bounded by Catherine Street, Exeter Street, Wellington Street and the Strand itself. The theatre entrance was at 345 Strand.

Evelyn Gardiner (Little Buttercup) and Leslie Rands (Captain Corcoran) in Act II

Before the theatre was built, the Strand Musick Hall had stood on this spot, sharing premises from 1864 onwards with 'The Gaiety' restaurant. When the time came to develop the site the name stuck, and a new theatre was built 'with every attention paid to public convenience and safety.' There were two public entrances giving access to both sides of the house and a private entrance from Exeter Street leading directly to the Royal suite and box. Large and elegant, this 'home of the sacred lamp of burlesque' had a seating capacity of almost 2,000. There were 28 private boxes which rose in tiers to the point where the balcony wings actually met the proscenium. Both the gallery and the pit were spacious by any standard, and it would be difficult to challenge the view expressed by *The Era* on 27 December 1868: 'a more elegant and commodious Theatre has never been seen in the Metropolis.'

The architect and designer were very conscious of the fact that fire was the greatest hazard of them all, for it had destroyed the previous theatre on the site and countless others in London and elsewhere over the years. So they decided not to use wood anywhere in the interior except for the floorboards. All corridors were made of cement and stone and the stairwells were framed in iron. Even the gas lamps had reversed burners which allowed them to burn downwards in comparative safety.

The first manager of the new theatre was none other than 'Honest John' Hollingshead, whose comments on rival establishments have already been noted. He started life as a journalist and for a short time worked for Charles Dickens. His views on most London theatres were not at all flattering, as can be seen from the following extract from an article he wrote for *Broadway* magazine in May 1868:

Dirty, defective and scanty, gas-hot, stifling air, narrow passages .. weak and unmelodious orchestras, delays that consume one-fourth of acting hours, and refreshment room keepers who sell nothing but the original firewater which exterminated the red man .. (these) are only some of the curious attractions provided for playgoers by miserly managers.

He was quite determined not to let such things happen at the Gaiety and he put to good use all the experience he had gained during his earlier years as a music hall manager. Many of his innovations were later, and incorrectly, attributed to Richard D'Oyly Carte. For example, he was the first theatre manager to take display space in newspapers instead of using the traditional playbills with their characteristic typography. He abolished all theatre fees for bookings, for cloakrooms and attendants. Programmes were given free of charge to every member of the audience and ladies in the boxes and in the stalls each received a perfumed fan as a souvenir. These were much prized in later years as valentines, and have become collectors' items. Performances started promptly at 7 p.m. so they would finish in reasonable time. In 1871, he introduced matinées on a regular basis: previously they had been given only for testimonials, or on gala occasions. 'Saloons' on each floor led into the restaurant next door, with the result that there were no drinking bars in the theatre itself, a unique feature in the London of those days.

A conviction Hollingshead shared with Carte was the superiority of electric light over all other means of illumination. So it comes as no surprise to learn that he was responsible for floodlighting the exterior of the Gaiety, the first time this form of showmanship had been seen in Great Britain. He imported a large number of arc lamps and had them put on a facing roof to bathe the whole of the Strand facade of the Gaiety in light. Unfortunately, they soon had to be switched off and removed after complaints that horses were being frightened.

John Hollingshead was also quite determined to give value for money, although his prices were by no means cheap. Orchestra stalls were 7/-, balcony seats 5/-, boxes £1-11-6d., pit 2/-and gallery 1/-. Every night he presented a programme of considerable variety ranging from burlesque items to Shakespeare. As well as his two leading stars, Nellie Farren and Fred Leslie, there was a repertory company specialising in popular opera and operetta. In the early years works by Offenbach, Auber, Verdi, Halévy, von Suppé, Donizetti and Delibes were performed.

The second Gaiety Theatre with Aldwych sweeping round to the left, after the major rebuilding of the area 1901–5

The handsome portico of the Lyceum Theatre has seen better times

The programme for the opening night of the Gaiety included *The Two Harlequins* by Jonas, a comedy by H.J. Byron entitled *On The Cards*, and a piece by Gilbert called *Robert the Devil, or The Nun, the Dun and the Son of a Gun*, a pun-ridden parody of Meyerbeer's *Robert Le Diable*, much in keeping with the ordinary burlesques of the period. In the glittering first-night audience was Arthur Sullivan, who knew John Hollingshead as a fellow-member of the Garrick Club. Hollingshead in turn was a close friend of Gilbert's, and it is entirely possible that he introduced the two men to each other for the first time on that auspicious occasion. That, of course, is conjecture: what we know beyond peradventure is that *The Era* review was approving, if not ecstatic:

> Mr W.S.Gilbert produced a very bright extravaganza, and most successfully managed to render the least promising of subjects for burlesque amusing.

Gilbert's close association with the Gaiety lasted for ten years. His comic drama *An Old Score* had its first performance on 26 July 1869, and then his operetta *Ganymede and Galatea* on 20 January 1872. In January 1878 he appeared in person, playing harlequin in a charity gala, and a month later on 14 February his pantomime *The Forty Thieves* was given.

The Gaiety played an important part in the history of the partnership for it was here on 26 December 1871 that Sullivan conducted the premiere of *Thespis*, their very first joint venture. It was a short item to follow H.J.Byron's *Dearer than Life*, and little more than a pantomime piece for Nellie Farren to display her talents as Mercury, with J.L.Toole as Thespis, Fred Sullivan as Apollo and the Payne Brothers providing the necessary slapstick routines as Stupidas and Preposteros. The Gaiety audience was, by all accounts, fairly noisy and vociferous, and some critics said that *Thespis* was a failure because Gilbert pitched his humour well over the heads of those in the gallery. Writing in Tom Hood's *Comic Annual* for 1873, Gilbert himself complained that too little time was allowed for rehearsal. Despite all this, *Thespis* outlasted five of the nine pantomimes then appearing on the London stage by running for 63 performances, one of which was graced by the presence of Sullivan's royal patron, the Duke of Edinburgh, on 9 January 1872. It was also put on as a benefit performance for Mlle Clary three months later: not bad going for a hurriedly-written piece intended as no more than a Christmas filler.

Whatever the audience may have thought of *Thespis* on the opening night A.E.T.Watson, writing in the *Standard* immediately after Christmas on 27 December 1871, had no doubts:

> There is no theatre in London where the kind of entertainment provided is more in accordance with the characteristic title of the house than at the Gaiety... Even at this time of year the able director, Mr. John Hollingshead, contrives to preserve a speciality for his theatre .. He has judiciously called on Mr.W.S.Gilbert to furnish him with an original opera-extravaganza, and entrusted its musical setting to Mr. Arthur Sullivan. From the association of these two names the most pleasing result has for some weeks past been anticipated, which the success of last evening fully justified.

> It was with an operatic extravaganza by Mr W.S. Gilbert that, just three years ago, the Gaiety Theatre opened its doors to the public and inaugurated a new regime in theatrical management which has borne good fruit. Independent, therefore, of his talents as a clever writer, delightful versifier and humorist, Mr. W.S. Gilbert has had the advantage of acquainting himself with tastes of the bulk of the Gaiety supporters, and of shaping his piece to suit the character of the house... We are not aware that Dr.Arthur Sullivan has previously written anything for the Gaiety, but by his musical setting of *Cox and Box* and by his opera *The Contrabandista* he has shown his talents for illustrating subjects demanding a fanciful conception, melodious strain, and humorous expression, together with skill in orchestral colouring and able musicianship.

Seymour Hicks and Ellaline Terris, Gaiety Theatre favourites, were among Gilbert's many friends

During the rest of his time at the Gaiety, Hollingshead managed to persuade Sullivan to write another piece for the stage – never an easy thing to do on account of the composer's indolence and reluctance to get involved with too much theatrical work. The commission was to compose incidental music for a Shakespeare production of *The Merry Wives of Windsor* on 19 December 1874, one which many closely associated with Sullivan might have regarded as far more suited to his talents and his stature than frivolous, light-hearted operetta.

After a long, slow decline in his health, undermined by an attack of rheumatic fever many years earlier, John Hollingshead decided to take a partner in 1885. His choice fell on George Edwardes who, within a year, took charge of the theatre completely. There followed a new, triumphant period for the Gaiety which has left a permanent mark on the history of the British theatre.

Edwardes followed a very simple principle – nothing but the best will do. He engaged such outstanding performers as Seymour Hicks, Ellaline Terriss and Hayden Coffin on long-term contracts, and in the decade between 1892 and 1903 the Gaiety gained world fame not only for its new style of musical comedy, but also for its chorus girls and the stage-door Johnnies who courted their favours. Many of these Gaiety girls, as they became known, married into the aristocracy. But for all the images and memories it has left behind it was a remarkably short-lived era. It came to an end, quite cleanly and firmly, on 4 July 1903 when, after a final performance of a show called *The Toreadors*, speeches were delivered from the stage by Henry Irving and others. The band played a selection of hits from 35 years of Gaiety shows, the audience joined in with *Auld Lang Syne* and then the lights were extinguished for the last time. The old theatre was pulled down to make way for offices, including those of the *Morning Post* also long-since gone from the London scene.

Four months later, on 26 October 1903, the New Gaiety Theatre designed by Norman Shaw on the corner of the Aldwych development, next to Bush House, was opened by King Edward VII and Queen Alexandra. It did not try to revive the tradition of its illustrious namesake, but in its own way it proved to be a very successful undertaking, moving into profit within nine months of opening. Unlike many of its contemporaries the New Gaiety Theatre remained a consistently profitable enterprise until its closure in 1939.

The Lyceum Theatre was built at 254 Strand in 1772 and for the first 30 years or so its reputation rested mainly on productions of opera, ballet, circuses, panorama and other forms of popular entertainment. In 1802 Madame Tussaud's waxworks opened here, but in 1830 the original building was completely destroyed by fire. The theatre was then rebuilt on a new site just round the corner from the old one. Part of the facade dating from July 1834 can still be seen at the end of Wellington Street, although it presents a rather sorry spectacle today. It is the Lyceum Theatre which has a longer association with Gilbert and Sullivan than any other.

Gilbert's first stage work, a 'comedietta' called *Uncle Baby*, played at the Lyceum from 31 October to 19 December 1863. It is by no means certain whether Gilbert or his father actually wrote the piece: but it can at least be credited to the Gilbert family. By Christmas 1867 Edward Tyrrell Smith had taken over the management and presented the theatre's first and only pantomime. Gilbert was responsible for the book and for this quite remarkable title:

Harlequin, Cock Robin and Jenny Wren, or *Fortunatus and the Waters of Life, the Three Bears, the Three Gifts, the Three Wishes and the Little Man Who Woo'd a Little Maid.*

The great actor-manager Sir Henry Irving and Ellen Terry, his leading lady at the Lyceum

It went very badly indeed, although in Gilbert's defence he had to squeeze rehearsals into an already over-crowded schedule, and was allowed only three weeks to do even that. To make matters worse, Tyrrell Smith insisted on adding spectacular effects including a snow-storm, a fountain and a grand ballet, none of which had anything to do with the plot. Gilbert took four days to write the book, and received a fee of £60 for his pains.

When the theatre fell on hard times in the 1870s a Colonel Hezekiah appeared on the scene and booked it as a vehicle for furthering the career of his daughter, a girl with unquenchable theatrical ambitions. To play opposite her the Colonel engaged a young, unknown actor from the provinces: his name was Henry Irving. A few years later it was Irving's own famous production of *The Bells* that saved the Lyceum from closure. He took over the management in 1878 with Ellen Terry as his leading lady thus starting a renowned stage partnership that lasted 21 years.

A revival of *Pygmalion and Galatea* was staged in 1883, in which Mary Anderson took London by storm. Gilbert was so impressed that he wrote a special one-act drama for her, which opened at the Lyceum on 26 January 1884. The piece, in which George Alexander also took part, was called *Comedy and Tragedy*. Gilbert later claimed that the plot had come to him while travelling on the Metropolitan Railway between Sloane Square and South Kensington stations. Another new actress, Julia Neilson, whose potential Gilbert recognised at an early stage, scored a considerable success in a further revival of *Pygmalion and Galatea* at the Lyceum in 1885.

Arthur Sullivan's links with the theatre also extend beyond the Savoy operas. Henry Irving commissioned him to write incidental music for a production of *Macbeth*, which he conducted on the opening night, 29 December 1888, and later for *King Arthur*, which he also conducted in person on 12 January 1895. Four years later in June 1899, when the Savoy Theatre was otherwise occupied, the D'Oyly Carte Company presented a brief twelve-night run of *The Mikado* at the Lyceum. It was during that same year that Henry Irving became part-owner of the theatre when he joined the syndicate of proprietors, but he was not allowed to enjoy his new status for long. The London County Council demanded extensive alterations to the building which went far beyond the syndicate's resources. And so the doors were closed in 1902, and by 1904 all that remained of the original structure were the rear walls and the existing portico.

Stoll then completely re-designed the interior as a music hall on which the Melville brothers took out a lease lasting thirty years, from 1907 to 1937. By this time the building was scheduled for demolition to clear space for the same development that swept away the New Gaiety Theatre in 1939. A final performance of *Hamlet* was presented with John Gielgud in the title role. Almost immediately thereafter the Second World War intervened: plans were shelved, the building was reprieved and in 1945 Mecca were granted a lease to run it as a dance hall. The interior stays fitted out as such to this day, but the exterior of the building has sadly been allowed to deteriorate.

There were two very well-known and popular restaurants in the Strand, both well patronised by members of the theatrical profession and their various hangers-on. One was Gattis at 436 Strand, and the other Romano's at 399. D'Oyly Carte was a regular customer of both establishments until he opened his own Savoy Hotel. In those days, no restaurant worthy of the name would think of closing its doors much before 3 a.m. As a result the Strand area was thronged until well into the early hours with lavishly-dressed young ladies escorted by

MESSRS. RUDALL, ROSE, CARTE, & CO.'S
LONDON OPERA, CONCERT, AND CHOIR AGENCY

(Under the Management of Mr. R. D'Oyly Carte),

20, CHARING CROSS, LONDON, S.W.

This Agency, for the engagement of *Artistes*, arrangement of Concerts, organisation of Tours, &c., was established by Messrs. Rudall, Rose, Carte, and Co., as a branch of their ordinary business, in the Autumn of 1868, and since that time has steadily extended its operations. Conducted by a house established for upwards of half a century in the Music Trade, as Musical Instrument Manufacturers to the Army and Navy, and Contractors with Her Majesty's Government, and known to every member of the Profession and Trade in the United Kingdom as Publishers of the *Musical Directory*, it was to be expected that the "Agency" would receive at once the confidence of a numerous *clientele*. This expectation has been fully realised. To give some idea to those Societies and *Entrepreneurs*, who have not already corresponded with Messrs. Rudall and Co., of the nature of their operations, a few of their most recent arrangements may be mentioned. Messrs. Rudall and Co. have been making engagements, by authority of J. H. Mapleson, Esq., for his Touring party, consisting of the following distinguished *Artistes*, headed by that world-renowned *Prima Donna* MADLLE. TITIENS:—

Madlle. TITIENS, Madlle. SINICO, Madlle. ROSA KANNENBERG (of the Grand Opera, Berlin, &c.), Signor FOLI, Signor CIAMPI (of the Royal Italian Opera), Signor VIZZANI (the greatly-admired new Tenor). Solo harp, Madlle. LOUISE JANSEN. Conductor, Signor BEVIGNANI.

Messrs. Rudall and Co. have had the Arrangement of Signor MARIO's Last Concert Tour, in which the following eminent *Artistes* have been engaged:—Madlle. LIEBHART, Miss ENRIQUEZ, Signor MARIO, Signor SIVORI (the celebrated Violinist). Solo Pianoforte, the CHEVALIER DE KONTSKI (Pianist to the King of Prussia). Conductor, Mr. WALTER MAYNARD.

Among the most important recent arrangements may be mentioned one with Madlle. CORANI (*Prima Donna*, from St. Petersburgh, the principal Italian Theatres, &c.), whose successful *début* last month at one of the Crystal Palace Concerts, and the Royal Italian Opera, will be fresh in the minds of concert-goers, and who has entrusted the management of her affairs to the Agency.

That universally celebrated Violinist, Signor SIVORI, who has been engaged on Signor Mario's Concert Tour, is now at liberty, and all communications respecting Concert Engagements for him are to be addressed to Rudall and Co.

Arrangements have also been made with that distinguished Composer, Conductor, and marvellous performer on the Contrabasso, Signor BOTTESINI, who will remain in England for some time.

Messrs. RUDALL, ROSE, CARTE, and Co., are prepared to make engagements with all the high-class artistes, and, among others, are specially authorised to make engagements for—

Madame RUDERSDORFF, Mdlle. NATALIE CAROLA, Madame LIEBHART, Miss BANKS, Miss BLANCHE COLE, Mdlle. SOFIA VINTA, Miss KATHERINE POYNTZ, Miss FANNY HOLLAND, Miss EMMELINE COLE, Miss EMILY SPILLER, Miss BERRY GREENING, Miss JESSIE ROYD, Madame ELENA, Miss DALMAINE, Miss ADA SINCLAIR, Miss MARGARET GALLOWAY, &c.

Madame PATEY, Miss JULIA ELTON, Mdlle. DRASDIL, Miss PALMER, Madame OSBORNE WILLIAMS, Miss ALICE FAIRMAN, Mdlle. DORIA, Miss ENRIQUEZ, Madame SAUERBREY, and Miss ADELAIDE NEWTON.

Mr. VERNON RIGBY, Mr. GEORGE PERREN, Mr. MONTEM SMITH, MR. WILBYE COOPER, Mr. NELSON VARLEY, Mr. WALLACE WELLS, Mr. E. LLOYD, Mr. FRANK ELMORE, Mr. G. T. CARTER, and Mr. ROBERT MASON.

Mr. PATEY, Mr. LEWIS THOMAS, Signor TAGLIAFICO, Mr. WINN, Mr. CHAPLIN HENRY, Monsieur WALDECK, Mr. LANDER, Mr. ORLANDO CHRISTIAN, Mr. RENWICK, and Signor CARAVOGLIA.

The Orpheus Glee Union, The Orchestral Soloists' Union, and Mr. and Mrs. German Reed's Entertainment.

INSTRUMENTALISTS.— PIANOFORTE : Mr. FRANKLIN TAYLOR, Miss AGNES ZIMMERMANN, Miss KATE ROBERTS, CHEVALIER DE KONTSKI, &c. VIOLIN: Signor SIVORI, Monsieur VIEUXTEMPS, Monsieur LOTTO, Mr. CARRODUS, Mr. HENRY HOLMES. and Signorina VITTORIA DE BONO. HARP: Mr. APTOMMAS, Mr. J. CHESHIRE, Mr. F. CHATTERTON, and Mr. ELLIS ROBERTS. FLUTE: Mr. A. COLLARD. Mr. DE JONG, Mr. RADCLIFF, Mr. BOCKSTRO, and Mr. BENJAMIN WELLS. CLARIONET: Mr. LAZARUS. TRUMPET: Mr. T. HARPER. &c., &c.

Although nearly all Engagements in Italy, France, Germany, and Spain, have long been arranged by Agencies, any extensive development of the "Agency" system, as applied to first-class musical performances, was unknown in England till introduced by Messrs. Rudall and Co.; but the rapidity with which the operations of the London Opera, Concert, and Choir Agency have extended shows that the advantages offered are widely appreciated; and there can be no doubt that before many years the whole musical business of the United Kingdom will be conducted on the continental system. Commerce is already much indebted to the system of "Agency." Stock and Share Brokers, Brokers of every article of wholesale consumption, Transfer Agents, Estate and House Agents, &c., take an important position in our commercial economy, and certainly the services which can be rendered by Agencies in the world of Art are not less considerable. To those who have not hitherto considered the matter, two points may be mentioned:—

First, Economy of Time.

The Agents being in the centre of the Metropolis, and *au courant* with all that is going on in the way of musical performances in every part of the United Kingdom, are able, at a few hours' notice, to name the best available talent for any date and place. These preliminary inquiries, as all *entrepreneurs* know, frequently drag their tedious length over many days, and sometimes weeks.

Second, convenience generally.

Messrs. Rudall and Co., being on the spot, have personal interviews with the artists when desirable, rendering journeys to London for their clients in the Provinces unnecessary. In the case of artists not of extensive reputation, and who may not be known by name to their clients, the recommendation of the Agency is a security as to their qualifications.

To *Artistes* the advantages of trouble saved in preliminary correspondence and business interviews with strangers, often without result, are obvious.

In furtherance of Messrs. Rudall, Rose, Carte, and Co.'s continental arrangements, a correspondence has been established with the principal Agencies of Italy, Paris, Germany, and Spain (including Cambiaggio e Ca. of Milan, Giacomelli of Paris, &c.), and arrangements can be made for English *Artistes* desirous of visiting the Continent, the Colonies, or America.

All arrangements as to terms are considered strictly confidential.

Artistes preparing for *début* can apply to the Agency, and can have an opinion as to their qualifications, from Twelve to Three daily.

Office Hours, Eleven to Four.

20, CHARING-CROSS, LONDON, S.W.

NINETEENTH ISSUE.

MUSICAL DIRECTORY, ANNUAL, AND ALMANACK, 1871.

CONTENTS.

Remarks on the events of the past year.

An Article on Beethoven's Life and Works (in commemoration of his Centenary Birthday), with an exact Chronological List of his works, by Mr. John Towers.

A Musical Almanack, with blank spaces for Memoranda.

Names and Addresses of all Professors of Music, Musicsellers, Instrument Manufacturers, &c., throughout the United Kingdom.

List of Bandmasters in the Army.

List (with Officers, &c.) of Musical Societies throughout the Kingdom.

A Record of the Operas, Festivals, Concerts, and Musical Events of the year 1870.

List of Copyright Music published throughout the United Kingdom during the year 1870.

A Tabular List of Advertisements of Concert Rooms, Theatres, &c., to let, with terms, number of seats, and particulars.

Musical Advertisements, Miscellaneous.

Price 2s.; by post, 2s. 3d. Bound in Crimson Cloth, 2s. 8d.; by post, 3s.

Rudall, Rose, Carte, and Co., 20, Charing-cross, London, S.W.

THE PROFESSOR'S POCKET-BOOK AND DAILY AND HOURLY ENGAGEMENT DIARY FOR 1871, compiled under the direction of M. JULES BENEDICT, expressly for Professors of Music, will be ready in a few days. Price, in roan cover, 3s.; free by post, 3s. 2d. Order at once.

Published by Rudall, Rose, Carte, and Co., 20, Charing-cross, London, S.W.

young army officers in their no less resplendent uniforms. Set against the exotic, gold-tasselled décor of places like Romano's, they presented a spectacle as glamorous and as attractive as the theatrical productions they came to see.

Make for the Strand Palace Hotel on the northern side of the Strand
Between 1831 and 1907 the Exeter Hall stood not far from the existing Strand Palace Hotel. There were in fact two halls in the building, in one of which oratorios were produced by the Sacred Harmonic Society in the 1840s and 1850s. In 1849 'the eminent musico' Jullien gave two concerts here, and three years later formed the New Philharmonic Society with the aim of presenting in the main hall popular music at popular prices. Later in the century, in 1882, the Exeter Hall was taken over by the Y.M.C.A. and used as its headquarters until 1907.

Since 1806 no fewer than four theatres have stood on the site which is now occupied by the Adelphi Theatre. The second of these, the Theatre Royal New Adelphi, with a seating capacity of 1500, opened in December 1858. Sullivan knew it well for it was here that his theatre music was first performed in public, at a matinée performance on 11 May 1867 of *Cox and Box*. Burnand and the staff of *Punch* had organised the occasion to raise funds for the family of C. Bennett, one of their colleagues on the magazine who had died quite suddenly. Sullivan conducted the performance after completing the orchestral parts the night before. Between 1859 and 1873 the Adelphi Theatre became famous for the great successes of Dion Boucicault. Then, in 1879, it was taken over by the Gattis whereupon it became a popular venue for melodrama and opera. From 1908 to 1917 George Edwardes scored hit after hit at the Adelphi with his musical comedies. During the following decade Gladys Cooper, Cicely Courtneidge and Tallulah Bankhead were among the many celebrated stars who appeared here, and when the theatre re-opened in 1930 C.B.Cochran presented a famous series of revues by Noel Coward and A.P.Herbert. After the Second World War Jack Hylton staged his radio comedies at the Adelphi, and in the 1960s Dame Anna Neagle danced her way through no fewer than 2,000 performances of *Charlie Girl*. And it was here that the old D'Oyly Carte Opera Company made its final appearance, 18 November 1981 to 27 February 1982, before it was disbanded.

Carry on to the Vaudeville Theatre
Just beyond the Southampton Street turning, where Gilbert was born, is the Vaudeville Theatre at 403-4 Strand, as elegant, spacious and as elaborately decorated as it was in his time. His *Rosencrantz and Guildenstern* was given its premiere here in a charity performance on 3 June 1891, before moving to the Court Theatre for its first professional run some ten months later. About 100 yards beyond the junction of Agar Street and Wellington Street stands the **Continue towards Trafalgar Square** impressive head office of the bankers William Coutts. The two original parts of the building were long neglected, but have been completely renovated and linked by an *atrium* in an uncompromising modern style. The bank traces its history on the site as far back as the 17th century, when a family firm of goldsmiths and money-lenders traded here. A century later the business was taken over and greatly developed by two Scots, Thomas and James Coutts. Arthur Sullivan kept an account at the Victoria Street branch of Coutts, and they are today bankers to Her Majesty the Queen. It was a name no less renowned in Gilbert's day: he mentions Coutts in his lyrics along with three other banking firms – Rothschild, Baring and Gurney.

From Trafalgar Square turn left into Whitehall
Almost opposite the Whitehall Theatre there is a small courtyard known as Craig's Court, after Joseph Craig who bought the land in 1674 from the Charing Cross Hermitage. In this tiny cul-de-sac, at 9a, Richard D'Oyly Carte joined his father's musical and dramatic agency business, after leaving the main family business in Berners Street. Many visitors associate Craig's Court with Charing Cross and expect to find it, not unreasonably, somewhere off the Charing Cross

Road. But that major thoroughfare had not been built by the 1870s and Charing Cross was a small, separate district in its own right and not merely an ill-defined end to Whitehall as it is today.

D'Oyly Carte's transfer to the agency business paid off almost at once. He promoted lecture tours by Matthew Arnold, Archibald Forbes, Serjeant Ballantyne and Oscar Wilde, in the provinces, on the Continent and throughout north America. On his books were the names of many famous stars of Covent Garden, including the tenor Signor Mario and four *prima donnas* of formidable reputation – Selina Dolaro, Bessie Sudlow, Pattie Laverne and Adelina Patti. The premises occupied by D'Oyly Carte were pulled down in 1880 to make room for a telephone exchange.

Left into Great Scotland Yard and then into Northumberland Avenue

The Playhouse Theatre, which in Gilbert's day was the Avenue Theatre, saw a production of his work translated from Offenbach's *The Brigands* on 16 September 1889, a fortnight after its first night in Plymouth. This theatre, not far from the Embankment Underground station, became a BBC recording studio in 1951 but then fell into disuse, presenting a very sad appearance for many years. Now, happily, it has been completely refurbished and from October 1987 the Playhouse has resumed its proper place among London's West End theatres.

A letter of introduction from Richard D'Oyly Carte written on behalf of one of his clients

44

Chapter 3

COVENT GARDEN AND ST.GILES

**Leicester Square
Underground: circular walk
allow 3 hours**

The neighbouring parishes of Covent Garden and St.Giles are full of history. Since well before 1632 and until a recent move across the river to Nine Elms, London's great fruit, vegetable and flower market was at Covent Garden, and for more than three hundred years London's principal theatre has been at Drury Lane. Many famous actors and actresses who have appeared there are commemorated in the names of surrounding streets – Betterton Street, Macklin Street, Garrick Street, among others. By far the most important venue for opera and ballet in London, the Royal Opera House, has been at Covent Garden since 1732. Immediately opposite is Bow Street police station, home of the first modern urban police force in the world. Next door is London's most famous magistrates' court, the seat of the Chief Metropolitan Magistrate. And within half a mile of all this splendour was one of London's worst Victorian slums, Seven Dials.

The name Covent Garden is, of course, a corruption of Convent Garden. The land once belonged to the Abbot of Westminster, and in 1632 Inigo Jones was engaged to design a church dedicated to St.Paul, and to lay out formal gardens. The nearby lanes became a fashionable residential area and it was in one of the town houses near the Strand that two hundred years later W.S.Gilbert was born, close to the famous church in which he was to be baptised. In the immediate locality there were three other theatres apart from the Royal Opera House and Drury Lane, and two gentlemen's clubs with which both Gilbert and Sullivan were eventually to become closely associated.

**From Leicester Square turn
east up Cranbourne Street,
over St. Martin's Lane to
Garrick Street**

The first of these, the Garrick, is to be found at 15 Garrick Street, an address known all over the world. Gilbert was a member here for many years and his portrait by Hubert Herkomer, which had previously hung in the drawing room of his house, Grim's Dyke, was bequeathed to the club by his widow on her death in 1936.

Arthur Sullivan was equally well known at the Garrick. For more than thirty years he treated it as a home from home, and much enjoyed dining and gambling in its convivial atmosphere, so full of Victorian bonhomie. Despite the references we find in Sullivan and Flower[1], and even in the highly authoritative Jacobs[2], the Club's records show that Sullivan was not elected to membership until March 1869, although he had been a very regular visitor for some time. Sir Francis Burnand, who became a member in 1865, recalls that he, Arthur Sullivan, Fred Clay, Harry Weldon with Captain Hawley Smart and one or two others, regularly dined together and were regarded as a pretty rowdy lot. They received quite a number of messages from the club president, Sir Charles Taylor, to tone down the conduct of 'their merry family'. Burnand goes on to complain that 'the

[1]Sullivan and Flower *Sir Arthur Sullivan, His Life, Letters and Diaries* London: Cassell, 2nd ed.1950 (p.58)
[2]Jacobs, Arthur *Arthur Sullivan, A Victorian Musician* Oxford: OUP, 1984 (p.56)

The actor-manager Sir Herbert Beerbohm Tree and leading artist of the day, Sir John Millais, close friends of Arthur Sullivan and fellow-members of the Garrick Club

At the end of Garrick Street turn right into New Row and then into St.Martin's Lane

Garrick in those days was certainly old-fogey ridden, and the glories of the social smoking-room in the old club had become a mere tradition.'[3] It certainly was the case that actors were being elbowed out by writers and academics, and that card games were over-encouraged.

When it was founded in 1831 the original aim of the Garrick Club had been to promote patronage for the drama, and to create a library which would specialise in works on theatrical costume. The first premises were in King Street, but soon after Garrick Street was built the club moved into its present building in 1864. It has a remarkable collection of theatrical portraits presented by Charles Matthews. Among the many past members of great distinction are Dickens and Thackeray, whose quarrel in the club resulted in an estrangement which lasted many years.

Sullivan frequently dined at the Garrick before moving on to other clubs in St.James's or in Mayfair in order to carry on gambling. He remained a member all his life, and celebrated at least two birthdays in the club. On the first of these occasions, 13 May 1879, he invited W.S. Gilbert to be his guest – a rare occurence, indeed. The party also included the Duke of Edinburgh, and after starting at the Garrick they moved on to Sullivan's flat. Fifteen years later, on a similar occasion, Gilbert was conspicuous by his absence. The Duke of Edinburgh (also by now the Duke of Saxe-Coburg) was among the guests once more, and so were HRH The Prince of Wales, Sir Augustus Harris, Sir Henry Irving, Sir Herbert Beerbohm Tree and Richard D'Oyly Carte. This time the party stayed on club premises and did not finish, or so we are informed, until 4.45 in the morning. Another good friend of Sullivan's, although not present on this particular ocasion, was the artist Sir John Millais.

Gilbert used to say that it took him so long to get elected because he was regularly blackballed by one of the committee in the mistaken belief that he was someone else. Whether there is any truth in this or whether this was one of his many after-dinner stories it is impossible to say at this distance of time, but club records show that he did not become a member until February 1906. Once inside the charmed circle his elevation came quickly enough, for in just over a year he found himself elected to the committee. The fact that he was now Sir W.S. Gilbert may have played a part in this change of fortune: club committees tend to regard knights of the realm with favour. Clearly they were not deterred by his attitude towards fellow-members, which was one of cantankerous irritability. He kept up one feud on club premises, with Forbes-Robertson, the actor, for more than thirty years. In his latter years, when he was not pursuing personal vendettas, he devoted an increasing amount of time to studying criminology, and it became his regular habit to leave the club each day in order to observe the long drawn-out trial of Dr. Crippen.

Not far from the Garrick Club is St.Martin's Lane where was once to be found the home of Baylis and Culpepper, whose establishment stood at the very head of London familiy magicians as a 'Noted House for Amulets' in Gilbert's *An Elixir of Love*. Near Trafalgar Square stands the Coliseum, built by Oswald Stoll as a music-hall in 1904. It occupies a site of an acre, has a 100ft frontage and can seat more people (2354) than any other theatre in London. It was here that the last premiere of any Gilbertian work was staged, on 27 February 1911. It was a one-act sketch about a prisoner in a condemned cell, entitled *The Hooligan*.

Everything about the Coliseum is on a grand scale by London standards. It not only has the largest, but at one time the only, revolving stage in Great Britain.

[3]Burnand, Sir Francis *Records and Reminiscences* London: Methuen, 1902 (Vol.I, pp 18 and 19)

With such resources it has for many years been able to attract companies to perform opera, operetta and ballet. The association with Sadlers Wells Opera began in April 1959, and ten years later the Coliseum became the permanent home of the company, who changed their name to the English National Opera in August 1974. *Patience* was taken into the repertoire in October 1969, and has since been revived in 1975 and 1979. In November 1986 the 1920s version of *The Mikado*, produced by Dr. Jonathan Miller, was presented with great success.

At the end of St. Martin's Lane turn left into King William Street and Chandos Place

Chandos Place, King William Street and Agar Street marked the bounds of another of London's most celebrated theatres, the Royal Charing Cross Theatre. Very few referred to it by that rather long name: most people called it, simply, Toole's. The entrance was at 24 King William Street. The building started life in 1840 as the Lowther concert rooms, which in 1855 became the Polygraphic Hall. It did not open as a theatre until the night of 19 June 1869 when, after speeches by E.L. Blanchard and Madge Robertson, the programme included the first performance of a burlesque by Gilbert, *The Pretty Druidess,* or *The Mother, The Maid and the Mistletoe Bough*. The following day *The Era* described the new theatre as an 'exceedingly elegant, handsome and commodious structure', and had this to say about the piece itself:

The famous beacon of Oswald Stoll's theatre, the Coliseum, the largest in London

> It was past eleven before Mr. W.S. Gilbert's new, witty and eminently whimsical musical extravaganza could be brought before the house; but the audience would not disperse until they had enjoyed the concluding entertainment, and their resolution was perfectly justified by the agreeable nature of the result ... The story is presented with great ingenuity, the lines are as remarkable for correctness of rhythm as for abundance of puns, and the parodies are written with unusual care to some of the prettiest melodies in the operatic and lyrical repertory ... although it was nearly half an hour after midnight before the curtain fell, jokes rattled off rapidly through continuous laughter, and Mr. Gilbert was summoned at the end to receive the congratulations of the house ... the first night of the Charing Cross has been pronounced an augury of a brilliant season, conveying the assurance of much future gratification being here in store for the London public.

Gilbert scored a further success at this theatre the following year on 26 May 1870, when *The Gentleman in Black* opened, with music by Fred Clay.

The 'Royal' prefix was dropped in 1872. After reconstruction ten years later Toole's, after the name of the manager, was formally adopted. In this way, popular tradition triumphed. In 1876 the Beef Steak Club was set up with its headquarters at the theatre, although later it moved to its own premises at 9 Green Street, W.C.2. Like its namesake the Sublime Society of Beefsteaks (1735-1867), which attracted leading luminaries and wits during the Regency, the new club had a select membership drawn from political, theatrical and literary circles, and it exercised much influence during its heyday.

Both Gilbert and Sullivan became members shortly after the club was formed, and it became one of Sullivan's favourite haunts. He took supper there on many occasions, and it was on Beef Steak Club notepaper that he wrote to George Grossmith in August 1877 offering him the role of John Wellington Wells in a forthcoming opera *The Sorcerer*. He used the club more than any other to discuss plans with Gilbert, and was often to be found there while working on *Iolanthe* and *Ruddigore*.

Gilbert was also a regular visitor to the club. On 25 May 1878 he gave a dinner party before the premiere of *H.M.S. Pinafore* and followed this with a late supper for a number of guests including Labouchère, Kendal, Frank Locker and others, but not Arthur Sullivan. When Gilbert was on speaking terms with them, Labouchère and Kendal were close companions of his but, like many other

47

Covent Garden Market as Gilbert would have known it, and the portico of St. Paul's church, where Professor Higgins and Colonel Pickering first encountered the flower-girl, Eliza Doolittle. Gilbert was christened here on 11 January 1837

From Chandos Place walk up Maiden Lane to Southampton Street

friends and acquaintances, they fell in and out of favour for no apparent reason. Most members of the Beef Steak Club were addressed either by their Christian names or nicknames, but Gilbert allowed no such liberties: he always insisted on his surname being used. He frequently took supper at the club after visiting the theatre, not returning home until 3 or 4 o'clock in the morning. But all this came to an end in 1908 when, for no apparent reason, he suddenly resigned his membership. The committee prevailed upon him to withdraw, but he rarely used the club thereafter.

At 17 Southampton Street, between Tavistock Street and the market hall, was Gilbert's birthplace. An office building stands on the site, the exact location of which has been the subject of much dispute. One authority[4] claims that it was the house in which his mother's doctor lived. On the other hand, Kate Field, an investigative journalist who wrote one of the first biographical articles about Gilbert, published in *Scribner's Weekly* in September 1879, suggests that he was not born in London at all but in the West Country. Gilbert himself, in an interview with Harry How, published in *Strand Magazine* in 1891, said that the house had belonged to his grandfather, a tea merchant.

To the left of the old Covent Garden market halls, across the piazza, stands St.Paul's Church, under the portico of which the famous opening scene of *Pygmalion* takes place. It became a landmark known all over the world after a film was made of the stage musical *My Fair Lady*. It was the 5th Duke of Bedford who commissioned Inigo Jones to build the church, and he imposed a very restricted budget. On one occasion, during a particularly difficult meeting with the Duke's advisers, Inigo Jones threw up his hands and declared, 'Gentlemen, if you want a barn, I shall build you the finest barn in Europe.' The description has survived, but not the original structure, for the church we see today was completely rebuilt in 1798 after a major fire. In later years, St.Paul's, Covent Garden, has become known as 'the actors' church', and many famous names can be seen on the memorial tablets. The ashes of Dame Ellen Terry are housed in a silver casket on

[4]Dark and Grey, op.cit. (p.1)

Cross the piazza to the junction of Russell Street and Wellington Street

Turn down Wellington Street to its junction with Exeter Street

The Gilbert and Sullivan pub

From the pub return to the junction of Wellington Street and Russell Street. Turn right: 50 yds on the right is the top end of Catherine Street

Return to the corner of Wellington Street and Russell Street and then turn right into Bow Street

the south wall, and among others buried in the church is Doctor Thomas Arne, composer of *Rule Britannia*. Here Gilbert was christened William Schwenck on 11 January 1837 – Schwenck after his maternal grandmother.

At the other end of the Flower Market, restored with such flair and imagination in recent years, stands the new Theatre Museum near the junction of Russell Street and Wellington Street. This houses the Gabrielle Enthoven collection, formerly at the Victoria and Albert Museum, and contains histories of the Royalty Theatre, the Opera Comique and the Savoy Theatre, as well as material on costume and set design and the development of stage management in the Victorian era. A standing exhibition features material on the Savoyards.

Another recent attempt to add to theatrical tradition, already rich in this part of London, has met with rather less success. The story starts in 1962 when the well-known brewers, Whitbreads, opened their pub *The Gilbert and Sullivan* at 28 John Adam Street, near the Savoy Hotel. With the assistance of Peter Goffin, and the blessing of the D'Oyly Carte Company, they gathered together a splendid collection which included *Mikado* costumes and fans, model sets of all the operas, specially-commissioned busts of the celebrated pair and other memorabilia. It was a haven for Gilbert and Sullivan enthusiasts, and many appreciation groups and societies held successful meetings and parties there until the premises closed after a serious fire.

With admirable intentions, Whitbreads decided to convert another of their pubs, *The Old Bell*, standing on the corner of Wellington Street and Exeter Street. They renamed it accordingly, transferred the greater part of the collection, and made every effort to create the right atmosphere. But the change seems to have been resisted by staff and customers alike. Pop music fills the air, and the items on display have been pushed aside by gaming machines. In other words, the transplant has not taken. Perhaps the regulars resented the imposition of middle-class entertainment and the values it represents: if so, there is a piquancy in the situation that Gilbert would have greatly relished.

Of all the great theatres in London, none is more renowned that the Theatre Royal in Drury Lane. It lies at the very heart of the history of British theatre. Charles II granted a royal patent for the first theatre in 1663 and his favourite, Nell Gwynn, made her stage debut here two years later. Between 1747 and 1776 David Garrick was actor-manager. He was succeeded by Richard Brinsley Sheridan, whose *School for Scandal* was first seen on 8 May 1777. After the theatre was attacked by a mob during the Gordon riots in 1770, a detachment of the Guards marched to Drury Lane every night to protect the building, a tradition which lasted until 1896. From 1788 to 1791 the Kembles and Mrs. Sarah Siddons took over the management, shortly after which the theatre was rebuilt for the fourth time. It is this building that has come down to us today. Lord Byron gave the opening address in 1812, and many other great names associated with the theatre's distinguished history are recorded in the foyer.

By the time Gilbert and Sullivan appeared on the scene, the Theatre Royal was managed by Augustus Harris, whose monument can be seen on the corner of Catherine Street and Russell Street. Harris was a remarkable man: as well as the Theatre Royal, at one time he also controlled the Royal English Opera House, which he bought from D'Oyly Carte, Her Majesty's Theatre and the Olympic Theatre. Under his management from 1879 to 1897, the Theatre Royal became renowned for spectacular drama, and for the Christmas pantomime featuring the popular comedian Dan Leno. It is a curious fact that although Gilbert was on the friendliest of terms with Harris, he wrote nothing for the Theatre Royal.

Not far from Drury Lane is Bow Street, where a Magistrates' Court has stood, on or near its present site, since 1748. Henry Fielding wrote *Tom Jones* here and served as Chief Magistrate together with his blind brother, Sir John. Their names, with those of five others who were resident in Broad Court, are recorded on a commemorative plaque. The Police Office, home of the famous Bow Street Runners, was formally established in 1829 by Sir Robert Peel as the Metropolitan Police Force. And it was here, 50 years later that D'Oyly Carte's stage manager, Richard Barker, took out summonses for assault against the directors of the Comedy Opera Company after their attempt to seize *H.M.S.Pinafore* properties on the night of 31 July 1879, an ill-judged adventure which led to rioting in the theatre.

Facing the Magistrates' Court is an even more famous building, the Royal Opera House. This foundation under royal patent dates back to December 1732: the first play to appear here was Congreve's *Way of the World*, which was followed by the *Beggar's Opera* by John Gay. In these early years it was not an opera house as we understand the term, but a theatre equipped to stage entertainments of many different kinds. The word 'opera' does not appear in its original title. Many leading actors of the time performed there including Garrick, Kean, Macready, the Kembles and Mrs. Siddons. By 1734, and during the following three years, Handel was closely associated with the theatre. He gave the first London performance of *Messiah* here and wrote six operas and sixteen non-operatic works for the theatre. The first building survived until 1808, when it was destroyed by fire. Rebuilding was put in hand without delay, and the second theatre on the site opened on 18 September 1809 with Mrs.Siddons and Charles Kemble in *Macbeth*. It was on this occasion that the 'Old Prices' riots broke out in protest against the increased admission charges.

By 1825 Charles Kemble had become manager, and he invited Carl Maria von Weber to become musical director and to compose an opera especially for London. Weber was too ill to take up the appointment, but he did write the opera *Oberon*, which he conducted at the first performance on 12 April 1826. By this time he was already critically ill, and he died not long afterwards.

When the lease became available it was taken up by Sir Michael Costa in April 1847. He immediately instructed an architect to transform the auditorium by adopting the horseshoe shape of the traditional Italian opera house. When the building works were completed, Costa re-opened the theatre as The Royal Italian Opera, Covent Garden. It did not long survive, for in 1856 fire intervened once more and all Costa's good works were destroyed. But nothing daunted he set about the task of rebuilding on the same site, although this time he was determined to create a fully-equipped opera house without compromise of any kind. He engaged as his architect Edward Barry, of the family that has left its very considerable mark on London. Barry senior designed the Houses of Parliament, while another of his sons was responsible for Tower Bridge. Edward Barry's building has changed very little since it was opened on 15 May 1858, although substantial development plans are now afoot. In 1946 the Royal Opera House, Covent Garden, became the permanent home of the Royal Opera and the Royal Ballet.

Interior of Covent Garden in 1813, and as it appears today

Costa was born in Naples and came to London as a young man and took out British nationality. He became the first permanent conductor of the Philharmonic Society and of the Birmingham and Leeds festivals. He went on to become one of the leading European conductors of his day, and his services to music were recognised when he received a knighthood from Queen Victoria.

The façade of the Royal Opera House, by Sir Edward Barry, has remained unchanged since 1858

Arthur Sullivan, on his return from Leipzig and with the help of some mutual friends, was able to watch the great man in rehearsal at Covent Garden. Costa took an immediate liking to the young musician and offered him the post of part-time organist. The duties were not onerous bearing in mind the operatic repertoire for the instrument at that time (or now, for that matter), but Sullivan did take part in productions of *Faust, Don Giovanni, William Tell*, and later works by Bellini and Verdi. In the 1870s the music of Wagner enjoyed great popularity although his works, including both *Tannhäuser* and *Lohengrin*, were sung in Italian. In 1892 the first complete *Ring* cycle in Britain was given at the Royal Opera House, under the baton of Gustav Mahler.

It was during Sullivan's engagement as organist that Costa asked him to write a ballet suite. It had to be scored to precise specifications to suit the style of the leading dancer, to take account of each entry and exit of the *corps de ballet* and to reflect the mood created by the scenery – all of which we take very much for granted today. Sullivan duly obliged with *L'Isle Enchantée*, which opened on 16 May 1864. But the work was not a success, and Sullivan soon relinquished his post.

Some 14 years later, however, with his reputation as a composer firmly established, Arthur Sullivan returned to Covent Garden at the invitation of the Gatti brothers who had, by then, taken over the management of the Royal Opera House. They were highly successful impresarios who had made their fortune from the sale of ice cream. They ran a restaurant in the Strand, and over a period of years they took out leases on a number of London theatres. They decided to

51

promote a series of classical concerts at reasonable prices, to attract the widest possible audience. Sullivan accepted their invitation to become principal conductor, choosing Alfred Cellier as his assistant. Sullivan conducted works from the classical repertoire and those of a religious nature, which gave him the rare opportunity of working with an orchestra of 80 players, many of whom were among the finest in England.

The young composer seized his chance with both hands, and made quite certain that his own pieces, including *Overture di Ballo* and the incidental music to *The Merchant of Venice*, received much-needed airings during the series of concerts, which opened in July 1878. Another work in need of support was *H.M.S.Pinafore* which, after a brilliant launch, had become becalmed. The hot summer and the smell of bad drains at the Opera Comique were affecting box office takings, and Sullivan decided to restore failing fortunes by including melodies from the opera, arranged by Hamilton Clarke, in the programme of a promenade concert he was due to conduct on 19 August 1878. His ruse succeeded beyond all expectation: almost overnight the bookings recovered and *H.M.S.Pinafore* went on to fulfil its earlier promise. Had Sullivan not carried out this rescue operation, the history of English light opera might well have taken a very different course, or have foundered altogether.

Continue up Bow Street to Long Acre

Close to the Royal Opera House is Long Acre, and here in a block which is bounded by Endell Street, Charles Street and Wilson Street stood the St.Martin's Hall and later, on the same site, the Queen's Theatre. St. Martin's Hall, which opened at 92 Long Acre in February 1850 as a venue 'for the development of choral singing', actually consisted of two halls – one a good deal larger than the other – together with classrooms and a catering room. It was in here in 1854 that Miss P.Horton started her 'Illustrative Gatherings': from April of the following year she was joined in this venture by her husband, Thomas German Reed. Their success was such that twelve months later they were able to take out a lease on 'The Gallery of Illustration' in what is now Lower Regent Street, where there began a long and fruitful association with W.S.Gilbert.

In 1858 Charles Dickens gave the first public reading of his work in St.Martin's Hall at a charity event in aid of the Children's Hospital, Great Ormond Street. This proved so successful that the author embarked upon a whole series of readings here before moving on to even larger audiences at the St.James's Hall and elsewhere.

Fire destroyed the Hall in 1860, and it remained closed for repairs until January 1862. Five years later it was converted into a theatre, renamed the Queen's Theatre, and in this new guise it opened its doors to the public on 24 October 1867.

In 1871 the husband of Henrietta Hodson, the radical politician and writer Henry Labouchère, purchased the lease of the Queen's Theatre to further his wife's acting career. In the event, it turned out to be a highly costly investment, which he was glad to get rid of a year later. Promenade concerts under Jules Rivière were the only presentations of any consequence during the final period of decline. Some say that the premiere of Gilbert's *The Fortune Hunter* was at the Queen's Theatre, but this is not correct. It took place, in fact, at the Queen's Opera House, which was a suburban music hall at Crouch End in north London. Closure of the Queen's Theatre came in July 1878 and in January of the following year the building became the University Co-operative Association Stores. In 1911 it was absorbed into a complex housing Odham's Press: today, an office block occupies the site.

Turn left along Long Acre towards Neal Street

In a westerly direction Long Acre leads to the ancient parish of St. Giles, now a part of fashionable Bloomsbury. The area takes its name from a hospital for lepers which was founded in 1101 by Queen Matilda, wife of Henry I. The hospital grew so wealthy that by the time of the Dissolution it had become an obvious target for Henry VIII, who granted it as a manor to the Dudley family, later Dukes of Northumberland. An old tradition survived for hundreds of years: criminals on their way to the gallows at Tyburn were allowed to stop at the gate for one last bowl of refreshment.

From Neal Street to Earlham Street, and on to Seven Dials

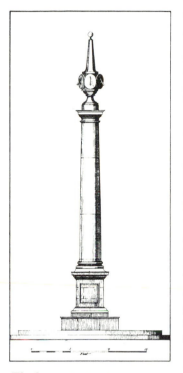

The Seven Dials column, designed by Edward Pierce in 1694

Within a stone's throw is Seven Dials, one of the most notorious areas in the whole of London. Its slums were deplorable even by 19th century standards, and for very good reason was the area cited as an example of the most abject poverty in *Iolanthe*. Its history dates back to 1693 when, with the approval of the Crown, new buildings were erected on the meadows to the north and west of Lincoln's Inn. Thomas Neale, who was an outstanding character of the period and moved freely in court circles, acquired land which was then known as Cock and Pie Fields, after an inn of that name in Long Acre. Neale had so firmly established himself that he was not only Master of the Mint but also Groom Porter to the King. He had the land laid out in a series of rectangles, with a circle in the centre from which radiated seven streets. At this central point he built a 40ft Doric column on which were mounted sundials facing each street. The scheme aroused great interest: Evelyn visited the site on 5 October 1694 and recorded the fact in his diary. Neale hoped that his properties would be snapped up by French emigrés arriving in London at that time, but in this he badly miscalculated, and his speculation ended in total failure. Nearly a century later, in 1773, rumours spread that Neale had buried a large treasure at the base of the column. A mob gathered and hauled it down finding, to their considerable fury, nothing whatsoever. The stones were then bought by a stonemason who sent them down to Sayes Court near Weybridge in Surrey. In 1822 they were re-erected on Weybridge Green as a memorial to the Duchess of York, who had died two years earlier. The sundials were replaced by a golden coronet. Attempts have been made to have the column put back where it belongs, and a Seven Dials monument appeal has been launched with the aim of building a replica on the original site.

With the demolition of the column the whole area went into a steady decline, and by the time of Dickens it had become little more than a squalid maze, as he tells us in *Sketches by Boz:*

> The Gordian knot was all very well in its way, so was the maze of Hampton Court. So is the maze of Beulah spa; ... but what involution can compare with those of Seven Dials? Where is there such another maze of streets, courts, lanes and Irishmen?

On the corner of Earlham Street and Short's Gardens now stands the Cambridge Theatre which opened in September 1930. In the late 1970s it was well-known to Gilbert and Sullivan enthusiasts for a highly successful production of *The Black Mikado*.

From Seven Dials into Monmouth Street and return to Leicester Square Underground

Within a few yards is Cambridge Circus where D'Oyly Carte opened his Royal English Opera House in 1891. A reviewer writing in the February issue of *The Lute* described the new theatre as 'an ornament of the district not long ago notorious for the filth and wretchedness of its dens.' The character of the neighbourhood first began to improve when Charing Cross Road cut through St.Giles to link Trafalgar Square to Tottenham Court Road. In more recent years great efforts have been made to improve Seven Dials still further. The main junction has been re-cobbled and many of the surrounding streets have been subtantially renovated. All that remains is for Neale's column, or replica, to be restored to its proper place.

*The Garrick Theatre in
1904 during the successful
run of Gilbert's 'Fairy's
Dilemma', which starred
Miss Violet Vanbrugh*

Chapter 4

LEICESTER SQUARE

Leicester Square
Underground to Piccadilly
Circus. Allow one hour plus
browsing time among the
bookshops and a visit to the
National Gallery

By London's timetable, Charing Cross Road was built only yesterday, but many of its original Victorian buildings have disappeared. The road runs northwards from Leicester Square underground station, through Cambridge Circus to Tottenham Court Road, and south towards Trafalgar Square. It is known to people all over the world as a centre for books, music, musical instruments and, more recently, discs and tapes. Some of the famous shops have gone, but many remain and there can be few more agreeable ways of spending a pleasant afternoon than by browsing among the bookshops and record shops in the area.

Leicester Square and its immediate surroundings became a major centre of entertainment in London while Gilbert and Sullivan, D'Oyly Carte and George Edwardes were alive. No fewer than five theatres play a crucial part in their story: the Garrick, the Criterion and the Prince of Wales, all of which can be seen today, together with Daly's and the Alhambra, which no longer exist.

**Walk south towards
Trafalgar Square**

At the southern end of Charing Cross Road on the left hand side there is a handsome, four-tiered, Italian Renaissance style building with an impressive 140ft frontage. This is the Garrick Theatre – the only one actually built for W.S.Gilbert. In the autumn of 1888 he conceived the idea of creating a new theatre not to stage his own works, but to lease it to the actor-manager John Hare, with whom he had recently patched up a long-standing quarrel. The leading theatre architect of the late Victorian era, Walter Emden, was brought in to design the building. His choice of Bath and Portland stone for the exterior cannot be faulted, but many difficulties arose during the construction. A stream, hidden since Roman times, was uncovered during the excavation works, causing serious flooding. Estimated costs rose from £30,000 to £44,000 and the project fell behind schedule. Gilbert said that at one time he wondered whether he ought to carry on building or to let out the fishing rights. In due course, however, all the difficulties were overcome, and on 24 April 1889 the new theatre opened with a production of *The Profligate* by Arthur Pinero which, among other things, included a song entitled *You Sleep*, with music by Sullivan. Hare's management of the Garrick Theatre lasted seven years. Gilbert thought he had done rather well fixing the annual rent at £5,000 but, according to Ellaline Terriss, as soon as the lease was in Hare's hands he sub-let the theatre for £25,000 per annum.

The Kendals took over the management in 1897, but the heyday of the theatre in Gilbert's lifetime was during Arthur Bourchier's regime from 1900 to 1915. Not that Gilbert was uncritical of the way things were run. While his last comedy *The Fairy's Dilemma* was in production, he wrote to a friend:[1]

'I've got to go to the Garrick Theatre for a rehearsal. They are all very civil and kind, but it is different from the Savoy, where everything went like clockwork. There's a sad want of method at the Garrick and I've had to put my foot down.'

[1]Dark and Grey *W.S.Gilbert: His Life and Letters* London: Methuen, 1923 (p.123)

The actor manager Charles Wyndham, after whom the famous theatre in Charing Cross Road is named

A contemporary magazine
features the Garrick
Theatre

The comedy had its first night on 3 May 1904, in an auditorium which has remained virtually untouched to this day. The original gallery has survived, there have been no major structural alterations, and the interior of the theatre is still very Victorian in character.

**Cross over to
St.Martin's Place**

Almost opposite the Garrick Theatre is St.Martin's Place and the National Portrait Gallery, an annexe of the National Gallery on the north side of Trafalgar Square. It was built in 1895 to bring together the national collection of portraits, protected by an Act of Parliament in 1856, which had previously been kept at the South Kensington Museum, the Bethnal Green Museum and at 29 Great George Street in Westminster. Among the many fascinating exhibits are portraits of Gilbert, painted by Frank Holl in 1886, and of Sullivan, painted in 1888 by Sir John Millais.

**Return to
Charing Cross Road**

**Along Irving Street to
Leicester Square**

Another very familiar landmark facing the Garrick Theatre is the statue of Henry Irving, which is said to occupy the site of the Old Curiosity Shop, immortalised by Charles Dickens, and not to be confused with the shop of that name in Portugal Street. Today, the small forecourt is a favourite haunt of pavement artists, escapologists and other street entertainers. From this point Irving Street can be seen on the left, giving access to the south-east corner of Leicester Square. Until the 16th century the land on which the Square stands was one of a number of open fields that stretched northwards towards a boundary now marked by Oxford Street, west to Piccadilly, east to St. Martin's Lane and south to Trafalgar Square. In 1657 the Marquis of Salisbury built a cluster of small houses along St.Martin's Lane, but the area north of the Square was not developed until the arrival of Huguenot refugees from France in about 1685. Over the years a footpath was created along the northern edge linking St.Martin's

Lane and Piccadilly. It made its way past the only building in existence at that time – a windmill, which gave its name to a military yard and later to Great Windmill Street and the Windmill Theatre, renowned for its proud wartime boast 'we never closed'. The footpath was known as Cranbourne Alley and it eventually became a large market-place for clothing of all kinds.

Make for the north-eastern corner of Leicester Square

The name of the Square derives from that of the landowner Robert Sidney, 2nd Earl of Leicester, who obtained a patent in 1671 to build himself a London residence on the open Lammas field. More houses soon followed and by 1678 it had become a handsome square among whose residents, at various times, were Sir Joshua Reynolds, William Hogarth, Sir Isaac Newton and Dr. Martin Burney. After an auspicious start the district went into decline towards the latter 18th and early 19th centures, and by 1840, when many of the houses were demolished to make way for Coventry Street and Long Acre, it was a slum.

On the eastern side of the Square the Odeon Cinema of the 1930s marks the spot where once stood the famous Alhambra, a theatre and music hall with a rich and varied history. 24-27 Leicester Square was the precise address, and the old premises started life in 1854-6 as an exhibition centre, the Royal Panopticon of Science and Art, where all the latest technological achievements of the age were to be shown. This worthy aim could not, however, be maintained and by 1858 the building had been converted to accommodate a circus, under the management of E.T.Smith. The name Alhambra was chosen to reflect the Moorish style of architecture. After two years the building underwent another transformation and became a music hall, one of whose early managers was John Hollingshead.

In 1870 a visiting group of French dancers, the Collona Troupe, took London by storm by including in their programme the *Parisienne Quadrille* otherwise known as the *Can-Can*. A public outcry followed, and in October of that year a renewal of the Alhambra's dancing licence was refused at the Middlesex Sessions. Three years later, however, the first London performance of Offenbach's *La Belle Hélène* received a rapturous reception at the Alhambra, and this was followed by another success from abroad, *Die Fledermaus*, by Johann Strauss. Home-grown entertainment at this time (1872-1878) was provided by the English Opera Bouffe, among whose stars were Kate Santley, Amy Sheridan and Selina Dolaro.

The building was then put to a wide variety of uses until fire broke out on 7 December 1882, destroying all the fittings, furniture, scenery and costumes. It seems so commonplace an event as to be hardly worth recording except, possibly, for the fact that the fire officer on duty that night in charge of the operations was Captain Eyre Massey Shaw, of *Iolanthe* fame.

Captain Eyre Massey Shaw

After rebuilding, the Alhambra opened the following year with an unsuccessful revival of Burnand's *Black-Eyed Susan*. By 1884 it had become a music-hall once more, with a growing reputation for first-rate ballet and pantomime productions In 1896 Arthur Sullivan was commissioned to write the music for Alfred Moul's ballet *Victoria and Merrie England*, which had been booked to open the Christmas season that year to herald the start of the Diamond Jubilee celebrations. It was a popular work that enjoyed considerable commercial success: Sullivan's diary confirms that it was still playing on 4 May 1899.

From 1893 to 1937, on the corner of Cranbourne Street and Leicester Court, stood Daly's Theatre, the home of musical comedy under that giant of the late Victorian and Edwardian theatre, George Edwardes. In many ways he surpassed his teacher, Richard D'Oyly Carte, in bringing to the public exactly what they wanted. He had learned the secret of success during his time at the Gaiety

Theatre under John Hollingshead and in the years that followed. Between 1895 and 1911 he produced no fewer than 11 highly successful shows at Daly's and elsewhere, including *An Artist's Model*, *The Geisha*, *San Toy*, *The Merry Widow* and *The Count of Luxembourg*.

Walk towards Piccadilly Circus

Coventry Street and the Prince of Wales Theatre are at the north-west corner of Leicester Square. The theatre is the latest in a long line to bear that proud name, but when it first opened on 18 January 1884 it was known simply as the Prince's Theatre. The first night audience saw a revival of Gilbert's *The Palace of Truth*, which ran for two months. In 1886 the Prince of Wales Theatre, off Tottenham Court Road, closed and the full title passed, almost by inheritance it seems, to the Prince's in Coventry Street. It soon became yet another home for musical comedy, and among the many distinguished names associated with the theatre we find Marie Tempest rubbing shoulders, as it were, with Mrs. Patrick Campbell and Forbes-Robertson. The existing theatre on the site is comparatively recent, having been completely rebuilt in 1936.

The last of the five theatres in this brief survey is the Criterion at 218-222 Piccadilly which, from its earliest years, is closely linked with Gilbert's career. Its origins are almost an exact reverse of those of the Savoy Theatre and the Savoy Hotel, in which the theatre was built first and the hotel afterwards. With the Criterion, a large hotel and restaurant was developed by Spiers and Pond in 1873 on the south side of what was then Regent Circus. It was later decided to build a theatre, partly in order to attract business to the hotel. A plot in the centre of the site was set aside for this purpose, and although built entirely below street level (even the dress circle is reached by a descending staircase) the theatre has access to natural light and ventilation.

The Criterion Theatre opened under the management of H.J.Byron with his own play *An American Lady*, which ran for 100 performances, and a one-act extravaganza by Gilbert called *Topsyturvydom*, with songs and additional music by Alfred Cellier. Between 1875 and 1877 Charles Wyndham's company, which included the young Ellaline Terriss, performed in repertory here.

It was at this time, following the success of *Trial by Jury* at the Royalty Theatre in Soho, that D'Oyly Carte opened negotiations with Gilbert and Sullivan with a view to staging a revival of *Thespis* at the Criterion for the 1875 Christmas season. However, he was unable to meet the financial conditions, so he dropped the idea for the time being and formed the Comedy Opera Company in the hope that the task of raising capital would be made that much easier.

On 3 April 1877 Gilbert's farcical comedy *On Bail* met with some success at the Criterion. It was, in fact, a rewritten version of *Committed for Trial*, which had played at the Comedy Theatre three years earlier. In December 1881 Gilbert's last farce (and, it should be noted, his 52nd stage play) *Foggerty's Fairy* was also given here. His final link with the theatre, however, was in 1893 when he translated the farce *Le Chapeau de Paille d'Italie* from the French and, with music and songs by Grossmith, turned it into the popular musical *Haste to the Wedding*. One reason why he involved himself in this venture was to help George Grossmith after he had decided to leave the D'Oyly Carte Opera Company to pursue his own writing and acting career. A different light is thereby thrown on Gilbert's character for although, as we have seen, he could be cantankerous and prickly, he could also be extremely generous to his friends.

SOHO

Tottenham Court Road to Piccadilly Circus Underground stations: allow 1½ hours

There is a good deal of controversy about the name Soho, but it seems to derive from an early 17th century hunting call, and first appears in written form in rate books dating from 1632. It is known that Huguenot refugees settled here after the revocation of the Edict of Nantes in 1685, and over the years Soho has attracted a large resident community of intellectuals including Dryden, Hazlitt, Leigh Hunt and Galsworthy. It is also a centre for pop music and the film industry, boasts some of the finest ethnic restaurants London can offer, and houses Chinatown, porn clubs, strip shows and the capital's red light district. Richard D'Oyly Carte was born in Soho and his great white elephant, the Royal English Opera House, was built here. Near at hand are the theatres of Shaftesbury Avenue, many of which have played a part in the Gilbert and Sullivan story.

From Tottenham Court Road station turn into Oxford Street. Take first turning left, Soho Street, into Soho Square

When it was first built in 1676 Soho Square was known as King Square after its designer, Gregory King. The Duke of Monmouth lived here and on the side of the gardens stands a statue of Charles II by Caius Cibber. By the 1870s it had become rather badly damaged, and the Soho Square Committee decided that they could not afford the cost of repairs. So they appointed one of their number

Soho Square, with Cibber's statue of Charles I in the foreground

Leave Soho Square by Carlisle Street: lst turning left is Dean Street

W.T.Blackwell (of Crosse and Blackwell fame) to give it away. An interesting problem: how does one actually set about the task of giving away a statue? How he managed it we do not know, but Mr Blackwell persuaded his neighbour in Harrow Weald, Frederick Goodall R.A., to accept the statue and, as we learn in a later chapter, it came into the possession of W.S.Gilbert. On his death, Lady Gilbert responded to many requests for its return by leaving it in her will to the residents of Soho Square. And so, after an absence of 60 years, good King Charles found himself being unveiled once again, in 1937, more or less on the spot where he had originally stood.

The Royalty Theatre at 73 Dean Street started life as an out-building of a large Georgian residence at that address. It was opened by Frances Maria (Fanny) Kelly, a comedy actress who left top billing at The Royal Strand Theatre to set up her own establishment which she called 'Miss Kelly's Theatrical and Dramatic School'. The theatre was built in the garden, but the only access was through some floridly-decorated public rooms and then an old stone staircase. It remained unaltered until well into the 19th century, but an increasing number of complaints from the audience and from the press about the discomforts of the place[1] bore fruit eventually, and substantial changes were made.

It re-opened as the Royal Soho Theatre in January 1850 but within a few years the interior was completely rebuilt and the name changed once again. It was as the New Royalty Theatre that it was re-launched in November 1861. Five years later Burnand's *Black-Eyed Susan* was presented here, a show which ran for 400 performances. This was followed by Gilbert's farce *Highly Improbable*, the first of a series of his works at the New Royalty to appear over a ten-year period. Next came *The Merry Zingara*, Gilbert's burlesque of Balfe's *The Bohemian Girl*, which ran from 21 March 1868. After her husband had given up the lease of the Queen's Theatre in Long Acre, Henrietta Hodson decided to try her luck at the New Royalty by taking over its management towards the end of 1872. Thus the scene was set for the huge and famous row with Gilbert which resulted in the circulation of privately-printed pamphlets, in which each vigorously and enthusiastically attacked the other.

Gilbert's first work under Hodson's management was *The Realm of Joy*, a burlesque on Meilhac and Halévy's *Le Roi Candaule* which he wrote, for reasons best known to himself, under the pen-name F.Latour Tomline. This production opened on 18 October 1873 and ran until Christmas. Meanwhile, Gilbert had written a comedy for Hodson, *Ought We To Visit Her?*, which achieved great success and enjoyed many revivals over the next 20 years.

The dispute arose over what we would now call stage direction although the term was not then in use. On the one hand Hodson felt that Gilbert had no business to interfere with the staging or casting of his pieces whereas the author, needless to say, considered that he had every right to do so. Another bone of contention was that Hodson always insisted on playing leading lady to her two seasoned actors, Wyndham and Toole. The quarrel grew increasingly bitter and although the play opened on the due date, 17 January 1874, Gilbert had quite made up his mind that Henrietta Hodson would not, from that time on, appear in any of his plays anywhere in London. He achieved this by withholding licences from theatre managements wishing to put one of his works unless they gave an undertaking that they would not under any circumstances cast Henrietta Hodson in any of the roles.

W.S. Gilbert at the age of 31

[1]Fitzgerald, Percy *The Gilbert and Sullivan Operas* Philadelphia: Lippincott,1894 (p.21)

*The radical politician
Henry Labouchère*

For any actor or actress to be blacked by Gilbert in this way in the mid-1870s was a very serious matter indeed, for his grip on London's theatrical life was formidable. In that year, 1874, to take just one example, he had plays, burlesques and other works on at the Haymarket, the Royalty, the Globe, the Court, the Criterion and at the Prince of Wales theatres. The ban on Henrietta Hodson lasted three years, by which time the dispute had reached a point where letters from solicitors were being exchanged, and threats to sue were very much in the air. One of the consequences of the whole affair was that, not surprisingly, he lost the friendship of Henrietta Hodson's husband, Henry Labouchère, who ran the influential radical magazine *Truth*.

After Hodson left the Royalty Theatre in 1875, Kate Santley became the sole proprietor, with Richard D'Oyly Carte as business manager. In the spring of that year Selina Dolaro took out a short lease on the theatre and asked D'Oyly Carte to manage on her behalf a season of light opera to include, among other works, Offenbach's *La Périchole*. This is a delightful piece but hardly full-length opera, and D'Oyly Carte decided that to give the audience their money's worth a filler was called for. He approached Gilbert and at 10 p.m. on 25 March 1875 theatrical history was made. The curtain went up at the Royalty Theatre to reveal an exact replica of a British courtroom, complete with wooden panelling, judge's bench and an overpowering coat-of-arms. It created a sensation: nothing like it had ever been seen on the British stage before. Not only were new high standards set in terms of scenery, costumes and sets, but the wit of the libretto was matched by the charm and elegance of the music. Audiences were swept off their feet, and *Trial by Jury* ran for 300 performances before being transferred first to the Opera Comique and then to the Royal Strand Theatre in April 1877.

A revival of Sullivan's *The Zoo* in 1878 is the final link between the Royalty Theatre and G & S: more structural alterations were carried out in 1883 and 1885, and in 1892, as the New Royalty Theatre, it saw the premiere of the runaway Brandon Thomas success *Charley's Aunt*. It stayed in business as a working theatre until November 1938 when the Lord Chamberlain revoked its licence. New building works were needed to conform with the safety regulations then in force, but these were not carried out. The empty building was severely damaged

*A scene from the D'Oyly
Carte Opera Company's
1939 production of
'Trial by Jury'*

Halfway down Dean Street turn left into Bateman Street, and then to Greek Street

Left into Old Compton Street, over Charing Cross Road and then turn first right (Stacey Street) to Shaftesbury Avenue

in the London blitz, and remained derelict until it was demolished in 1953. Six years later an office block was built on the site, and the only reminder of the past is the name of the new building, Royalty House.

The derivation of Greek Street has nothing to do with the nationality of some of the restaurants there, but comes from Greg Street by which it was known until the 18th century. Here, Richard D'Oyly Carte, whose father ran his business in Berners Street just five minutes walk away, was born on 3 May 1844.

When the new Shaftesbury Avenue was cut through the upper end of St. Giles in the 1880s many decaying properties were pulled down. Planners at that time decided that if there were to be new theatres they should be built in this part of London rather than in the Strand/Kingsway area. But it took more than 40 years for their policy to bear fruit, and then only one new theatre appeared, the Saville in 1931. Here the D'Oyly Carte Opera Company presented Christmas seasons in 1965/6 and again in the following year. Now, the Saville has become ABC Cinemas 1 and 2.

The success of his venture into light opera assured, Richard D'Oyly Carte turned his attention to his next project which was nothing less than the rebirth, as he saw it, of English grand opera. The first thing to be done, of course, was to build a new theatre, and his eye fell on the corner site created by Shaftesbury Avenue at its junction with Cambridge Circus and bounded by Greek Street and Romilly Street. There D'Oyly Carte gave shape to his dream and built the Royal English Opera House which, as the Palace Theatre, has survived to this day, its facade virtually unchanged. Both Gilbert and Sullivan were present when Helen D'Oyly Carte laid the foundation stone on 15 December 1888.

Designed by Colcutt and Holloway, the new theatre was built in three tiers of red Ellistown brick and Doulton terra-cotta, with arcaded windows and deep balconies. The grand staircase was supported on columned arches and the proscenium finished in green Italian marble, Mexican onyx and alabaster. An independent generator provided electric power for 2,000 lamps, the sole source of light. Every available luxury was lavished on the interior furnishings and the latest stage machinery was installed. The galleries were cantilevered, and a royal retiring room was specially provided. The building took two years to complete, and by the time it opened in January 1891 two quite opposing views had emerged. On the one hand, we find *Theatre Magazine* saying:[2]

> ... if grand opera in England is ever to succeed, now is its chance. It is provided with a house as admirably arranged and as sumptuously furnished as any audience could desire.

On the other hand, *The Star* theatre critic wrote on 16 August 1889 that a new opera house in London was unnecessary when there was already an enormous wastage resulting from the inefficient use of Covent Garden, Her Majesty's Theatre, Haymarket, and the Theatre Royal in Drury Lane. The name of the critic was George Bernard Shaw.

Much to D'Oyly Carte's great disappointment many clouds hung over the launch of his new venture. The quarrel with Gilbert over finance was now out in the open. He had condemned the choice of site for the new theatre and predicted its failure. He declined to provide a libretto for an opening production and even turned down an offer of free tickets for the gala first night. D'Oyly Carte found himself in an extremely difficult position because he had intended to transfer all Gilbert and Sullivan productions to the new theatre, and lease the Savoy Theatre

[2]Fitzgerald, St.J.Adair *The Story of the Savoy Opera* London: Stanley Paul, 1926 (p.160)

The Palace Theatre c.1908, Carte's ill-fated Royal English Opera House, now extremely successful under the management of Andrew Lloyd Webber

on extremely favourable terms. But Gilbert's refusal to have anything to do with the Royal English Opera House completely thwarted his plans.

To make matters worse, D'Oyly Carte had commissioned Sullivan to write a new work for the grand opening night. Sullivan was flattered but somewhat embarrassed, as he was already heavily involved in composing *The Gondoliers*. However, working in his summer retreat at Grove House in Weybridge, he devoted time which he felt he could ill afford to the new project, which was nothing less than a setting of *Ivanhoe* to a libretto by the novelist Julian Sturgis. He completed the task between May and December 1890. The work consisted of three acts with nine scenes, each of which required a different set. D'Oyly Carte set out to provide only the best. He engaged a team of four designers working under Irving's set designer, Hawes Craven, and he recruited two complete sets of principals of international reputation to give performances on alternate nights, with a chorus of 72 singers and an orchestra of 63 players.

The opening night on 31 January 1891 was, indeed, a brilliant success. According to a report in the *Boston Sunday Herald*, 10,000 applications were received for the 1,976 seats available. At the end of the first act many of those standing in the auditorium were asked to leave because of the dangerous crush. At 8 p.m. the royal party arrived, including the Prince and Princess of Wales, Princess Victoria and Princess Maude, and the Duke and Duchess of Edinburgh. Cellier conducted the national anthem and then Sullivan took the podium for the rest of the evening. During the first interval he joined the royal party, and after the performance returned in triumph at 4 o'clock in the morning.

Ivanhoe ran with great success to about its 100th performance, which Sullivan returned to conduct. But thereafter attendances dwindled, quite slowly at first

Sir Augustus Harris, most powerful theatre magnate of his day

and then more rapidly. After the 155th performance, at the end of July, the theatre closed. A new work Carte had commissioned from Frederic Cowen, *Sigma*, was not yet ready, so he had to fall back on a production of Messager's comic opera *La Basoche*, the rights of which he had acquired earlier, and with this he re-opened his theatre in November. The new production, interspersed with a few more performances of *Ivanhoe*, survived for only ten weeks, until January 1892. In a final bid to save the situation D'Oyly Carte engaged Sarah Bernhardt for Sardou's *Cleopatre*, but this only ran for four weeks.

By this time D'Oyly Carte had lost £32,000 and by July he had no alternative but to sell out to a consortium led by Sir Augustus Harris, which already controlled Covent Garden, the Olympic Theatre and Her Majesty's Theatre. £200,000 was raised by a public flotation advertised in the *Financial Times* which enabled the consortium to take over the Royal English Opera House and, within a matter of weeks, convert it into the Palace Theatre of Varieties. And as the Palace Theatre or, simply, the Palace, it has played a major part in the theatrical life of London ever since.

In 1908, Maud Allen gave a performance in *Salome* which not only created a great scandal but also resulted in litigation. Two years later in April 1910 Pavlova made her less controversial London debut at the Palace. In the late 1920s and early 1930s C.B.Cochran, with his famous young ladies, staged his reviews here, and throughout the war years Jack Hulbert and Cicely Courtneidge appeared in a number of successful shows. From 1951, for a period of twenty years, the theatre was in the hands of Emile Littler: his great triumph was undoubtedly a production of that much-loved *Lilac Time*. In the 1970s and 1980s the Palace has enjoyed the enormous popularity of a series of musicals by Andrew Lloyd Webber, whose company now owns the theatre.

Keep Palace Theatre on the left. Walk along Moor Street to Old Compton Street. Then turn into Frith Street and return to Shaftesbury Avenue

As for the building itself, remarkably little has changed. The amphitheatre was rebuilt in 1908, the roof and some of the offices repaired after war damage and the seating capacity reduced to 1,450. But the atmosphere created by Richard D'Oyly Carte's sumptuous decor is very much in evidence. He would feel quite at home here today, were it not for the music.

Not far from the Palace is another link with the past of a much more tenuous nature. On the corner of Frith Street and Old Compton Street stood the premises of the very high-class costumiers and drapers, Sewell and Cross. They were well-known, highly fashionable and counted among their customers the Empress Eugénie. The business closed in 1870 after *The Princess* appeared, but well before the Savoy operas.

Frith Street (originally Thryft Street) leads back into Shaftesbury Avenue: from this point westwards to Piccadilly Circus three theatres were built during the redevelopment of this part of London, only one of which is of interest to the Savoyard. That is the Lyric Theatre at 29 Shaftesbury Avenue, the second of three theatres to be built with a frontage occupying a whole block from Great Windmill Street to Archer Street. It opened on 17 December 1888 not with a new production, but with a transfer of Cellier's highly popular *Dorothy*. It was the 817th performance, and the show went on to break the record previously set by *The Mikado* for the longest non-stop run.

Continue to Piccadilly Circus Underground

Two of Gilbert's later comic operas were produced at the Lyric Theatre neither of them scored by Sullivan. The first, *The Mountebanks* concerned a magic lozenge, an idea Sullivan had strenuously opposed for many years. The second, *His Excellency*, Sullivan refused to set to music because Gilbert insisted that the

leading part should be played by Nancy McIntosh, an actress whose lack of acting ability, in Sullivan's eyes, was responsible for the comparative failure of *Utopia Limited* in 1893.

The Mountebanks, which opened on 4 January 1892, was a triumphant success, and put paid to the notion that Gilbert could not write good comic opera without Sullivan. However, by an unhappy coincidence both his musical collaborators died during the production. Alfred Cellier just before the opening night, and Arthur Goring Thomas during the run. Thomas had originally accepted the commission from Gilbert, but later retired on account of serious mental illness. Alfred Cellier completed the work and then turned his attention to the overture, which he managed to finish just a few days before he died in December 1891.

Towards the end of the run, which lasted eight months, the manager of the theatre, Howard Sedger, tried to economise by sacking 18 girls from the chorus. When he heard about this Gilbert was furious. He threatened Sedger with legal

65

action and made certain that the girls were paid for a further week beyond their original engagement. They sent a charming note of appreciation in return.

By the time *His Excellency* was ready for production George Edwards had taken over the management of the Lyric Theatre. He asked Ellaline Terriss to take the lead at the end of her run in *The Shop Girl* at the Gaiety Theatre. Gilbert chose as his collaborator Osmond Carr, but the show was not a financial success. He had other problems as well. There were fierce arguments with Edwardes about payments which he said were due on translation rights, and he also felt obliged to bring an action against *The Star* for revealing the plot before the opening night.

Taking one consideration with another, Gilbert's association with the Lyric Theatre was certainly not a happy one.

Chapter 6

BLOOMSBURY

Oxford Circus to Tottenham Court Road Underground stations: allow 2½ hours plus plenty of time for a visit to the British Museum

The unusual and rather beautiful name of Bloomsbury, home of the group of writers and artists who achieved fame in the 1920s, comes from the Manor of Blemundsbury, which belonged to the De Blemontes family in the 13th century. The manor house stood roughly where the Senate House of London University stands today. Bloomsbury refers to that area bounded, west to east, by Tottenham Court Road and Southampton Row and, north to south, by Euston Road and Shaftesbury Avenue. Among the many outstanding buildings in this part of London is the British Museum, where most of Gilbert's diaries and manuscripts are kept.

From Oxford Circus underground take the exit signposted 'Oxford Street North/Regent Street East' and walk up Regent Street to Langham Place

Langham Place, just north of Oxford Circus, is now dominated by Broadcasting House, but before 1941 three important concert halls were to be found here. Two of them were at the Queen's Hall, which had a large auditorium capable of seating 2,492 people, and a smaller recital room for an audience of 500. The building occupied a site between Mortimer Street, Riding House Street and Langham Place itself. The third venue was St.George's Hall, where now stands St.George's Hotel and Henry Wood House, where some of the BBC's offices are situated.

The Queen's Hall, still remembered with affection by many musicians today, is where the original Promenade Concerts took place. In 1941 German bombs brought to an end a great tradition of music-making, and there are those who say that its loss as a concert hall has yet to be made good in London. In St. George's Hall, which was destroyed on the same night, some of the music of young Arthur Sullivan was first heard. It was opened as a concert hall by the New Philharmonic Society on 24 April 1867, but by December of that year the lease had been taken over by Thomas German Reed, who renamed the building St.George's Opera House. Here he presented a season of light opera, opening with a piece he had commissioned from Frank Burnand and Arthur Sullivan after seeing a charity performance of their *Cox and Box*.

The result was *The Contrabandista* or *The Law of the Ladrones*, which proved something of a flop – not surprising, perhaps, when we find that it was written, rehearsed and produced in just over a fortnight. Not even a first-rate 40-piece orchestra and a large chorus recruited from Her Majesty's Theatre and the Royal Italian Opera could save the day. Other shows followed, including *The Beggar's Opera*, Auber's *L'Ambassadrice* and Offenbach's *Ching Chow Hi*, but after three months German Reed had to close down and the hall reverted to its original title. His one consolation came later: so impressed had he been by *Cox and Box* that he acquired the rights and when he staged a revival at St.George's Hall it ran for over 300 performances.

Two of Gilbert's works were also seen here: his farce *A Medical Man*, on 24 October 1872, and *Eyes and No Eyes*, a 'comedietta', on 7 May 1875. The German Reeds retained an interest in St.George's Hall until 1895, but after an interior refit in 1897 it became the Matinée Theatre, a music hall for high-class vaudeville. From 1903 it was used for a short time as one of the first recording studios. Edward Elgar made some of his earliest recordings here. Two years later the building was taken over by the conjurer John Maskelyne who ran his Magic Show at the St. George's Hall for twenty years with great success. Then, in 1933, the BBC moved in and converted the hall into a main variety studio, which remained in use until the outbreak of war in September 1939. A year later it was hit by incendiary bombs and then in May 1941 it was reduced to an empty shell, together with its neighbour the Queen's Hall, never to be rebuilt.

From its very early days the BBC has regularly broadcast the Savoy operas, but the very first Sullivan work to go out over the 'wireless' was his grand opera *Ivanhoe*. This was in 1929, and the broadcast was made in two parts, with a libretto available for listeners who wished to follow the work closely. Six months later Rupert D'Oyly Carte allowed *Cox and Box*, one of the operas in the current Savoy season, to be broadcast in its entirety on Christmas Eve. After this cautious start, works from the main Gilbert and Sullivan repertoire followed in succession. And so the microphone created another huge and world-wide audience, a process already set in motion by the gramophone and to be accelerated still further by the invention in Britain of television in the years ahead.

Turn right behind All Souls into Langham Street and then into Great Portland Street leading to Oxford Street. Turn left into Berners Street

Langham Hall at 48 Great Portland Street was once a very fashionable venue for recitals and chamber music, much as the Wigmore Hall is today. D'Oyly Carte hired the premises in March 1885 for *Mikado* rehearsals, while the sets were actually being built at the Savoy Theatre. Another link with the past in this part of London is at 6 Berners Street, where Richard D'Oyly Carte's father ran an instrument-making business. As Rudall Carte and Company they supplied military bands and published a musical directory every year. The name was very well-known in the music world and carried a lot of influence and goodwill: not unhelpful when the time came for Richard to run the family's concert agency business on his own account.

At the top of Berners Street turn right into Mortimer Street and into Cleveland Street, and right again into Tottenham Street

On the right-hand side of Tottenham Street, just beyond its junction with Scala Street, there once stood the Prince of Wales Theatre which gave its name to the present theatre in Coventry Street. Theatrical and musical entertainment in one form or another had been provided on this site since 1772, when Francis Pasquali built a concert hall which became variously known as the King's Concert Rooms, Tottenham Street Rooms, New Rooms and the Ancient Concert Rooms. In 1810 it became the New Theatre, but by 1831 when George Macfarren tried unsuccessfuly to revive English opera here, the name had been changed yet again to the Queen's Theatre. One more transformation was to follow – the Fitzroy Theatre – before it became the Prince of Wales. In Gilbert's time the theatre was run by Edgar Bruce, who commissioned the 30-years-old dramatist to write a farce. The result was *Allow Me To Explain*, which ran with moderate success from 4 November 1867. It was the fourth play of Gilbert's to be performed.

Marie Wilton, later Lady Bancroft

By the time he returned to the Prince of Wales Theatre seven years later Gilbert was a much matured author. Now he was presenting his 40th play, a lively comic drama entitled *Sweethearts*, which became one of his most popular pieces. It opened on 7 November 1874 and during the run Marie Wilton, who later became Lady Bancroft, took over the lead part. By the time *Trial by Jury* opened at the Royalty Theatre, *Sweethearts* had already achieved more than 100 performances. It was followed in its turn by yet another of Gilbert's plays, *Tom Cobb*.

The Prince of Wales Theatre closed in 1886 and nearly 20 years were to pass

The British Museum

Tottenham Street to Tottenham Court Road, cross over to Chenies Street. Turn right into Gower Street leading to Bloomsbury Street. Take either Montague Place or Great Russell Street to reach the British Museum

before another, The Scala Theatre, was built on the site. Several seasons of opera were given here, including one by the D'Oyly Carte Company in 1938, while the Prince's Theatre was being refurbished. After the war, the building was converted into a cinema and is now used as a hostel run by the Salvation Army.

Nearby, on the corner of Scala Street and Wheatfield Street, is a shop to which every lover of theatre should make at least one pilgrimage, if not many more. It is the home of Pollock's Toy Museum, where a fascinating collection of toy theatres can be found and cut-out models can still be purchased. Those printed in colour, as might be expected, cost more: hence the origin of the expression 'tuppence coloured: penny plain'. Gilbert was an ardent toy theatre enthusiast and had many fine models in his collection.

The British Museum, built in 1759, houses the national collection of rare treasure drawn from all parts of the world. It had its beginnings in three great private collections: the books and manuscripts of Sir John Cotton; the manuscripts of Sir Robert Harley, Earl of Oxford, and the unique collection of Sir Hans Sloane which included prints, medals, antiquities, coins, precious stones and natural history specimens. King George IV gave the money needed to build the King's Library in 1823, after which the rest of the building was greatly enlarged and the fine, impressive portico added in 1847. Two more wings were built following a major bequest in 1884, and at the same time the natural history section was moved into its own new building in South Kensington.

In the vast collection of manuscripts and literary works belonging to the British Museum are the Gilbert Papers – diaries, plot-books, manuscripts, correspondence and photographs. He bequeathed these to Lady Gilbert who, in

69

turn, left them to Nancy McIntosh. Her executors sold most of the collection to the museum authorities and the rest to the Pierpont Morgan Library in New York. There is still a certain amount of unpublished material, the copyright of which is vested in the Royal General Theatrical Fund.

From Bloomsbury Street cross New Oxford Street and bear left across the traffic island

The most southerly point in Bloomsbury is the Shaftesbury Theatre, which stands at the top of Shaftesbury Avenue. Built in modern renaissance style, it opened on Boxing Day 1911 as the Prince's Theatre, one of the first in which D'Oyly Carte revivals were staged, and one of the most successful, other than the Savoy Theatre itself. Between 29 September 1919 and the end of January the following year the company put eight of the operas into repertory, and mounted the first revival of *Princess Ida* since its first run in 1884.

The 1921/2 season, from 3 October to 8 April, included a revival of *Cox and Box*, the first since 1896, and the first revival of *Ruddigore* since it first appeared in 1887. For this production Geoffrey Toye was commissioned to write a new overture, which today is more frequently performed than the original. In the same season King George V and Queen Mary attended a performance of *The Gondoliers* on 10 March 1922.

The Princes Theatre sustained the Gilbert and Sullivan tradition for many more years to come: 1924, 1926 (when a short extract from the first night, with Dr. Malcolm Sargent conducting, was actually broadcast: one of the first outside broadcasts ever to be attempted), 1942, 1956, 1958, 1959 and 1960. Queen Elizabeth paid an informal visit to the theatre on 10 March 1959 to attend a performance of *Ruddigore*. In the 1960s the theatre was closed for restoration and on re-opening it adopted its present name, achieving almost instant notoriety with *Hair*, a musical which presented full frontal nudity on the British stage for the first time. The foundations of British society were shaken but not undermined, more than can be said for those of the theatre itself, for at the end of the run it was found that an underground stream had been eroding the foundations of

Take St.Giles High Street to return to Tottenham Court Road Underground station

the building for many years. Another long closure followed while these structural matters were attended to. Happily, in recent years the Shaftesbury has taken on a new lease of life as the home of the successful Theatre of Comedy company.

Chapter 7

MAYFAIR

Oxford Circus to Green Park Underground stations: allow 2½ hours

The district bounded by Park Lane, Regent Street, Oxford Street and Piccadilly has for more than 100 years enjoyed the reputation of being by far the most fashionable part of London. Yet until the early 18th century there was little to be found here except green fields and an open lane, following more or less the route now taken by Piccadilly, known from about 1550 as the 'way to Redinge'. The only feature of any interest was an annual fair, held in fields to the north of where Regent Street now stands, which opened on May Day of each year and lasted for 15 days, and for which royal permission had to be sought from James II. It is perhaps just as well that His Majesty did not, as far as we know, grace any of these occasions with his royal presence, for they were by all accounts extremely riotous and rowdy affairs. There was none of the legitimate trading usually to be found at country fairs of this kind. Instead, the whole time seems to have been given over to music and dancing, to drinking and wenching, gaming, lotteries, stage plays and 'droleries' of every sort. It was a most popular event which attracted the nobility as well as the peasantry. And it was called, it need hardly be said, May Fair.

From Oxford Circus Undergrounds take the exit signposted 'Regent Street East/ Oxford Street South.

Although Gilbert acquired considerable wealth during his lifetime, he never aspired to join the high society and Court circles so beloved by members of the aristocracy. But he understood well enough the motives of those who did so aspire. He knew all about the hopes and the plans of the middle-aged matrons who came to shop – not in exclusive Bond Street, still beyond reach – but in one or more of the popular shops in the Regent Street area. His wife was almost certainly one of their number, and when the time came to choose material for costumes, it was to Regent Street drapers, haberdashers and milliners that he sent Richard D'Oyly Carte. One of the best known of these is Liberty's, with its famous mock-Tudor frontage and the moving clock set above the archway over Kingly Street.

Arthur Lasenby Liberty was a mere lad of nineteen when the wonders of oriental design were revealed to him at the 2nd Great International Exhibition at South Kensington in 1862. Japan was still a closed country in those days, unknown to the Western world. But in Paris in 1856 a French dealer, Braquemand, came across bundles of discarded colour prints that had been used to wrap a consignment of Chinese porcelain. They were by the master, Hokusai, and when Braquemand put them on display they created a sensation, especially among early Impressionist painters. Chinese and Japanese goods soon became all the rage, and a shop opened in the Rue de Rivoli which was patronised by Baudelaire, Tissot, Fantin-Latour, Degas, Zola, and a young American artist who was then studying in Paris, J.M. Whistler. And it was Whistler who brought the Oriental revolution – for it was no less – to London in the early 1860s.

Young Arthur Liberty got himself a job at the Regent Street store of Farmer and Rogers, and in due course was promoted to the managership of the oriental

Liberty's supplied costumes and materials for the original productions of 'Patience' and 'The Mikado'

Go down Regent Street to its junction with Great Marlborough Street

Turn right: cross Regent Street into Hanover Street and then into Hanover Square

department, which specialised in Indian shawls, but also stocked Japanese prints, drawings, lacquers and bric-a-brac. By 1875 Liberty felt confident enough to branch out on his own and opened a shop at 218a Regent Street with one assistant and a porter. Success came immediately. Within a very short time Liberty's customers included Carlyle, Ruskin, the Rossettis, the architect Norman Shaw, Charles Keane, Whistler, Watts, Burne-Jones, Leighton, Millais and Alma-Tadema. Even trade rivals like William Morris called regularly to buy exotic fabrics quite unobtainable elsewhere. In less than twelve months Liberty had to take premises next door to cope with the demand. The opening of the Grosvenor Gallery in 1877 set the seal of social acceptability on his fabrics and prints and Liberty, for his part, actively supported Aestheticism and the Pre-Raphaelites by developing fabric designs, interior decor and even occasional furniture very much in accordance with their tastes and precepts.

By 1881 Gilbert had completed *Patience*, his satire on Aestheticism and all its works, and called on Liberty's to find suitable fabrics for the ladies' chorus. He took his own sketches, which bore a remarkable resemblance to the style of Burne-Jones, and as well as dress fabrics purchased authentic drapes, beads and pottery ware. Never one to miss a business opportunity, D'Oyly Carte followed up by securing from Liberty a full page advertisement in the *Patience* programme for its entire run.

George Edwardes said that in *Patience* Gilbert had managed 'to catch the very spirit of Aestheticism and hold it up for the world to laugh at ...the occasional chair, the Liberty curtain from the East ...' But even he had to admit, somewhat ruefully, that his wife had insisted on furnishing their new home throughout with fabrics purchased from Liberty's.

Happily for Gilbert and Sullivan the vogue for Japanese designs and all things Japanese persisted, and by the time they were ready with *The Mikado*, some three years later, the fashion was still at its height. For the principal characters antique robes and kimonos were borrowed from Japan, but the rest of the cast were dressed in fabrics from Liberty's who, once again, obligingly took advertising space in the programme.

The Hanover Square Concert Rooms, which were opened at 4 Hanover Square on 1 February 1775, occupied a unique position in the London concert scene for nearly 120 years. Most of the famous singers and soloists of the period performed here at one time or another. Johann Christian Bach gave regular concerts in the Rooms from 1776 to 1782, and another famous series, the Salomon subscription concerts, followed soon after between 1786 and 1794. From 1785 onwards an annual performance of *Messiah* became part of an established tradition that endured for more than 60 years, and from 1833 to 1869 the Philharmonic Society, leading promoters at that time, used the Hanover Square Concert Rooms for their annual seasons, in each of which eight concerts were presented. The Royal Academy of Music also gave occasional concerts here between 1823 and 1874.

The concert hall, which had a seating capacity of 900 and was said to have excellent acoustics, was on the first floor of the building. Below were a wide foyer, a tea room and various offices. The Rooms could be hired not only for concerts, but also for balls, masquerades and banquets. The arched ceiling was decorated with paintings by such well-known artists as Gainsborough aand Cipriani. It was later embellished, in 1845, with medallions showing the heads of composers such as Byrd, Bellini, Cherubini, Donizetti, Gluck, Palestrina and Pergolesi.

In 1856 a split in the ranks of the Philharmonic Society led to the formation of the Musical Society of London, which remained in existence for some time. It was an exclusive group that catered for a select audience by keeping seat prices high and this, in turn, meant that they could command the services of performers of the calibre, for example, of Clara Schumann, a friend both of Sir George Grove and of Sir Arthur Sullivan. Among its honorary members the Musical Society of London numbered Auber, Berlioz, Joachim, Rossini and Spohr, many of whom made personal appearances at the concerts.

Meanwhile, the Philharmonic Society followed the normal practice of the day by presenting programmes consisting of a wide variety of items drawn almost at random from the orchestral, instrumental, choral and even operatic repertoire. Major works would be interspersed with shorter pieces of no apparent relevance whatever, in a manner which modern audiences would find completely baffling. It was at one of these concerts, in 1855, that Arthur Sullivan sang one of his own pieces with Sterndale Bennett conducting: later that same season Richard Wagner made his London debut as a conductor. In 1875 the freehold of the building was sold, and the concert hall became the Hanover Square Club. By then, the Philharmonic Society had already transferred their concerts to the St. James's Hall. Later, they moved to Queen's Hall.

The church of St. George in Hanover Square has for more than 200 years been one of the most fashionable in London for marriages within the Church of England, and probably has more members of the aristocracy in its congregation than that of any other church in the country. Its parish certainly represents the most valuable piece of real estate in Britain. It was in this church on 29 December 1820 that Richard D'Oyly Carte's paternal grandfather married for the second time: the only thing known about his bride is her name, Mary Large.

Cross Hanover Square to its north-west corner, at its junction with Tenterden Street

Until 1912 the Royal Academy of Music stood on the corner of Hanover Square and Tenterden Street. Founded in 1822 under the patronage of King George IV the Academy was to have provided residential places for 80 mixed students, but when it opened in March 1823 only 21 boys had been registered. This was an unhappy portent of things to come, for during the first 40 years of its existence the Academy was beset by financial difficulties. A royal charter was granted in 1830, and four years later William IV decreed that one quarter of the proceeds from the annual music festival at Westminster Abbey should be given to the Academy. The rest of the funding came mostly from donations and scholarships. One of these, the Mendelssohn Scholarship, financed by the proceeds of a memorial concert given by Jenny Lind, enabled Arthur Sullivan, then aged 14, to attend as a scholar, and he remained in close touch with the Academy throughout the rest of his musical career.

It was not until 1868 that the Academy received any financial help from the state, and when it came it was meagre in the extreme. Under Gladstone's government an annual grant of £500 was awarded, and even this was promptly cancelled on Disraeli's return to power. But despite all the problems and the pressures the Academy grew in reputation and in stature, so much so that when the time came to leave Hanover Square in 1912 it was able to move into new, custom-built premises in Marylebone Road.

Sullivan won his scholarship in open competition with 14 other boys, all his senior. He studied harmony and counterpoint under John Goss, and the piano under Sterndale Bennett, with whom he dined at his home in Russell Street. He was popular with his tutors, his scholarship was renewed for three years in succession, and his outstanding merit was recognized by the Academy. Special arrangements were made for Sullivan to go to the Leipzig Conservatoire to enable him to extend his studies.

Return to the western side of Hanover Square and turn into Brook Street. Turn left at the traffic lights into New Bond Street

In February 1875 Sullivan returned to the Academy as a part-time professor, a post he held for two years. During this time he was also musical director of the Royal Aquarium and, later, director of the National Training School for Music. This new institution came into being, ironically enough, largely as a result of criticism levelled at the Academy to the effect that talented students unable to pay the fees were being turned away, and that too few orchestral musicians were being produced.

Thomas Bond, Comptroller of the Household of Queen Henrietta Maria, and who was later given a baronetcy, was the man who gave his name to Bond Street and to New Bond Street. He bought the estate from the Earl of Clarendon and laid it out in a formal manner with Bond Street as one of its main thoroughfares. It soon became one of the most fashionable streets in London. Lord Nelson lived for a short time at No.14, the author, Laurence Sterne, lived and died at No.41 and a good deal later, in 1877, Sir Coutts Lindsey built a residence at No.135 to Italian Renaissance designs by Soames which required a Palladian doorway to be brought all the way from Venice. This remarkable building was a picture gallery much more than a house. It was built more or less as an annexe to a restaurant next door, in which an inaugural banquet, attended by the Prince and Princess of Wales, was held in May 1877. As the Grosvenor Gallery it became a meeting-place for aesthetes and Pre-Raphaelites. The works of Dante Gabriel Rossetti, Burne-Jones, Holman Hunt and Whistler were regularly exhibited, and other celebrities of the day, including Swinburne, William Morris and Oscar Wilde, were frequent visitors. They treated the place as a club, for such it had virtually become, and made regular use of its facilities including a lending library. Lindsay's aim was to:

'afford to pictures and sculptures the advantage they receive in private homes from the background of harmoniously patterned walls and appropriate furniture.'

He also promoted an annual exhibition of works rejected by the Royal Academy for their summer show, and the two institutions became serious rivals as arbiters of artistic taste in London.

'I'm a Waterloo House young man', from the 1939 production of 'Patience' by the D'Oyly Carte Opera Company

The walls of the Grosvenor Gallery were painted green and gold – greenery-yallery. Among the paintings in the opening exhibition were eight by Burne-Jones, including *Merlin and Venus*, and Whistler's *Nocturne in Black and Gold: The Falling Rocket*, which provoked Ruskin's attack and the subsequent libel action. Such boldness enabled the Grosvenor to establish a leadership among members of the avant-garde movement during the 1880s. Millais first exhibited his portrait of Sullivan on 28 April 1888, but we know from his diary that the composer was far too nervous to attend the opening and chose to see the painting quietly the following day. Two years earlier Sullivan had played host at a reception given at the Grosvenor Gallery in honour of Franz Liszt on his first visit to England. In 1890 the exhibitions were transferred to the New Gallery and the two adjacent buildings, 134 and 135 Bond Street, were used exclusively as a social club for gentlemen, known as the Grosvenor Club, until its closure 12 years later.

Take the 2nd turning left (Conduit Street) into Regent Street. Turn right into Regent Street

At the corner of 193-7 Regent Street and 60-65 Conduit Street stood another well-known firm of silk mercers, Lewis and Allenby. The owner, Arthur Lewis, and his wife gave house parties at their home at Moray Lodge on Campden Hill, from which came the Moray Minstrels, the amateur group for whom Frank Burnand and Arthur Sullivan wrote *Cox and Box*. Two other firms should be mentioned at this point. The first is the well-known milliner, Madame Louise, who had premises at 210-210a and at 266-268 Regent Street, and the celebrated

74

outfitters Swears and Wells, who occupied 192 Regent Street before moving to Oxford Street in the 1920s.

Another familiar landmark in Regent Street is the Café Royal, an elegant restaurant and banqueting suite that flourished during the Edwardian era, especially after Romano's and Gatti's closed down in the Strand. With its magnificent reception hall and sumptuous balcony encircling the splendid restaurant under a gold-embossed cornice, the Café Royal was described by George Edwardes as a place 'where love birds stole a march on their chaperones'.

During the last two years of his life Gilbert lunched regularly at the Café Royal with the Dramatists Club. Other favourite haunts were the Criterion Restaurant and the Burlington Hotel, where he could often be seen in the company of other writers such as Arthur Pinero, R.C. Carton, Anthony Hope, J.M. Barrie, Cecil Raleigh and a very young Somerset Maugham.

Continue to Piccadilly Circus

Until the 1880s the circus at each end of John Nash's great thoroughfare was known as 'Regent's Circus', a source of considerable confusion. What we now know as Piccadilly Circus was for many years dominated by Swan and Edgar's, which became a favourite place of rendezvous in this part of London. The store closed as recently as 1983 when the Debenham Group sold the site, now occupied by Tower Records. Of all the grand and fashionable drapers and costumiers mentioned by name in the Savoy Operas Swan and Edgar's were the last to survive and are very much missed.

The Swan and Edgar building, now Tower Records, at Piccadilly Circus

At the heart of Piccadilly Circus is the Cupid-like figure of Eros which was originally poised above a fountain erected in memory of the much-loved philanthropist Anthony Ashley Cooper, Earl of Shaftesbury. Until his death in 1885 he campaigned vigorously against the appalling conditions under which far too many women and children were employed in Victorian England, and he set up a number of charities to help them. He is further remembered, of course, by the avenue that bears his name, cut through the slums of Soho in 1896. The statue of Eros was designed by Alfred Gilbert to point up Shaftesbury Avenue, but after being restored recently it has, mysteriously, been put back facing the wrong way.

The word 'Piccadilly' is said to derive from 'pikadil', which was a starched collar invented in 1617 by a highly successful tailor, Robert Baker. He made his fortune in the reign of James I and, having done so, he built himself an imposing house on the country lane leading westwards out of London at its junction with Hedge Lane, now Coventry Street. Local country bumpkins, presumably much amused by the pretensions of this social upstart, promptly dubbed the new house 'Pickadilly Hall', and it is by this nickname that is identified in some contemporary records. From 1624 to 1683 the house was used for gaming purposes other than during the days of the Commonwealth, and as other houses came to be built (there were eleven houses and two inns by 1651) the original house gave its name to the area as a whole.

Turn right immediately up Swallow Street and right again into Vine Street

Between 1664 and 1670 the Lord Chancellor, Lord Clarendon, built a large mansion at Piccadilly, which was later purchased by the 2nd Duke of Albemarle, and by the early years of the 18th century Sir Thomas Bond appeared on the scene, and much of his planning survives to this day. During the 1880s Piccadilly became an extremely fashionable shopping and residential area: many of the houses have since been converted into hotels, offices or clubs. It also became a favourite promenade during the summer season especially when, as now, the annual exhibition of paintings is on at Burlington House. Despite many changes

*The Classical Monday
Popular Concerts were
held in St. James's
Hall from February 1859
to March 1901*

**Return to Piccadilly
and turn right**

in recent years, Piccadilly and Piccadilly Circus remain major tourist attractions in London.

The London headquarters of the international carriers, Pickfords, were for many years at 5 Vine Street. Established in the 1740s, Pickfords had become a household name, with offices and depositories all over Britain and extensive wharfage along the Thames. One of their advertisements claimed, about 100 years ago, that they were 'general carriers and agents to the London and North Western and other railway companies, shipping and custom house agents, town carmen and furniture removers.' Or as their slogan, quoted by Gilbert, put it rather more succinctly, 'We carry everything'.

Where the Piccadilly Hotel now stands was the site of the St. James's Hall, occupying the whole block and with entrances at 73 Regent Street and 28 Piccadilly. The main hall, with a seating capacity of 2,127, was the largest in central London. As a result, seat prices were lower than at the Hanover Square Concert Rooms or at the St. George's Hall. In the winter season of 1858-9 the music publisher, William Chappell, launched a series which he called 'Classical Monday Popular Concerts', with seats at 3/- and 1/-. The venture proved very successful and came to occupy centre stage in London's musical life. Many distinguished soloists from continental Europe were engaged, Clara Schumann and Joachim among them, and it was at one of these concerts that Sullivan first met Sir George Grove, with whom he formed a close friendship. From 1862 until well into the 1890s St. James's Hall was also regularly used by the splinter group from Hanover Square, which now called itself the Philharmonic Society.

It was not only music that was in demand. Charles Dickens drew large audiences here every week at his public readings of such works as *David Copperfield*, *A Tale of Two Cities* and *Great Expectations*, for which the admission charge was four shillings.

*Arthur Sullivan
as a young man*

Arthur Sullivan made his first major appearance at the St. James's Hall on 11 July 1866 when, under the sponsorship of Jenny Lind, he conducted a 'Grand Orchestral Concert' in a programme of his own works. These included four songs, the overture *The Sapphire Necklace*, the *Bush Dance* from *Kenilworth*, and his E major Symphony. The following year, in May, his song *Oh, Hush Thee My Babie* was performed by Barnby's Choir, and in June 1867 the overture *Marmion* was included in a programme. Sullivan himself conducted *The Martyr of Antioch* on 18 March 1881 and *The Golden Legend* on 23 November 1886.

His earlier appearances at St. James's Hall were of less consequence to him as a composer. On 29 July 1880 he performed the sad task of delivering an eulogy at a concert given in memory of Sir George Grove, 'that lovable and delightful man.' On 27 May 1881 he accompanied Mrs Ronalds who sang *The Lost Chord*, a piece he came cordially to dislike as his career progressed. In 1885 he conducted a concert for the Philharmonic Society which featured none of his own music but did include a Brahms symphony (No.3 – written just a year earlier) and the Beethoven violin concerto. On 9 April 1886 he met Franz Liszt once more, at a concert to honour the distinguished guest, and afterwards escorted him to a party given by the Prince of Wales.

The reference to St. James's Hall in *Utopia Limited* is made in a much less exalted context referring, as it does, to the smaller of the two halls, in which

*Burlington Arcade in
the heart of fashionable
Mayfair*

entertainments of a very different kind were presented. These included Moore and Burgess's Christy Minstrels, much in vogue at the time, blacked-up entertainers named after E.P. Christie's Virginian Serenaders who had originally come to London in 1842 under the aegis of a showman with the resounding name of George Washington Moore. Their successors opened at St. James's Hall in 1871 and they were still playing, both there and on tour, when *Utopia Limited* was staged more than twenty years later. On the whole, their antics and some of their material were frowned upon by respectable members of society, and Gilbert's reference to them in his libretto was none too well received.

In many different ways St. James's Hall served its London audiences faithfully and well, and its demolition at the turn of the century was one of many omens signifying change and the end of a great era. The hotel now standing in its place, designed by Norman Shaw, was started in 1905 and completed three years later. On the southern side of Piccadilly is yet another famous name to conjure with, Fortnum and Mason, whose reputation for excellence is world-wide. Of particular renown is their food hall, in which you will find a large clock with a 24" cylinder musical box which plays extracts from *The Mikado*. The clock is actually named after the opera, and was made in 1886 by Symphonium of Leipzig under licence from Richard D'Oyly Carte.

Turn right up Sackville Street and then left and right into Savile Row

Savile Row, for many years the home of bespoke tailoring in London, takes its name from Dorothy Savile, wife of the Earl of Burlington. Two houses of interest are No. 14, where Richard Brinsley Sheridan lived, and No. 23, where the Alpine Club of *Thespis* was established. Near at hand is Burlington Arcade, built in 1815 for Lord George Cavendish to designs by Ware. This has become famous for its 'small shops and tall beadles' and is a favourite haunt of tourists to London of all nationalities. The 'Beadles of Burlington' came into being in 1819 as a three-man force to prevent any disturbance or unseemly behaviour in the Arcade. Whistling is still prohibited and it would be a brave Londoner, or an even braver tourist, who would dare to disturb the tranquillity of this most dignified of all pedestrian precincts.

Return to Burlington Gardens and turn right. Turn left into Burlington Arcade. At the far end turn right for Green Park Underground station

Chapter 8

ST.JAMES'S

**A circular walk from
Piccadilly Circus
Underground: allow 2 hours**

The name by which this fashionable part of central London has long been known goes back as far as the 11th century, when a hospital was founded for 'maidens with leprosy' and dedicated to St.James the Less, Bishop of Jerusalem. Four hundred years later King Henry VIII made the hospital administrators an offer which it would have been imprudent to have refused, and so it came about that they exchanged their land for a royal estate in Suffolk. The King lost no time building an attractive brick mansion around several courtyards: the gatehouse, or clock tower, with its original doors with linenfold panelling is now one of London's most familiar landmarks.

On the Dissolution of the Monasteries (1536-9) Henry seized from the Abbot of Westminster an adjacent plot of land, 93 acres in all, which he enclosed to form the royal park of St.James's. However, by this time he seemed to be more interested in Whitehall Palace and he made that his formal London residence. It was not until Whitehall burned down in 1698 that St. James's Palace took over the central role. The court became the 'Court of St.James's', a title by which it is known today and to which ambassadors from abroad are still accredited, despite the fact that Buckingham Palace has been the royal residence since Queen Victoria came to the throne in 1837.

With such an auspicious background and favoured location it is not surprising that St. James's, often described as 'the heart of London's clubland', has over the years upheld its reputation for high fashion and elegance. As well as numerous clubs, other fine buildings house foreign embassies or have become the London headquarters of many professional and commercial organisations. Others now

The royal park of St. James's, with the buildings of Whitehall in the background, c.1900

Take the Lower Regent Street exit: walk down the east (left-hand) side

have luxurious shops at ground floor level, often with well-appointed offices or flats on the upper floors. It is, above all, a district which breathes an air of style and affluence. In Lower Regent Street stands the BBC Radio Paris Studio where some of today's London-based radio shows, including *My Music*, are produced. Tradition has it that near this spot, in the Gallery of Illustration at 14 Regent Street (as it was then) Gilbert and Sullivan first met. They were introduced to each other, or so the story goes, by their mutual friend Fred Clay. Gilbert later produced his rather tedious anecdote about confusing Sullivan with a meaningless musical question.

All this is said to have happened on 21 November 1869[1], but there are other dates on which it is claimed that their first meeting took place. Eden[2] puts it on or about 11 July 1870, but more likely is December 1868 at the Gaiety Theatre, or earlier at either the Savage or the Beefsteak Club. Whichever date is correct, the Gallery of Illustration plays an important part in the Gilbert and Sullivan story because it was here that the young librettist developed dramatic skills which produced those later *coups de theatre* which only the brilliance of Sullivan's music could match. In February 1856, as we have seen, the conductor of the Theatre Royal orchestra, Thomas German Reed, and his wife Priscilla Horton, who had acted and sung at Covent Garden and the Haymarket Theatre, transferred her 'Illustrative Gatherings' to 14 Regent Street which they called the 'Gallery of Illustration'. These quite remarkable productions offered a style of family entertainment unique to the London stage.

Plays were called 'illustrations'; roles 'assumptions'; audiences were known as 'gatherings'; acts 'parts'; while the set was always referred to as the 'drawing room'. Musical accompaniment either on the piano or harmonium was of much less importance than the words of the plays, which were also known as 'chamber dramas'. And although they had more than a touch of Victorian religiosity about them, they were in their own way of very good value. The Gallery in which they presented was little more than a bijou theatre but the stage could be seen from every seat in the house, which is more than can be said for some London theatres even today. Admission charges were moderate, but the productions proved so popular that the German Reeds were able to attract leading writers and scenic artists of the day, Telbin, Beverley and O'Connor among them. According to Fitzgerald:[3]

'these elegant little dramas .. provide a harmless pleasant sort of show to which a worthy 'Dr Daly' from the country or the strictest matron can bring their children without fear of damage.'

So, from his comparatively humble beginnings as an orchestral musician Thomas German Reed had become by the late 1860s a successful impresario who had had the good sense to acquire a gifted, enterprising wife and who, to be fair, brought to the partnership many talents of his own. For example, he wrote the scripts for some productions and the music for others. On 11 April 1867 he went to a charity performance at the Adelphi Theatre where he saw the production of *Cox and Box* that made such an impression on him. He lost no time in acquiring the rights from Burnand and Arthur Sullivan, although for reasons not entirely clear he did not mount his own production of the piece immediately, as might have been expected. Instead, he gave them a new commission for a major work to

St. James's Theatre c.1840 and in 1957

[1]Wilson, F.W. *The Gilbert and Sullivan Birthday Book* Dobbs Ferry, New York: Cahill and Co.,1983
[2]Eden, David *Gilbert and Sullivan – The Creative Conflict* London: Associated University Presses, 1986
[3]Fitzgerald, Percy *The Gilbert and Sullivan Operas* Philadelphia: Lippincott, 1894

be presented at St. George's Hall. When it arrived it turned out to be a flop despite its promising title, *Contrabandista*.

Cox and Box opened at the Gallery of Illustration on 29 March 1869 to the delight of audiences, and ran for 300 performances. On the same bill appeared *No Cards*, for which Fred Clay wrote the music to words by W.S. Gilbert. It was in this way that his name first appeared with Sullivan's on the same programme, but not against the same work. On 22 November 1869 Clay and Gilbert followed *No Cards* with another successful production, *Ages Ago*, which played for well over 350 performances, more than the initial runs of some Gilbert and Sullivan operas such as *Trial by Jury*, *The Sorcerer* and *H.M.S.Pinafore*. German Reed wanted Sullivan to write the music for Gilbert's next piece, *Our Island Home*, and when the composer declined he settled down and wrote the full score himself. Two more successful pieces by W.S.Gilbert followed: *A Sensation Novel* in January 1871 and *Happy Arcadia* in October 1872. Two years later the lease of the Gallery of Illustration expired and the German Reeds had to find a new home for their entertainments. They chose St George's Hall (*see Chapter 6*) and took with them their star comedian Corney Grain. In later years their business passed into the hands of their son, but it did not survive his death in 1895.

On the south-east corner of Lower Regent Street and Charles II Street, previously numbered as 7-9 Regent Street, were the premises of Messrs. Howell and James, fashionable Victorian drapers. The firm started out as court jewellers and added its drapery department later: it is listed in 1881 as selling 'jewellery, silverware, artwork and pottery'. The firm was well-known for its exhibitions, held between May and July of each year, of 'Paintings on China by Lady Amateur Artists'.

Unlike Liberty's, who created their own designs, Howell and James followed fashion, but did so with considerable success. Their most famous coup came ten years or so after *The Mikado* when, within hours of the opening at the Gaiety Theatre of the musical comedy *The Geisha*, which was to prove outstandingly popular, the store put on prominent display all kinds of Japanese designs and souvenirs. A post with Howell and James was so much sought after that to become a sales assistant it was said that the applicant had first to pay a premium of £100 to cover the cost of training, and then to work without salary for the first six months.

Howell and James closed down in 1904. The building with which their business was most closely connected was Waterloo House, which seems to be confirmed by the fact that just beyond Charles II Street is Waterloo Place. Other authorities insist that Waterloo House was to be found in Cockspur Street, housing other drapers, Halling, White, Pearce and Stone. But nowhere in the trade directories of the 1860s or 1870s is there any reference to a Waterloo House in Cockspur Street.

Until the 1st World War, the Portland Club was at 9 St.James's Square. Unlike other clubs in the vicinity it was exclusively a gaming club, and by 1885 Sullivan was a very regular visitor, sometimes gambling at cards the whole night. On one occasion he rose from the table at 6 a.m. having won £102 playing bezique with Sir Charles Russell, Lord Chief Justice. Gambling had become such an obsession that even after the first night of *The Mikado* instead of joining the celebrations he rushed back to the Portland in order to resume his card game.

Near the corner of King Street and St.James's Square, where the office block 'St.James's House' now stands, there was one of the most elegant playhouses in the whole of London. For most of its 120 years it was known as the St.James's

Make for the south-east corner of Lower Regent Street and Charles II Street

Corney Grain, the German Reeds principal comedian

Turn right into Charles II Street and into St.James's Square

Make for King Street on the opposite side of St.James's Square

Theatre but there were two short periods when it had other names. Between April 1840 and February 1842 it was called the Prince's Theatre, and between October 1869 and October 1879 it was the Theatre Royal, St. James's. Here in November 1866 Henry Irving scored his first London success in a play by Dion Boucicault and Holcroft, and four weeks later, Gilbert made his writing debut in this same theatre.

He had a dramatist friend, Tom Robertson, who allowed Gilbert to drop in at rehearsals. The licensee of the St. James's, a Miss Herbert, asked Robertson at rather short notice to write a novelty programme for the Christmas season. He declined, but recommended Gilbert who within ten days completed a burlesque on Donizetti's *L'Elisir d'Amore* which he called *Dulcamara, or the Little Duck and the Great Quack*. After a week of rehearsal it opened on 29 December 1866 with Frank Matthews in the leading role, and ran successfully until Easter 1867. This gave Gilbert the confidence to turn to full-time writing, and the funds he needed to take a wife: two ambitions he had cherished for some time.

Rutland Barrington

When his next work appeared at the St. James's Theatre in 1875 Gilbert was a writer with a well-established reputation. The new lessee, Marie Lytton commissioned him to write a comedy: he duly obliged with *Tom Cobb, or Fortune's Toy*. It turned out to be the most successful production during the whole of Miss Lytton's management. It opened on 29 April 1875 as part of a triple bill, and for a short period in June of that year one of its companion pieces was *The Zoo* by Stephenson and Arthur Sullivan, which ran for 18 days before moving on to the Theatre Royal, Haymarket. And so, once again, the names of Gilbert and Sullivan briefly appeared on the same theatre bill.

More than a decade later, just before the opening of *The Yeomen of the Guard*, Rutland Barrington left the D'Oyly Carte Opera Company to take over the management of the St. James's Theatre. His opening night was a disaster, and Gilbert stepped in as soon as he could to rescue him with a new play, *Brantinghame Hall*, which opened on 29 November 1888. Despite this gallant attempt, Barrington's ambition to become an independent producer was not fulfilled. Not long afterwards Oscar Wilde made his debut at this theatre with *Lady Windermere's Fan*, which opened on 20 February 1892. For another sixty years the St. James's was a familiar and attractive feature of London's theatrical world, but in the 1950s it fell victim to the pressures of rising land values and the relentless thrust of West End property development.

Turn right along King Street

The Savage Club, now in Fitzmaurice Place just off Berkeley Square, had premises at 37 King Street, although it would be more accurate to say that they had one of their premises at that address, as Hollingshead explains:

> The Savage is little more than a glorified tap room, a day and evening club, peripatetic from necessity rather than from choice, moving from pot-house to pot-house when the landlords discovered that they could use their 'long rooms' for a more profitable purpose than as a house of call for lower Bohemians.'

Among its other addresses were Adelphi Terrace, the Savoy Hotel and No.1 Carlton House Terrace. The club was founded in 1857, and when Gilbert joined some seven years later the annual subscription was still only £1. His playwright friend Tom Robertson was one of the most active members. As the years went by the membership became more and more distinguished, so that by the time the 25th anniversary was reached we find the Prince of Wales presiding over their celebratory dinner. Sullivan, as well as Gilbert, was a member of the Savage and so too were J.L. Toole, Sir Frederick Leighton, G.A. Sala, Sir Squire Bancroft, G.A. Henty, Sir John Gilbert, Lord Kitchener, Lord Roberts and, until his accession to the throne, King George V.

At the end of King Street turn left into St. James's Street and on to St. James's Palace

The Chapel Royal in January 1858, as Sullivan would have known it during his last year as a boy chorister

St. James's Palace

The best-known landmark in this part of London is certainly St. James's Palace, with its familiar clock tower and sentries from the Household Division on duty in the gateway. The present clock was installed when the original was moved to Hampton Court Palace during the reign of William IV. On the other hand, the Guard Room, the Chapel Royal and the Presence or Tapestry Room, bearing the initials of Henry VIII and Anne Boleyn, are all part of the original fabric of the building. At various times the Palace has been the residence of Edward VI, Elizabeth I and Mary, also the birthplace of Charles II, James II, Mary II, Anne and George IV. It was here that Charles I spent the last night before his execution in the Guard Room, where one of his retainers scratched an inscription on a glass window.

In Friary Court the Changing of the Guard takes place daily when the Queen is in residence at Buckingham Palace. Overlooking the Court is the balcony from which the Proclamation is read on the death of a monarch. To one side is the Ambassadors Court, where credentials are presented, and next to that is the Presence Room, with its William Morris ceiling, where until 1865 Queen Victoria received each season's debutantes. It was this 'coming-out' ceremony that

Gilbert seized upon in his most lavish scene in Act II of *Utopia Limited*. A parquet floor was built to cover the entire stage, five costumiers were hired to make the costumes and a deportment teacher to put the young ladies of the chorus carefully through their paces. After the public dress rehearsal, this spectacular scene became the subject of a good deal of gossip. Cellier and Bridgeman say that the exact and faithful representation of the ceremony gave rise to a lot of displeasure in the English Court and among the Establishment of the day[4]. On the other hand, Audrey Williamson says there is no evidence that the royal family were offended:on the contrary, note was taken of the fact that the poor girls had nothing to eat or drink, with the result that the 'cheap and effective innovation' of providing tea and biscuits to the debutantes followed shortly afterwards.[5]

In Gilbert's day St.James's Palace fulfilled more than purely formal or ceremonial functions, for within its walls were the offices of the Lord Chamberlain in whose department was the Censor of Stage Plays. In 1907 he banned a revival of *The Mikado* to avoid any possibility of offending Prince Fushimi of Japan during his state visit to Britain.

Take Marlborough Road to the Chapel Royal

At one time the Chapel Royal was attached to the main Palace, but in 1809 a road was cut through the grounds after a fire had damaged part of the structure. The 32 gentlemen choristers and 16 choirboys who belong to the Chapel Royal have enjoyed royal patronage since the early 16th century. Henry VII, Henry VIII, Edward VI and Mary each maintained the Choir from private funds. But it was during the reign of Queen Elizabeth I that the Choir became largest and the most renowned in the land. The singers were paid more than three times the average national wage of the day and the children were placed under 'the governance of a Master'. The golden age of Elizabethan church music had dawned, and the traditional excellence of the choir was maintained right up until its closure in 1923. It was here that Arthur Sullivan sang both as a member of the choir and as a treble soloist.

Behind and slightly to the right of the Chapel is Marlborough House, standing in its own grounds and protected by a high wall. It was built for the 1st Duke of Marlborough, victor of Blenheim, and remained in his family until it passed to the Crown in 1817. It was occupied by Leopold I of Belgium until his accession in 1831 and then by Queen Adelaide. After her death in 1849 it became the official residence of the Prince of Wales and, although he much preferred York House, he moved into it when he married Alexandra in 1863. By this time Sullivan had become one of Edward's many friends and was a frequent visitor to Marlborough

Back along Marlborough Road and turn right into Pall Mall

House where the royal couple remained until Queen Victoria died in 1901. Young Prince George was born here in 1865, and when he succeeded to the throne his mother returned to Marlborough House to spend the rest of her days.

Facing the gates of Marlborough House and Clarence House on Pall Mall, which owes its name to the Tudor game of pell mell, was the Marlborough Club which was by far the most exclusive of the many gentlemen's clubs to which Sullivan belonged. Proposed by Prince Christian and seconded by the Duke of Edinburgh he was duly elected in January 1881. After paying his entrance fee and first year's subscription of £42 he first dined as a full member on 23 January and a few weeks later, on 12 May, he threw a party in the club to celebrate his 39th birthday. His guests included the Duke of Edinburgh, the Duke of Connaught,

[4]Cellier and Bridgeman *Gilbert, Sullivan and D'Oyly Carte* London: Isaac Pitman & Sons, 1914
[5]Williamson, Audrey *Gilbert and Sullivan Opera – A New Assessment* London: Rockliff, 1953

Fred Clay, Michael Costa, Alfred Rothschild, Rueben Sassoon, Edward Hall, George Lewis, John Millais, W.S.Gilbert and Tom Chappell. A later diary entry tells us that on 22 December 1886 he dined in the club privately with the Prince of Wales, the Duke of Cambridge and Alexander Mackenzie. Exalted circles indeed.

Further along Pall Mall, at No.42, were premises of a very different kind belonging to the well-known clock-makers Lund & Blockley who, in August 1886, made the special bells required in *The Golden Legend*. At 30 Pall Mall the Junior Carlton Club opened its doors in 1868 and almost immediately Gilbert enrolled as a member. From that time onwards he seems to have regarded himself as a Conservative although there is no evidence to suggest that he ever took an active part in politics. Gilbert was probably more interested in the fine library and collection of portraits at the Junior Carlton, and he kept up his membership there until the day he died. Indeed, on that fateful day, 29 May 1911, he took lunch in the Club, patching up a quarrel with the Kendals which had gone on for many years, before returning to Grim's Dyke where he met his end.

Carry on to the corner of Pall Mall and Waterloo Place

On the corner of Pall Mall and Waterloo Place stands one of London's oldest and most prestigious clubs, the Athenaeum. The reference we find in *Ruddigore* is, however, not to these august premises but to a number of provincial centres for scientific and literary pursuits which adopted the name.

Turn left out of Pall Mall at the traffic lights into the Haymarket

At 7-8 Haymarket stands the Theatre Royal with its famous Corinthian portico which was added by John Nash in 1820. Formerly it was called the Little Theatre in the Haymarket – a delightful name – and received its royal patent in 1766 in rather a bizarre manner. The manager at that time, while in the presence of the Duke of York, met with an accident in which he had the misfortune to lose a leg. The Duke intervened on his behalf and obtained the letters patent, which was no mere formality as the legal status of the establishment was in some doubt.

The original building dates back to 1720 and thanks to its location it managed to survive the fire scourge which ravaged so many other theatres over so long a

Gilbert's longest club membership was with the Junior Carlton in Pall Mall

The Theatre Royal,
Haymarket

period. Indeed, it often accommodated companies who had been rendered
temporarily homeless. The enterprising Thomas German Reed held his post as
musical director here from 1838 to 1851 before moving on to St.Martin's Hall.
The manager was the comedian J.B. Buckstone, who after 34 years in the job was
succeeded by Sir Herbert Beerbohm Tree. Under Buckstone's management the
theatre kept to its outmoded business and retained its very old-fashioned atmosphere. There were no stalls; the pit occupied all the space in front of the stage.
The auditorium was lit by candles, and Buckstone would appear every evening
resplendent in court dress accompanied by ushers bearing candelabra. At the end
of each performance it was solemnly announced from the stage that 'the play
would be repeated every night until further notice'. All in all, the Theatre Royal,
Haymarket, remained a charming 18th century survival. Authors were paid £50
an act for original works, plus 96 seats for each performance. At 9 p.m. the doors
were opened to allow people in at half-price. Actors were paid on a fixed salary
scale: up to £20 a week for the leading roles, a small fortune in those days. The
one concession Buckstone made to modernity was to allow regular matinées at 2
p.m., following the example set by the Gaiety Theatre, and during 1873 even
some morning performances were put on as an experiment. It was in this theatre

86

that Gilbert scored his greatest non-operatic successes. Over a period of ten years he wrote seven plays for Buckstone which, with later revivals, kept his name on the billboards in the Haymarket for nearly twenty years, quite apart from all the other theatres that regularly staged his work.

The first piece produced here, on 6 July 1867, was a burlesque on *Robinson Crusoe*, but it was his success at the Olympic Theatre with *The Princess* four years later that caught Buckstone's attention. A commission quickly followed and the result was the first of the 'fairy comedies', *The Palace of Truth*, which opened on 19 November 1870. Every night Gilbert now found himself with 96 tickets he had no idea what to do with, so he decided to take steps to end this antique arrangement and to receive a cash payment in lieu: four guineas a performance for the first three months, and two guineas thereafter.

The Palace of Truth, written in blank verse like *The Princess*, was suggested by an idea of Palgrave Simpson. With Buckstone and Madge Kendal in the leading roles it ran for 150 nights, but even this success was eclipsed by Gilbert's next production at the theatre. This was his comic drama *Pygmalion and Galatea*, also starring Buckstone and the Kendals, which opened on 9 December 1871 and ran for 237 performances. During the course of the year Gilbert had no fewer than seven of his plays on the London stage, at the Court Theatre, the Gaiety Theatre, the Gallery of Illustration, as well as the Theatre Royal itself. *Pygmalion and Galatea* went into standard repertory and over the next 20 years earned Gilbert an estimated £40,000. It also provided a vehicle for such rising stars as Mary Anderson, Lillie Langtry and Julia Neilson. Two years later *The Wicked World* was presented. This was the play which drew a most hostile review from 'Enoch' in the *Pall Mall Gazette*, against which Gilbert brought a libel action attracting a lot of publicity and doing no harm, presumably, to box office takings. A year later almost to the day a serious drama specially written for the Kendals, *Charity*, had its first night on 3 January 1874.

In late 1876 Gilbert wrote two contrasting pieces for Marion Terry, his latest protégé: the drama *Dan'l Druce*, which had its premiere on 11 September, and a farcical comedy called *Engaged*, which first appeared in October with some success. In 1877 a revival of *Pygmalion and Galatea* fuelled the row between Gilbert and Henrietta Hodson, to whom Buckstone had promised the female lead. The author would have none of this, and since by this time he wielded a great deal of influence at the Theatre Royal, his view prevailed. Ten years later Buckstone found the management of the theatre too much of a financial strain and handed over to Beerbohm Tree, who promptly put on yet another successful revival of *Pygmalion and Galatea*, this time with Mary Anderson in the leading role. Two years later there was a revival of a production first seen in 1874 of *The Merry Wives of Windsor* for which Sullivan's incidental music was again used.

At the top end of Haymarket the road bears left to Piccadilly Circus The old pit at the Theatre Royal survived until 1904, when stalls were at last fitted and the whole of the interior redecorated. Nevertheless, the handsome building Gilbert knew is still very much with us and he would almost certainly endorse the view that it is, after Drury Lane, the most important theatre in the whole of London.

Westminster from the air

WESTMINSTER AND VICTORIA

Westminster to Victoria Underground stations: allow 2½ hours

The City of Westminster as it stands today occupies an area of about four square miles with Kensington and Chelsea to the west, Paddington, Holborn and Marylebone to the north, the City of London to the east and the Thames to the south. In medieval times it consisted of little more than land around Westminster Abbey and the royal Palace of Westminster. In accordance with the custom of the times sanctuary was granted to fugitives in the Abbey precincts, with the inevitable result that many vagabonds and other unsavoury characters gathered there: hence Little and Broad Sanctuary as well as Thieving Lane.

From Westminster Underground cross Westminster Bridge Road and walk round the Palace of Westminster

The dwellings occupied by these people and their successors came to be known as the Westminster rookery. Many of them were swept away when the broad boulevard of Victoria Street was created in 1851, the year of the Great Exhibition. Immediately to the north was an enclave of refugees from France, a fact commemorated by the name Petty France. Sullivan lived in Victoria Street for nearly twenty years, and it was an area Gilbert knew well during his early years at the Bar.

In the shadow of Big Ben and of Westminster Hall is New Palace Yard, now an enclosed car park for members of Parliament. Gilbert's precise stage directions for the second act of *Iolanthe* specify New Palace Yard as the setting. Walter Emden followed these instructions exactly, and depicted part of the front of Westminster Hall for the first production. In 1901 Gilbert wrote to Helen D'Oyly Carte suggesting that for all future productions this set should include a representation of the face of Big Ben showing the actual time, and that the tower should show a light when the House was actually sitting, an innovation introduced in reality in 1893. For once, Gilbert's suggestions were not taken up: they were thought to be too costly. In any case there is some inconsistency here: if accuracy is the sole aim, should not Private Willis be a Metropolitan Police constable or a member of the Special Branch, bearing mind that New Palace Yard is never guarded by troops in peacetime? For the 1977 silver jubilee production of the opera given by the D'Oyly Carte Company Gilbert's stage directions were ignored altogether for a new set was used showing the riverside of the Houses of Parliament, and featuring the famous terrace where members entertain their constituents and supporters to strawberry teas during the summer season.

Paradoxically, New Palace Yard refers not to Barry's mock-Gothic building which aroused so much controversy at the time, but to the much older Palace of Westminster which was built before 1066 by Edward the Confessor, on some foundations which date even further back to the time of King Canute. This small area has been a seat of government for well over a thousand years. Buildings have risen and have been replaced in a haphazard way over the centuries. Simon de Montfort summoned the first Parliament here in 1265 and subsequent meetings were held in the chapter house of the Abbey until their own council chamber was built. The House of Lords met in a hall next to St. Stephen's Chapel, which was

Westminster Hall, where the royal courts of justice were housed for 600 years

known as the Court of Requests, or White Hall. Henry VIII took this name when he decided to build his own sumptuous palace immediately next to the precincts of Westminster. Some centuries later in 1834 the old Palace of Westminster was destroyed by fire, leaving only part of the cloisters, St. Stephen's Chapel and, mercifully, Westminster Hall still standing. Rebuilding plans provoked a great deal of discussion. King William IV offered the government Green Park and even Buckingham Palace as possible alternative sites for new parliamentary buildings, but the Duke of Wellington expressed a preference for the riverside site because it could be more easily defended if ever the need arose. This view prevailed. Barry was appointed chief architect and from 1837, over a period of twenty years, the present building rose steadily on the site of its predecessor. The east or river frontage is 940ft long, Victoria Tower 336ft high and the clock tower housing Big Ben 316ft high. The famous bell weighs 13½ tons and was named after Sir Benjamin Hall who was Commissioner of Works when the clock, made by Dents, was installed in 1859.

Impressive though Barry's creation undoubtedly is, nothing in the Palace of Westminster can match the beauty and nobility of Westminster Hall, which is by

*Westminster Abbey,
the nation's church*

**From the Palace of
Westminster make for
Westminster Abbey**

far the most important survival from medieval times. Designed by Henry Yevele, who built the naves of Westminster Abbey and of Canterbury Cathedral, the Hall is 240ft long, 68ft wide and 92ft high to the centre of its twelve-bay hammerbeam roof. This is made of English oak and is considered to be the finest of its kind in the world.

Until the 14th century, Westminster Hall was used by the reigning monarch, when in London, for state banquets and to entertain ambassadors from abroad. From the latter part of the 13th century until 1825 it also housed the chief courts of English law. Many great historical events have taken place here. In 1305 the Scottish patriot, Sir William Wallace was condemned to death in the old hall, and in 1327 Edward II forced to abdicate. Other notable trials include those of Perkin Warbeck in 1498, Sir Thomas More and Bishop Fisher in 1535, Lord Protector Somerset in 1551, the Earl of Essex in 1601, Guy Fawkes and the seven conspirators in 1606 and the Earl of Strafford in 1641. There followed the trial of Charles I in 1649 and the installation of Cromwell as Lord Protector four years later. Titus Oates was convicted here in 1685, and the seven bishops acquitted in 1688. The impeachment of Warren Hastings ended with his acquittal in 1795, after a trial lasting seven years.

When the Hall was not used for formal occasions it was divided into a number of courts of superior jurisdiction – the King's Bench, Common Pleas, Exchequer, Chancery and Master of the Rolls. These were separated from each other by low partitions, with the corridors thus created full of shops selling not only law books and stationery, but also such things as toys, millinery, ale, coffee, sweetmeats – and even paintings. This chaotic state of affairs, which grew steadily worse throughout the 18th century, prevailed until the early 19th century, when a special annexe was built. Later, in 1882, the new Royal Courts of Justice were opened in the Strand, and it is in this building that for the past hundred years or so the dignity of English law has been upheld in a more seemly manner and to the satisfaction of successful litigants. During the early part of his career, Gilbert knew the courts well. He used to visit them frequently with Sir Charles Watkin-Wilkins, his pupil – master in 1863-4. Later, in October 1873, as his own litigant in the Court of Common Pleas at Westminster Hall, he sued Enoch, drama critic of the *Pall Mall Gazette*. In November 1878 he visited two very different trials in the same Court, those of Whistler v Ruskin, and Robertson v Labouchere. Three years later the action against the Comedy Opera Company concerning rights in *H.M.S.Pinafore* also came before the Court of Common Pleas, which found in favour of Gilbert and Sullivan.

It will be recalled that in *Trial by Jury* Gilbert refers to the Court of Exchequer, which was a common law court established by Edward I to deal with financial disputes between the Crown and ordinary citizens. It was abolished by the Judicature Act of 1873, so the reference is an anachronism. But perhaps the librettist should be allowed a certain amount of poetic licence in this case, since it is far easier to find rhymes for the word 'Exchequer' than it is for the names of the other courts of superior jurisdiction.

Westminster Abbey, or the Collegiate Church of St.Peter to use its full designation, is the nation's church, founded by Edward the Confessor on the site of a much earlier Benedictine Abbey. Every Coronation since that of William I in 1066 has taken place in the Abbey, which was largely rebuilt during the reign of Henry III. He, and all his successors up to and including George II, are buried here. It is quite beyond the scope of this book to describe the magnificent architecture of the Abbey and its precincts: each and every visitor must be left to make their own discoveries.

Cross Broad Sanctuary to Middlesex Guildhall

A comparative newcomer to Parliament Square is Middlesex Guildhall, built in 1906-1913 as the administrative headquarters of the County. No longer used for that purpose, the building has been converted to house the Middlesex Sessions, or Crown Court. Until 1913, these were held in the Sessions House at Clerkenwell, which was the venue Gilbert clearly had in mind when setting the stage for *Trial by Jury*.

Go to the north side of Parliament Square: turn left into Parliament Street

Within easy reach of the Houses of Parliament is Downing Street, named after its speculative builder Sir George Downing, who graduated from the University of Harvard in 1642. One of his assistants, Samuel Pepys, described him as a 'perfidious rogue'. He certainly managed to hold a post in the Treasury under Cromwell and to get himself knighted by Charles II after the Restoration. Downing Street itself was described as a 'pretty, open space, especially at the upper end where there are four or five very large and well-built houses fit for persons of honour and quality, each house having a pleasant prospect into St.James's Park.'[1]

Pass the Cenotaph in Whitehall, with Downing Street on the left

After the Glorious Revolution of 1688 all properties owned by the Earl of Lichfield, a retainer of James II's who joined him in exile, became forfeit to the Crown. No.10 Downing Street was among these. George I assigned it to one of his Hanoverian ministers, Baron Bothmar, upon whose death the house reverted to the Crown. George II offered it to his prime minister Sir Robert Walpole, who asked that it should not be a personal gift but one attached to the office. No.11 Downing Street is now the official residence of the Chancellor of the Exchequer, and No.12 houses the Government Chief Whip.

The offices of the Privy Council are in the building standing on the corner of Downing Street and Whitehall, where Gilbert spent a 'wretched' four years from 1856 to 1860. He had obtained by competitive examination a post as assistant clerk in the Education Department at a salary of £120 per annum, which amount placed him very firmly in the ranks of the lower middle class, as befitted his station in life. It was during his time in the Department that he wrote a letter to the *Times*, published on 3 October 1860, complaining about an assault in the street by guardsmen, in which he described himself as 'Lieutenant, Civil Service Rifles.'

Carry on to the Horse Guards

Horse Guards, named after the four regiments of cavalry raised by Charles II as his personal bodyguard, stands on a site which Inigo Jones intended to use for his great Palace of Whitehall, of which only the banqueting hall had been built at the time of his death. The present building, with its low arch beneath a clock tower, dates from 1747-1752 and is the headquarters of the Commander-in-Chief of the British army. The guard is mounted by the Household Cavalry of the Queen's Life Guard and is changed each day at 11 a.m. In the small courtyard immediately behind the sentries is the entrance to the Admiralty as Nelson would have known it, and where his body lay in state after it had been brought home from Trafalgar. The building is hidden by an elegant screen built to a design by Robert Adam in 1760. Horse Guards Parade looks out over St.James's Park and makes a very impressive setting for the ceremony of Trooping the Colour, performed each year by the Brigade of Guards and the Household Cavalry on the Queen's official birthday.

Through the archway into Horse Guards Parade

Cross Horse Guards Parade into St.James's Park. Turn left and exit into Birdcage Walk. Cross over to Queen Anne's Gate. At the Petty France junction turn left and cross over into Tothill Street

The land seized by Henry VIII for St. James's Park remained more or less desolate until the reign of James I, who showed great interest and actually started a menagerie. After the Restoration, Charles II called in the celebrated French

[1] Kent, William *An Encyclopaedia of London* London: J.M.Dent, 1951

landscape gardener Le Nôtre to draw up plans for the gardens, to include a canal feeding a lake which has survived to the present day. John Nash completed the work and built the first bridge over the lake, now a sanctuary for birds of many different species. Among the most popular residents are the pelicans, who are fed every day at 4 p.m. by their house near the path running along the western edge. Not many years ago a group of penguins proved a great attraction for the many visitors to the Park. In Gilbert's time, as now, the gates were kept open at night, with the result that in the 1870s St.James's Park became notorious as a meeting place for prostitutes and their clients. This fact is noted by possibly the most risqué line in all the Savoy operas.

Return to Broad Sanctuary: turn right up Victoria Street

Central Hall, Westminster, built in 1912, stands on some of the land previously occupied by the Royal Aquarium, the Summer and Winter Gardens and a large complex that also housed the Imperial Theatre. Under the patronage of the Duke of Edinburgh, the Royal Aquarium was intended to be a miniature Crystal Palace in the heart of London, where amusement could be tempered with instruction – a very Victorian ideal. The Winter Garden was a vast conservatory containing palms and exotic plants, trees, shrubs and fountains. The great hall measured 340ft by 160ft, and there was a promenade covered by an iron and glass roof. In the Aquarium were 13 large tanks for marine and freshwater specimens of all kinds. On 22 January 1876 the official opening ceremony took place with Arthur Sullivan, according to a report in *The Era*, conducting the concert hall's 'splendid band.'

But this was by no means all. The complex also had a roller skating rink, with its own band, a large reading room, a library, separate rooms for writing, chess and billiards, an art gallery, a restaurant, a telegraph office and a House of Commons division bell. The Royal Aquarium Theatre opened on 15 April 1876, but became the Imperial Theatre three years later. It was possible to buy a ticket on the Metropolitan Railway for 2/6d. covering the cost of a return journey and admission to the complex – little enough by today's standards, but still more expensive than the rival Crystal Palace. It was hoped by this and other means to keep out the riff-raff: a forlorn hope as it turned out for, by keeping the doors open until 10 p.m., the complex attracted as many ladies of the night as did St.James's Park. Probably many more when it rained.

The Duke of Edinburgh made certain that the post of musical director of the Royal Aquarium should first be offered to Arthur Sullivan, who found the prospect of conducting a permanent and salaried orchestra of 40 players irresistible. He travelled to the Continent to recruit his players and appointed as his deputy George Mount, who soon found himself responsible for two popular concerts a day. This left Sullivan free to concentrate on more demanding items for the regular Thursday afternoon concerts, which provided some notable firsts including, the London premiere of Schubert's incidental music to *Rosamunde*, and Wagner's *Tannhäuser* Overture. Sullivan soon became disenchanted with the way things were going at the Royal Aquarium. He considered that a growing number of side-shows was having a bad effect on the general standard of entertainment and that as a result, musical standards were slipping as well. He was also under fresh pressure from his royal patron, this time to accept the post of director of the National Training School for Music. In the end it was the riff-raff who tipped the scales: Sullivan decided he could no longer afford to be associated with a venture of such increasingly unsavoury reputation. He resigned in August 1876 and was succeded by his deputy.

The Imperial Theatre was chosen by the Comedy Opera Company for the rival production of *H.M.S.Pinafore* after the riot at the Opera Comique. A scratch

93

company was hastily put together but after 91 performances, first at the Imperial and then at the Olympic, the run collapsed. On 6 August 1879 Gilbert wrote to Sullivan: 'I hear the performance at the Aquarium was wretched and that very few audience were present.' Shortly afterwards the management of the Imperial was taken over by Marie Lytton, but not even she was able to stave off the inevitable closure which came in 1889. One attempt, lasting ten months, was made to re-open the theatre nearly ten years later, but it was then completely restored and refurbished for yet another opening ceremony on 22 April 1899, which was performed by none other than Lillie Langtry. But three years later the final blow was delivered by the Methodists, who purchased the site and effectively forced a closure on 16 June 1906. The whole of the Royal Aquarium was then pulled down: some of the interior mouldings and panelling from the theatre found their way into the Royal Albert Music Hall in Canning Town, but everything else was reduced to rubble to make room for the new Central Hall. Where one Victorian ideal had failed, Victorian non-conformity was about to succeed.

Victoria Street was built between 1845 and 1851. Nests of alleyways and courts were demolished, and a colony of almshouses and cottages known as Palmer's Village, with its own chapel and school, was swept away, to be replaced by one of the most forbidding streets in London. The high, Italianate facades were overpowering in their effect. As Besant noted in 1902, 'the solid uniform buildings on either side of the street have a very sombre aspect; they are used mainly for offices.[2]

The redevelopment of the area in recent years has been dramatic and, on the whole, beneficial. The new offices are light, and somewhat varied in style, and the new piazza in front of Westminster Cathedral has revealed an elevation hidden from view for far too long. One bright spot in the original Victoria Street has fortunately been left intact – the Army & Navy Stores, whose fame and reputation were carried all over the world with the final flowering of Britain's

[2] Besant, Sir Walter, ed. *The Fascination of London* London: Adam and Charles Black, 1902

94

imperial power. It was established in September 1871 as the Army & Navy Co-operative Limited to enable its members, drawn from Her Majesty's forces, to buy goods of the highest quality at the keenest possible prices. Indeed, for much of its existence the Army & Navy has been run more like a club than a high-class department store. Rules were drawn up for those qualifying for membership and those who did not. Officers on the Army and Naval lists, active and retired, were eligible, as were their families. Surprisingly for those class-ridden times, non-commissioned officers, petty officers and their families also qualified. Then came Peers of the Realm; Privy Councillors; Lords Lieutenant and Deputy Lieutenant; members of the diplomatic corps and Foreign Office; ministers of the Crown and departmental heads; members of the Royal Company of Scottish Archers; Royal Irish, Indian and Colonial Constabulary; civil officers of the Government of India and secretaries of naval and military messes and canteens. The sinews of Empire in a single mailing list.

Members agreed to leave money on deposit, or to pay cash only, thereby creating substantial working capital. This meant that suppliers could be paid promptly and substantial discounts obtained. The system worked very well, and soon a lot of prestige attached itself to the name 'Army & Navy'. Early catalogues make fascinating reading today and reveal an astonishing range of goods and services. Fully paid-up members living within reach of Victoria Street could have their port delivered and decanted in time for dinner, and all the clocks in the house properly wound up by a suitable-qualified craftsman. Those were the days!

Not far from the Army & Navy, between Artillery Row and Strutton Ground, stood Albert Mansions where, at No. 8, Sullivan had his first London flat. Gilbert called on him here to read the libretto of *Trial by Jury* in February 1875 in the very early days of their partnership, and it was in this flat in August 1877 that Grossmith was auditioned for his part in *The Sorcerer*. Not long after his brother's death that year Sullivan moved into the flat next door (No. 9): there survives a piece of mourning notepaper bearing this address on which Sullivan confirmed to

The entrance hall of Sullivan's flat at No. 1 Queen's Mansions

Sullivan's bedroom

Fanny Ronalds

D'Oyly Carte his acceptance of terms. The flat Sullivan vacated was promptly occupied by his secretary Walter Smythe, and together the two men stayed at Albert Mansions until 1881. *Patience* had by then run for over 500 performances and the revenue from this success, and others, had improved Sullivan's financial position to such an extent that he was able to move into a new flat in Queen's Mansions, more or less opposite the Army & Navy Stores. He took out leases on Nos.1 and 2, moved Walter Smythe into No.2 in July 1881, but delayed his own removal until the following year. He sought the advice of Fanny Ronalds on interior decor and furnishings, and the end result was described by some of his friends and contemporaries as 'extremely comfortable'. As was the custom of the time, the flat was filled with bric-a-brac from all over the world – Persian carpets, silk wall hangings and tapestries, oriental lamps and lanterns, antique Egyptian screens, divans, palms and other potted plants and a parrot he was very fond of but which he called, with great lack of originality, Polly. Many of these curios were trophies from his visits abroad.

With Fanny Ronalds acting as hostess he gave his first party in the new flat in May 1882, celebrating his 40th birthday. Three weeks later, however, there occurred a tragedy which cast a shadow over his life for some time. His mother was taken ill while lunching with him and died soon afterwards: immediately Sullivan went into deep mourning which lasted almost a full year.

Telephones were becoming highly fashionable at this time, and Gilbert persuaded his partner to follow his example by having one installed in the new flat. On Whit Sunday in 1883 Sullivan asked a number of friends round to listen through his 'electrophone' to extracts from *Iolanthe* transmitted direct from the stage of the Savoy Theatre. Among his guests were the Prince of Wales, the Duke of Edinburgh, Ferdinald Rothschild, John Millais and Gilbert himself. Sullivan now threw himself into social activity with renewed vigour. He decided to create a *salon*, as Fanny Ronalds had done, and launched a series of lavish parties, usually on the first Sunday of the month. On 8 June 1884, for example, he gave a dinner party for a small number of distinguished guests, most of them of aristocratic birth, and they were joined later by a group of 20 or more guests from the world of the arts. The departure of the last guest is carefully recorded: 2.30

a.m. A month later, on 6 July, the Duke of Edinburgh, Lord Wolseley and Richard D'Oyly Carte were among the dinner guests. They were entertained by George and Weedon Grossmith supported by a musical group and a conjurer.

As Sullivan's stature as a musician grew so did his reputation as a social lion, and he became much in demand by the fashionable hostesses of the day. Consequently, during the height of the season his flat became little more than a *pied-a-terre* in which he could relax for an hour so so before getting himself ready for the next engagement. Like Gilbert, Sullivan was a realist when it came to money: he understood quite clearly the foundation on which his growing fortune rested. It was no accident that for the telegraphic address of his London flat he chose the simple words 'Pinafore:London'.

Early in 1884 Sullivan wrote to the American librettist Bret Harte saying that he would not be writing any more operas but devote his time to 'more serious work' instead.[3]. A few weeks later, in May, he turned down yet again Gilbert's idea of a magic lozenge. By February of the following year, however, we find the two settling down to put the finishing touches to *The Mikado* before releasing copies to the cast for their first read-through. Another happy occasion in the Queen's Mansion flat was Gilbert's visit bringing about a reconciliation after the long and bitter carpet quarrel.

This final stage in their relationship was destined not to last many years. In the autumn of 1900 Sullivan went on holiday to Thusis, in Switzerland, where he contracted a chill from which he failed to make a full recovery. On returning to England he visited Cellier in Tunbridge Wells to work on *The Emerald Isle*, but his illness grew worse and he was forced to go back to London on 15 October. The next day he sent an encouraging letter to Helen D'Oyly Carte saying that his health had improved, but the truth was sadly otherwise. Over the next three or four weeks his condition continued to deteriorate and it was decided to call in the Queen's physician, Sir Thomas Barlow, with whom an appointment was made for the morning of 22 November. Sullivan spent a wretched night and at 6 a.m. rang for his valet and his maid. The crisis followed almost at once, and he died in the arms of Herbert, his nephew, before either Barlow or Fanny Ronalds could reach him. He was 58.

Queen's Mansions, 58–60 Victoria Street, where he lived from 1881

That morning, and for several days thereafter, the curtains at No.1 Queen's Mansions remained firmly shut against the failing winter sunshine. The last piece of notepaper from the flat was used in March of the following year when Herbert wrote to one of the pall-bearer, Sir Frederick Bridge, offering him a personal momento. Many years later, in October 1928, the LCC placed one of their blue plaques near the Queen's Mansion entrance, bearing the simple inscription 'Sir Arthur Sullivan (1842-1900) Musical Composer Lived Here.'

[3]Goldberg, Isaac *The Story of Gilbert and Sullivan* New York: Crown, 1935

Chapter 10

LAMBETH AND SOUTHWARK

Lambeth North to Waterloo or Embankment Underground stations: allow 2 hours

Turn right out of Lambeth North station, cross over and walk to the next set of traffic lights about 200 yards ahead. Turn into Lambeth Road: first turning left is Lambeth Walk. Halfway along it is crossed by Lollard Street. Gibson Road is on the left.

Sullivan's birthplace at 8 Bolwell Terrace in Lambeth

Throughout their long histories the ancient boroughs of Lambeth and of Southwark on the south bank of the Thames have always presented a face of poverty in the sharpest contrast to their affluent neighbours across the river, the cities of Westminster and of London. It is in Lambeth we we find the birthplace of Arthur Sullivan and in Southwark his father's place of employment for six years.

About 50 yards down Gibson Road in Lambeth there is a right-hand bend followed by one to the left. This is where Bolwell Street once passed through to Lambeth Walk, and where began a small terrace of houses which has long since disappeared under the playing fields of the local school. The houses, described as 'mean, ugly and austere', were typical of the mass-produced artisan dwellings of the 19th century. Built for railway workers in this instance, they consisted of a basement, two floors each with two rooms, and a flight of five stone steps with a double handrail leading up to a dignified front door. It was at No.8 Bolwell Terrace, otherwise known as Bolwell Street, that Arthur Seymour Sullivan was born on 13 May 1842.

When Thomas Sullivan took possession of his house in 1839, the area in which it stood was brand-new, but it soon became shabby and run-down. He had got a job playing the clarinet at Davidge's Surrey Theatre at a salary of one guinea a week, just enough to meet the annual rent of £20 on the house, with a little left over for food, heat, clothing and other expenses. But soon the first child, Fred, was born and when Arthur arrived his mother was forced to have him 'minded' while she went out to earn a little extra cash as a governess. In 1845 Thomas Sullivan decided that he would not find fame and fortune on the streets of London after all, and took his growing family back to the more agreeable environment of Sandhurst which he had left some years earlier. It is a testimony to the remarkable stability of money and property values in Victorian times that more than 60 years after it was built the house in which Sullivan was born still had a rateable value of only £28 per annum. After the composer died a memorial tablet, donated by the Incorporated Society of Musicians and unveiled on 20 July 1901, was placed on the house, which survived until 1965. Then it was demolished in a major redevelopment which produced the Ethelred Housing Estate and a playing field for the Lilian Bayliss School. Bolwell Street no longer exists: the entire character of the district, even the famous Lambeth Walk, has been changed beyond all recognition by insensitive planning decisions. The old squalor has given way to modern ugliness and lack of character.

One small relic remains thanks to the intervention of Spike Milligan. During the demolition work he went to the site and with the help of a £5 note managed to acquire the front door of the Sullivans' house which he later presented to the Museum of London, where it is now on permanent display. No trace remains of the memorial plaque which was presumably carted away in the rubble or buried under the new works.

At the end of Gibson Road turn right along Black Prince Road to the Albert Embankment. Proceed to Lambeth Palace St. Mary's Church

Nearby on the Albert Embankment are the headquarters of London's Fire Brigade and moorings for fireboats. One of these sank in October 1987, carrying with it the proud name of 'Eyre Massey Shaw', hero of the Alhambra fire and doubtless many others, into the Thames mud. Beyond the roundabout at the foot of Lambeth Bridge stands the residence of the Archbishop of Canterbury, Lambeth Palace. The former parish church of St. Mary's is immediately adjacent, and it was here that Arthur Seymour Sullivan was christened on 31 July 1842. Fourteen years later he paid a special visit to the church in order to play the organ. The baptismal register dates back as far as 1539 and is now in the hands of the parish authorities following the deconsecration of the church in 1978.

There has been a church on the site since before the Norman Conquest, as is confirmed by an entry in the Domesday Book. However, apart from the 15th century tower, the vestry door and some interior bosses, the present building is a mid-Victorian reconstruction in the Gothic style. No fewer than six archbishops are buried within the precincts and in the graveyard can be seen memorials dating back to 1504. Vice-Admiral Bligh, commander of *H.M.S. Bounty*, is buried here as are the Tredescants, the distinguished family of botanists whose collection of plant specimens from all parts of the world caught the attention of Charles I and which, in 1682, was given to the Ashmolean.

It is the work of the Tredescant family that has kept St. Mary's alive today, for after deconsecration it was planned to demolish the church and to sell the land for office development. But the Tradescant Society mounted a campaign to save the building, to clean and restore it, and turn it into a museum. All this has been achieved most successfully: apart from the many items of interest on display there is a bookstall as well as a refreshment counter.

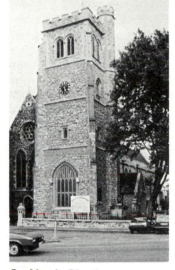

St. Mary's Church, Lambeth, where Sullivan was christened on 31 July 1842

There appears to be a direct link between St. Mary's and the D'Oyly Carte family, for on the wall above the bookstall there is a memorial tablet to a D'Oyly from Kent, described as 'philanthropist to the poor of the parish.' During the fund-raising campaign to save the church, principals from the D'Oyly Carte Opera Company gave two concerts here in January 1979.

Return to Embankment: carry on to the Royal Festival Hall. End the tour at Waterloo or cross the river via Hungerford Bridge to Embankment Underground

From the Embankment on the Lambeth side of the river the postcard view of the Houses of Parliament presents itself. The members' terraces can be clearly seen – red awnings for the House of Lords and green for the House of Commons – and just visible in the gardens is Rodin's celebrated statue of *The Burghers of Calais*. On the south bank are the following buildings: St. Thomas's Hospital; the impressive County Hall, until recently London's administrative headquarters; Jubilee Gardens, where the Festival of Britain was held in 1951; and just the other side of Hungerford Bridge is the major arts complex consisting of the Royal Festival Hall, Queen Elizabeth Hall, Purcell Room, Hayward Gallery, the National Theatre and National Film Theatre.

At a cost of only £2 million the Royal Festival Hall was built for the Festival of Britain and gave London a much-needed concert complex that soon replaced the Albert Hall as the main venue for classical music. The first D'Oyly Carte Opera season here was not given until 1971, but a year later the Company played to full houses during a four-weeks season in July and August, as part of the Greater London Council's South Bank Arts Festival. In 1975, from 17 June to 9 August, the Company mounted an ambitious centenary season in which all the Savoy operas were presented, including a revival of *Utopia Limited*. Since then there have been more performances of the operas either in full or in concert form, and the RFH is, at the time of writing, the London base for the 'Magic of D'Oyly Carte'. This is the rump of the old D'Oyly Carte Company which, before its

dissolution, was supported by the arts committee of the GLC. Gilbert's own work has been given on the South Bank in recent years, for in 1977 there was a successful revival of *Engaged* at the National Theatre. As part of the campaign against the abolition of the GLC two very free adaptations of Gilbert & Sullivan's works appeared during the summers of 1984 and 1985 at the Queen Elizabeth Hall. Written by Ned Sherrin and Alistair Beaton, the first was called *The Ratepayer's Iolanthe*, which was followed by *The Metropolitan Mikado*.

To reach Blackfriars Road go to the Elephant and Castle Underground and take the Bakerloo line exit. Cross St. George's Circus for the southern end of Blackfriars Road

A brief footnote will complete the Sullivan story so far as buildings in this part of London are concerned. 124 Blackfriars Road marks the site of the old Surrey Theatre which in the 1830s was a music hall under the management of a man named Davidge. After he left the army in 1839 Thomas Sullivan came to London to improve his prospects, but without any success. He was engaged by Davidge to play the clarinet in the pit band and persevered in this demeaning post for six years during which time, as we have seen, his son Arthur was born. On his return to Sandhurst he re-enlisted, and rose to the rank of sergeant bandmaster. Thomas and Mary Sullivan were intensely musical people, and there can be no doubt that their home background had a most profound influence both on Arthur and his elder brother.

Chapter 11

HOLBORN AND THE INNS OF COURT

Temple to Chancery Lane
underground stations:
allow 2½ hours.
Please note that the Inns of
Court are private property.
Visitors are generally
welcomed but some of the
entrances are closed at
weekends and after
7 p.m. on other days

From the station turn left
along Victoria Embankment
to Middle Temple Lane

Follow the lane until half way
up the hill. Turn right at the
barrier into Crown Office Row
and so into Inner Temple

For nearly 700 years the Temple in London has been closely associated with lawyers and the law. The name derives from the Order of the Holy Sepulchre of Knights Templars, military crusader knights who lived by the flank wall of the city of London. They were a very powerful group of men who gave protection to the neighbouring monasteries belonging to the Whitefriars, Carmelites and Blackfriars, commemorated among other means by street names in the area, and who had dealings both with the Carthusians at Smithfield and with the Knights of the Order of St. John at Clerkenwell.

In 1161 the Knights Templars moved to the Temple, the precincts of which then ran right down to the bank of the river Thames, because their numbers had outgrown the original commandery south of Holborn. They then successfully petitioned to build a church after the design of St. Sepulchre's in Jerusalem, and by 1185 the Temple church had been built and was consecrated by the Patriarch of Jerusalem himself.

In the years that followed the Templars grew vastly rich and powerful, so much so that they were seen to pose a serious threat to a number of European thrones. This was not a situation the Church could tolerate and in 1312 the Order was dissolved, and all its property and assets were handed over to a rival Order, that of St. John of Jerusalem, later known simply as the Knights of Malta. This became a secular body in 1800 very much concerned with humanitarian work of various kinds. Under their rule students in the Temple were encouraged to read and practice secular law. So by the time of the Reformation, when Henry VIII abolished the rest of the knightly orders, it was perhaps inevitable that the ownership of the Temple should pass into the hands of the lawyers, where it has remained to this day. By 1501, the first date for which administrative records have survived, the four Inns of Court had in effect become secular monasteries, each self-regulating and run by a self-perpetuating body of benchers. To these Inns were attached all attorneys of the higher courts as well as practising advocates, non-ecclesiastical judges and their respective students of the law.

The names Inner and Middle Temple indicate their proximity to the city wall. There was also once an Outer Temple to the west, but the land on which is stood has long since been used for other purposes. Inner Temple with its tranquil courtyards, halls and lawns, is an oasis of peace in the noise and bustle of a modern city. It has seen a great wealth of English history, and members of its societies have become leaders of nations in many parts of the world.

At the age of 19, W.S.Gilbert enrolled as a student of the Honourable Society of the Inner Temple on 11 October 1855, two years before he took up his post as a clerk in the Education Department of the Privy Council. The Bar seems to have been a second choice of career for him, for he had sought military service in the Crimea. In the event, his name stands in the roll of the larger of the two Temple

At the end of Crown Office Row turn left. Then left again under the archway into the courtyard of Temple Church

Inns, founded in about 1440, alongside those of Coke, Seldon, Erskine, Judge Jeffreys, Cowper, Lamb, Boswell and, in modern times, Mahatma Gandhi, to mention only a few.

On the left is Inner Temple Hall, the third building of that name to occupy the site. Its immediate predecessor was destroyed by German bombs on 10 May 1941. Gilbert knew the original building which dated back to the reign of Edward III. Here he ate the required number of dinners each term before being called to the Bar on 17 November 1863. Three years later the medieval building was pulled down to make way for a Victorian Gothic 'improvement'. The inner walls of the present hall are lined with with the armorial bearings of Readers of the Inn dating back over seven centuries. There are also portraits of later members of the House of Stuart and, by way of contrast, the House of Orange as well. Over most doorways and at the rainheads of many of the buildings may be seen Pegasus, symbol of the Inner Temple. The corresponding symbol of the Middle Temple is the Paschal Lamb. The Inner Temple Library contains more than 90,000 books and manuscripts from the 14th century onwards, but the centrepiece of the Temple is undoubtedly the church with its famous Round built in 1185, and the

Cross the courtyard and under the archway into Pump Court

Quire which was added later in 1240. During World War II the roof was damaged and many of the stained glass windows were lost, but otherwise the church survived the bombing which destroyed the adjacent Lamb Court, Pump Court, Cloisters and Inner Temple Hall, all of which had to be rebuilt in the early 1950s. Regular services take place in the church, which is open to visitors. At the back is a narrow lane, where Johnson first met James Boswell, which leads to a graveyard in which the tomb of Oliver Goldsmith may be found.

Gilbert spent his pupillage at No. 4 Pump Court, which he later used as the setting for 'My Maiden Brief'

Pump Court gets its name from four water pumps that stood there, one against each wall, strategically placed as a ready source of water for fire-fighters who had

Return to Middle Temple Lane and turn left. Some 20 yards on cross over in front of Middle Temple Hall

to deal with frequent blazes in medieval times. It is one of the oldest of all Temple courtyards. In its time is has housed such distinguished names as Henry Fielding, Cowper and Blackstone. W.S. Gilbert spent his pupillage here, either at No.4 or 5, under Sir Charles Watkin-Wilkins. He set his story *My Maiden Brief* in these chambers.

Middle Temple Hall, built in 1576, was frequently visited by Queen Elizabeth I, whose sea-dogs Drake, Raleigh, Frobisher and Hawkins often met here as well. They did so as members, for they were all lawyers at one time. Beneath the magnificent double hammerbeam roof, itself 400 years old, stands a table – called the cup-board – made from the timbers of the *Golden Hind*. The high table was made from Windsor oak given by Elizabeth I and floated down the river Thames. Above hangs the superb equestrian portrait of Charles I by van Dyke. The first performance of *Twelfth Night* was given in this Hall in 1601, with Shakespeare playing one of the parts. In our own times, Queen Elizabeth the Queen Mother visited the Hall on 6 December 1978 to attend a performance of *Trial by Jury*, given by the D'Oyly Carte Opera Company, to celebrate the 100th concert presented by the Bar Musical Society.

Carry on to Middle Temple Gardens. Keep the fountain on your left and take the steps leaving the Temple via Judge's Gate. Turn right along Devereux Court to the Strand

To return to weightier matters. Middle Temple has produced many great men including, among others, Edmund Burke and John Dickinson, the man who actually drafted the American Declaration of Independence. It is a remarkable fact that of those who signed that regrettable document, no fewer than five were members of this Inn.

The Royal Courts of Justice in the Strand, resplendent after all the restoration and cleaning work of recent years, is another building which reflects the late Victorian enthusiasm for mock-Gothic architecture. It is of cathedral-like proportions: the Great Hall alone is 280ft long and 80ft high. Altogether it took six years to build, and on its completion in 1882 all the higher courts and their attendant offices, which had for so many years functioned in a state of chaos at Westminster, were at last brought together under one roof. A visit to the Law Courts is well worth making: at the time of writing the building is open from 10 a.m. to 4 p.m., but before making plans it would be advisable to check these times and to make sure that no temporary restrictions are in force.

Enter the Royal Courts of Justice. Pass through the Great Hall and make for the stairway at the far end on the left. This leads up to the main court floor and to the rear exit into Carey Street. OR if the building is closed follow its perimeter anti-clockwise through Bell Yard and into Carey Street

Return along Carey Street to Chancery Lane

As litigants both Sullivan and Gilbert came to know the court-rooms that form a tier in the Great Hall. The quarrel over who should pay for the front-of-house carpet, to which frequent references have been made, ended up as Gilbert – v-Carte in the Chancery Division during August and September 1890. Gilbert returned to this court four years later to bring his successful action against *The Star* for revealing the plot of his forthcoming production at the Lyric Theatre. March 1898 saw the famous libel action in the Queen's Bench Division in which Gilbert sued another newspaper, *The Era*, which described him as a 'grand llama or sacred elephant'. And in January 1910, once more in the Chancery Division, the indefatigable Gilbert sued C.H. Workman for breach of contract.

At the back of the Royal Courts of Justice is an alley leading from Carey Street separating the building from the neighbouring London School of Economics. At the end of the alley is Clements Inn Passage, which is all that now remains of the tiny Clement's Inn where Gilbert took his tenancy in chambers after his call to the Bar, at a cost of £100. Clement's Inn was among the many buildings demolished in 1874 to make way for the Royal Courts of Justice. Clement Scott makes much of Gilbert and of the Inn:

Clement's Inn ! . . . the curious old Inn-of-court by which one proceeded in old days from the busy Strand, through the slums of Clare Market, straight to the delightful peace and quiet of Lincoln's Inn Fields . . . No one, as far as I can

*The Royal Courts of
Justice, 1882, the last
major public building
in the Victorian
Gothic revival*

see, has noticed that Clement's Inn was the scene of the very earliest labours of
one of of our most distinguished dramatists and humorists, William Schwenck
Gilbert.

Tucked away in the angle-corner of old Clement's Inn, on the ground floor,
were the chambers from which W.S. Gilbert gave his admiring friends his very
earliest work. He had been a Clerk in the Education Office but the work was
distasteful to him. His temperament would not brook dictation or control, as
well as all of us know by this time. Gilbert has often told me that when he broke
away from the 10 to 4 drudgery at the Education Office, he purchased a quire
or so of blue foolscap paper, a packet of quill pens, and a few wood blocks, and
commenced to fire away with pen and pencil, mainly for the comic papers. He
had a small berth in a correspondentship to a Russian newspaper, handed over
to him by his relative Sutherland Edwards, which caused either envy or awe to
many of us in those days ...

I always wanted to live, if Fate favoured me, at ... Garden House, Clement's
Inn, always to my mind the most delightful *rus in urbe* in our mighty London.

104

Turn left and walk the length of Chancery Lane

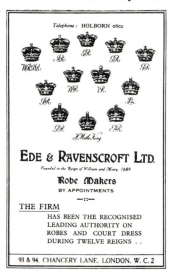

Court robemakers Ede & Ravenscroft made judicial court costumes to Gilbert's order

Running from Fleet Street to Holborn, Chancery Lane over the centuries came to be regarded as the centre of legal London. In medieval times the office of the Lord Chancellor was held by the Bishop of Chichester whose palace was at Lincoln's Inn. Part of his establishment was the old writ office, situated in what is now Chancery Lane. Later, the courts and the offices for the Court of Chancery were to be found here: furthermore, it formed an important link between the Temple and Gray's Inn and Lincoln's Inn. Nowadays Chancery Lane is of less importance, but it remains close to the hub of affairs. On the right stand the offices of the Law Society which represents the interests of solicitors, and which were dubbed by Gilbert as 'The Institute'. Opposite is situated the Public Records Office where the Domesday Book and Magna Carta are kept, among many other important historical documents. Immediately to the north of the Public Records Office is a passageway, Rolls Gardens, which is what remains of Master of the Rolls Court as Gilbert knew it. It was here that counsel for Carte and for the Comedy Opera Company met on 1 August 1879, each side trying to prevent the other from producing *H.M.S.Pinafore*, and each claiming sole rights in the work. At 93/4 Chancery Lane are the premises of Ede and Ravenscroft, of whom the unique claim is made that they are the oldest bespoke tailors in the world. They and those who have gone before them have supplied ceremonial robes and regalia since 1689, under royal warrants granted by each of the thirteen monarchs since that date. Foreign courts have also been served by them, as have peers of the realm, local authorities, livery companies, the academic world and, of course, the legal profession.

Joseph Ede was clearly a man of great enterprise. In 1820 he took out a partnership in an established concern, Webb, which soon carried his name, and helped to prepare coronation robes for George IV. Next he turned his attention to the matter of matrimony, and paid court to the daughter of Burton Ravenscroft, the famous wig-maker of Lincoln's Inn. It was Ravenscroft who had patented in 1822 his 'forensic wig', still worn today. Ede's wooing was crowned with success and in due course we find the firm of 'Ede & Son' trading in Serle Street, Lincoln's Inn. Merger with the Ravenscroft business duly followed, and in 1894 Ede and Ravenscroft took possession of the premises they still occupy, in which can be seen an impressive display of robes, regalia and the royal warrants signed by Lords Chamberlain over the past 300 years.

The finale of Act II of 'Iolanthe', with Lorraine Daniels, Suzanne O'Keefe and John Reed

105

No hard evidence exists to prove that Gilbert ordered costumes and robes from Ede and Ravenscroft for the first production of *Trial by Jury*, but there must be a very strong probability that this is what occurred. There is no doubt at all that costumes for the revival of *The Sorcerer* in 1885 came from them, as did the judicial robes for later productions of *The Gondoliers* and *Utopia Limited*. But it was *Iolanthe* that provides the most remarkable link between the firm and the Savoy operas. Gilbert called at the Serle Street premises to order replicas of the robes worn by peers of the realm 'authentic to the last detail', many bearing the insignia of various orders of chivalry. It was the fact that they were so authentic that really upset the office of the Lord Chamberlain. *The Era* reported in October 1882, characteristically in advance of the event:

> Messrs. Gilbert and Sullivan's new comic opera will be graced by some of the most remarkable costumes ever seen upon the stage. Several of the characters in the opera are supposed to be peers of the realm, and Messrs Ede and Son, the famous robe-makers to Her Majesty, the House of Lords, the Archbishop of Canterbury &c., have been commissioned by Mr. Gilbert to prepare robes of the most splendid kind. They will be of the same quality and make as worn by peers on state occasions, and, having seen a specimen robe at the establishment of the above eminent firm, we can testify as to the richness of the materials and the excellence of the workmanship. The robes will be of the finest velvet, of various colours, blue, crimson, green &c., and they will be trimmed with ermine, while embroidered satin vests and breeches, with silk stockings, and all other details of a state costume, will be included, the most costly materials being included throughout. Therefore when these personages appear in the opera they will be dressed in exactly the same style as peers at a real Court ceremonial. Other costumes in which gold lace, delicate fringes, &c., are used will also be very beautiful, and Mr. Gilbert has personally superintended their production. When we add that the cost of some of these elaborate dresses will not be far short of fifty pounds each some idea may be formed of the splendour with which the new opera will be placed upon the stage.

Beyond Ede and Ravenscroft is a gateway from Chancery Lane into Lincoln's Inn through which can be seen the old Hall, built in 1489, and the Chapel which

Before he gave up the Bar altogether, Gilbert's last chambers were at 1 Verulam Buildings

Cross Holborn and into the courtyard immediately opposite into Gray's Inn Place. Turn right along Field Court, and under archway into Gray's Inn Square

dates from 1623. It was in this Hall that the Lord Chancellor held occasional court: at other times it was occupied by an appellate court. Among the many famous students here was Thomas More.

Gray's Inn takes its name from the manor of the de Gray family which flourished during the reign of Queen Elizabeth I. It numbers among its members Francis and Nicholas Bacon, the Earls of Southampton and of Essex, Gresham, Burghley, Walsingham and Romilly. In modern times Gray's Inn has produced thinkers and writers of the calibre of Hilaire Belloc and Sidney Webb, and future prime ministers including Winston Churchill, Edward Heath and Robert Menzies.

South Square, formerly known as Holborn Court, is dominated by Gray's Inn Hall. It is renowned partly for its revels, and partly for the fact that *A Comedy of Errors* was first performed here in 1594. Most of the Hall came through wartime bombing unscathed, and what damage was caused to the fabric of the building was completely made good thanks to the generosity of the American Bar Assoociation. Appropriately enough, it was in Gray's Inn Hall that Winston Churchill first met President F.D. Roosevelt. Another survivor of World War II was No.1 South Square, where Charles Dickens spent a miserable apprenticeship as attorney's clerk in chambers with the firm of Ellis and Blackmore from May 1827 to November 1828. The south-west corner of South Square, Nos.2 to 9, was completely destroyed by bombs.

It was at No.3 South Square that Gilbert took chambers late in 1866 or early in 1867. They soon became the haunt of a group of young critics, dramatists and journalists who called themselves the 'Serious Family'. The members paid a two-guinea subscription and the list included Tom Hood, who was 'head of the family', Henry Byron, Clement Scott, Arthur Cecil, Tom Robertson, Artemus Ward, E.L.Blanchard, Jeff Prowse, Henry Leigh, Paul Gray and several others. They met regularly every Saturday to exchange, doubtless in a convivial atmosphere, the social, political, legal and literary gossip of the day. Gilbert retained these chambers until some time after his marriage, using them as a writing den. Here he wrote some of his earliest plays and the *Bab Ballads*. The chambers were also used for entertaining his friends, including fellow contributors to *Fun* magazine, and his particular mentors Henry Byron and Tom Robertson.

Take the passage leading to Verulam Buildings, and then into Gray's Inn Road. Turn right for Chancery Lane Underground

These were not the first chambers he had occupied at Gray's Inn. For a short time during the late summer and autumn of 1866 he was to be found at No.1 Verulam Buildings after his return to London from the north, where he had tried his hand at practice on the Northern Circuit both at Liverpool and at Manchester under the sponsorship of a family friend, Sir John Holker. This first real encounter with the legal world outside the cloistered calm of Clement's Inn soon convinced him that where he was concerned the Bar was unlikely to yield handsome dividends, and that he would be far better advised to pursue a literary career.

Whether the first part of that proposition was well-judged or not we shall never know. But as to the outcome of the second part there is no possible doubt whatever ...

107

108

Chapter 12

THE CITY

A series of three walks and a visit to the Standard Theatre in Shoreditch. The first walk is from the Barbican to Blackfriars Underground stations: allow four hours including visits to the London Museum and St. Paul's Cathedral

Within the Barbican complex, built in the early 1970s, are a number of places of historical interest, including the remains of London's Roman and medieval wall, and the Museum of London itself, full of fascinating exhibits. There is also the Barbican Centre for the performing arts with exhibition halls, a cinema, a library, art galleries, a theatre used by the Royal Shakespeare Company as their permanent London base and a fine concert hall, present home of the London Symphony Orchestra, which is a regular venue for concerts given by the London Savoyards. Also in the Barbican complex, quite apart from the large-scale housing development, is the newly-built Guildhall School of Music, the third of London's music academies. It was from the original Guildhall School of Music, it may be recalled, that Gilbert recruited female students for the chorus in *Fallen Fairies*.

The Museum of London, which can be reached by following the signs from the Barbican underground station, formerly occupied part of Kensington Palace. Since moving to the Barbican it has won many awards for the outstanding displays showing the unfolding of London's social history from pre-historic times to the present day. Among the galleries devoted to London life in Victorian times we can find displayed the front door of Arthur Sullivan's birthplace in Lambeth, rescued from the demolishers by comedian and conservationist Spike Milligan. Also in the museum are pieces of furniture from 'Grim's Dyke', Gilbert's house in Harrow Weald, which were presented in 1954 by Nancy McIntosh. Among them was his much-prized 9ft grand piano made of satinwood. This and other items have not been on display since the move to new premises and are, presumably, kept safely in store.

From the Museum descend to London Wall. Turn right then left into St. Martin's Le Grand. Bear left past the underground station into New Change. Turn right through the Cathedral gardens in Paternoster Row. Make for the main entrance facing Ludgate Circus

St. Paul's Cathedral has been described as 'the spiritual heart of the City of London'. Seat of the bishopric of London, St. Paul's is by far the largest and most famous of all the City churches, and the commanding site on which it stands at the top of Ludgate Hill has been a centre of Christian worship since Saxon times. It was here that Mellitus was consecrated bishop of the East Saxons by Saint Augustine in 604. Later that century Bishop Erconwald rebuilt the cathedral in stone, but this was destroyed by Viking raiders in the 9th century. The next church survived for little more than 100 years, having been destroyed by a fire which swept through the city in 1087. Then followed a long period of further rebuilding, with many interruptions and reverses, which came to an end with the Great Fire of London in 1666.

At first it was thought that the ruins of 'Old St. Paul's' could be patched up and repaired, but in 1668 a royal commission decided that the site should be cleared and an entirely new church built to plans by Sir Christopher Wren. The new cathedral, with its magnificent dome rising to a height of 365ft to the top of the cross surmounting it, was to prove Wren's crowning masterpiece and dominated the London skyline for nearly 300 years.

St. Paul's Cathedral

The funeral of Sir Arthur Sullivan in St. Paul's Cathedral took place on 27 November 1900

The strong choral music tradition at St.Paul's, which dates back to the patronage extended to the Choir both by Henry VIII and Elizabeth I, was enhanced in later years by a succession of great organists, whose names and whose works would certainly have been well-known to Sullivan from his student days onwards. Names such as Jeremiah Clarke (1695-1707) and Attwood (1796-1838). Then, in Sullivan's own time, Goss (1838-1872) and Stainer (1872-1888). Handel and Mendelssohn had both, in their day, played the magnificent organ in the cathedral.

Although it took some time for Sullivan's choral music to make its mark, his extensive output of hymns and anthems during the 1860s would certainly have been known to the Cathedral choir. Towards the end of his life the composer was commissioned by the Dean and Chapter to write a *Te Deum* for a thanksgiving service marking the end of the Boer War. As it happened, Sullivan died almost a full year before that event, but he had already composed the work in advance, and it was duly performed in the cathedral on 2 June 1902.

In a document dated 18 August 1882 Sullivan expressed a clear wish to be buried in the same grave as his parents and his brother at Brompton Cemetery. He also asked that his own service should take the same form as that used for his

Sullivan's memorial, designed by Goscombe John, is to be found not in the crypt, but in the north transept, next to a list of cathedral organists

mother's funeral and that, if possible, both the anthem from *The Light of the World* and the funeral march from *The Martyr of Antioch* should be played. When the melancholy time came the authorities at Brompton Cemetery responded to these wishes without delay, and the family grave had already been opened when news came of an offer by the Dean and Chapter of St. Paul's of a resting place for Sir Arthur in the cathedral crypt. Events followed rapidly from that point on. The Queen let it be known that Sullivan's personal preferences were to be disregarded and ordered a semi-state funeral starting in the Chapel Royal at St. James's Palace. When the doors were opened at 11.30 on the morning of Tuesday, 27 November 1900, the chapel was seen to be filled with white lilies and chrysanthemums. Two large palms had been placed before the altar, and the Master of the Queen's Music, Sir Walter Parratt, representing Her Majesty Queen Victoria, carried a wreath which bore the following inscription:

a mark of sincere admiration
for his great musical talents
Victoria Regina

The congregation included representatives of the Prince of Wales, the Kaiser, foreign ambassadors, many members of the aristocracy and almost everyone of any consequence from the world of music, opera and drama. A notable exception was Gilbert, who was in Egypt. After the first part of the burial service, the cortège started its slow, solemn procession to St. Paul's led by the band of the Scots Guards playing the *Dead March* from *Saul*. Thousands stood in silence along the route, which passed down Pall Mall, along Northumberland Avenue and on to the Victoria Embankment on the north side of the Thames, before turning up Queen Victoria Street and so to the final resting place. Flags on all public buildings were flown at half-mast, and the life of the Empire's capital city came to a virtual standstill.

On arrival at St. Paul's the coffin was carried to the catafalque by the pall-bearers – Sir Squire Bancroft, Francois Cellier, the Royal Equerry Colonel Collins, Sir Frederick Bridge, Sir George Lewis, Sir Alexander Mackenzie, Sir George Martin and Sir John Stainer. The burial service was repeated in full and under Cellier's direction the choir sang the anthems Sullivan had specified, with others thrown in for good measure, while on the organ was played the *andante espressivo* from the Symphony in E.

The composer's grave is ornamented by engravings of emblematic birds entwined among foliage, which serves a border to an otherwise plain copper tombstone on which the following inscription appears:

Sir Arthur Sullivan, Mus.Doc., M.V.O.
Born 13 May 1842 Died 22 November 1900

Down Ludgate Hill take first turning right, Maria Lane, to Warwick Lane, at the end of which turn left into Newgate Street

Sullivan's memorial is in the north transept, facing that of Sir John Stainer and immediately next to a list of cathedral organists. Designed by Goscombe John, and unveiled on 22 November 1902, the tablet shows a full-length female figure holding a lyre, above a medallion of the composer in three-quarter length profile. Laurel leaves form a border, with a cherub on each side. The simple gravestone inscription is repeated on the tablet.

On the corner of Old Bailey and Newgate Street stands the most famous criminal court in the world. The word 'bailey' derives from *ballium*, or enclosure of the City wall in medieval times. The building incorporates stones from its predecessor on the site, the notorious 800-years-old Newgate Gaol, which was finally pulled down in 1902. The previous 'Old Bailey', which occupied a site slightly to the north of the present building, was erected in 1539 in an attempt to afford some protection to the King's Justices and the City Aldermen against the

*Work on the Central
Criminal Court was
started in 1902, and
completed in 1907*

dread diseases and pestilence that were only too often to be found in the hall of
Newgate Gaol, where trials were previously held. In 1750, the Lord Mayor of
London, two judges, an alderman, an under-sheriff and fifty others died from
typhus contracted from prisoners. Thus began the tradition whereby on the first
two days of each session and on Red Letter days, judges at the Old Bailey and the
Sheriff's party carry posies of sweet-smelling flowers to smother the evil odours
emanating from the prison building.

It was the original Old Bailey, or Central Criminal Court to use the designation
it was given in 1834, to which Gilbert refers in *Trial by Jury*, *The Pirates of
Penzance* and *Ruddigore*. Some have held that the pirates ought to have been tried
at Bodmin Assizes, but Gilbert had more than enough law to know that in 1834
the Central Criminal Court had been given Admiralty jurisdiction to hear trials of
crimes committed on the high seas.

Gilbert was in practice at the Bar when over 50,000 people packed Old Bailey
and Smithfield to witness in 1864 the execution by hanging of the first railway
murderer, Franz Muller. The scaffold, which was set up near the site of the
present main door, then the Debtors' Door to the prison, was overlooked by the
inn which can still be seen today, *The Magpie and Stump*, where window seats
changed hands at 20 guineas each. The last public execution in England took
place four years later, in May 1868.

In recent years pressure of work inside the Central Criminal Court has
increased so much that a new extension providing 20 new courtrooms was added
to the Old Bailey in 1972. At the highest point of the building stands one of the
best-known and most frequently-reproduced symbols in the world – Frederick

Go down Old Bailey back to Ludgate Hill and turn right. Cross Ludgate Circus into Fleet Street

Pomeroy's gilded bronze figure of the Lady of Justice. She stands 12ft high, the span of her arms is 8ft, the length of her sword is just over 3ft and she is *not* (and it is worth emphasizing the point) blindfolded.

Ludgate Hill was originally called Fletestrete, but the modern version of that name is nowadays applied only to the short but renowned stretch of road that links Ludgate Circus to the Strand. In the latter part of the 17th century Ludgate Hill was famous for its bookshops and for its auction rooms. The scientific society of which Benjamin Franklin was a member regularly met here. The roadway was widened in 1864 when Ludgate Circus was built. A century later in 1964 there was a great outcry when new office development at the top of the hill threatened to spoil one of the most spectacular of all the views of St.Paul's Cathedral. After much pressure a compromise was reached, and the developers were persuaded to move back the frontage to some extent. But there are still many people today who consider that the new block is obtrusive, and that planning consent for its construction should not have been granted.

In Victorian times there was a shop on Ludgate Hill trading under the resounding title of 'The Commercial Plate Glass Company'. It was here in 1861,

The main hall of the Old Bailey

Ludgate Hill in the early years of this century

113

in a small back room behind the shop, that a certain Mr. Maclean founded a new satirical journal under the title *Fun*. Its editor was Henry Byron, a dramatist who wrote the most successful farce of the period, *Our Boys*. From the very early days one of the most regular contributors to the new journal was W.S.Gilbert.

Other writers whose work often appeared included Francis Burnand, Jeff Prowse and John Hollingshead, with Gilbert frequently doubling-up as the drama critic. Within a short space of time this new venture began to pose a threat to *Punch*, and it quickly outgrew its modest office behind the looking-glass shop. It moved premises to 80 Fleet Street, on a site now occupied by Barclays Bank. It was from this address that the first bound volume appeared in 1862.

Return to Ludgate Circus. Turn right into New Bridge Street for Blackfriars Underground station

The magazine attracted other contributors including Clement Scott, who became drama critic of *The Daily Telegraph*, Tom Robertson, Gilbert's mentor in revolutionary stage production techniques, George Augustus Sala, the leading journalist of the day, George Sims, who went on to found *The Referee*, and two American writers – the humorist Artemus Ward and the formidable Ambrose Bierce, perhaps best known for his remarkable collection of short stories *In the Midst of Life*. Lastly, there was Harry Leigh, who vied with Gilbert in writing comic verse. Late in his career Sims fondly recalled the 'glorious' days of working on *Fun* magazine. Writers were paid at the rate of £1 a column, with fractions of a column paid *pro rata*. Whether it was prose or verse made no difference, neither did the writer's standing in his profession. Raw novices and seasoned journalists were all paid the same flat rate by the cashier, who solemnly measured each contribution on the printed page with a piece of string and calculated the fee accordingly. In due course Maclean sold his magazine and it eventually passed into the hands of the Dalziel brothers, whose offices were at 153 Fleet Street in a building which still stands to this day.

The Tower of London

At Tower Hill Underground
station take the subway and
turn right for the Tower of
London ticket office and
main entrance

During the past 900 years the Tower of London has, at various times, served as a royal palace, prison, mint, execution ground, garrison headquartes, museum, zoo, armoury and arsenal. Immediately on his accession in 1066 William the Conqueror started to build the keep both to protect and to subdue the citizens of London. At that time the river Thames was wider at that point than it is now, and London was therefore vulnerable to naval or marine assault. William chose his site carefully with these strategic considerations very much in mind. Work on the new fortress was continued throughout his reign, and many of his successors added to the fabric of the building, or made alterations, to produce the familiar landmark which possibly more than any other single building has come to symbolise the nation's capital. The Tower of London is, beyond doubt, the oldest fortress, palace, prison – call it what you will – in Europe, pre-dating both the Doge's Palace in Venice and the Kremlin in Moscow by 300 years or more.

Most of the construction work, which involved curtaining the original fortress with walls, nineteen towers, a moat and seven gates, was done during the reigns of Henry III, Richard I and Edward I. All reigning monarchs up to Queen Elizabeth I lived in the Tower of London and held court within its impregnable walls. An extensive cleaning programme has recently been completed with the result that the building looks even more splendid than it did in Victorian times. But no amount of cleaning can wash away its grim and blood-stained history of murder, torture and execution – three topics which Gilbert found especially fascinating.

The idea for an opera based on the Tower came to him while waiting for a train at Uxbridge station. A poster for the Tower Furnishing Company featuring a beefeater caught his eye, and he decided to carry out some research. His reading took him to Harrison Ainsworth's novel *The Tower of London* (1840) and Wallace's *Maritana* (1845) which gave him gave him characters, an escape plot, and a firm conviction that the action should take place in Tudor times. As for the setting of the piece there was an embarrassment of riches, but he eventually selected Tower Green, Tower Wharf, the Beauchamp and Cold Harbour towers, the Little Ease dungeon and the Chapel Royal of St.Peter ad Vincula. The choice of a name for the opera proved to be a far more difficult matter, and is a point of some controversy even today. The project started life as *The Tower of London* but after eight months or so, in September 1888, it was renamed *The Tower Warder*. Then it became *The Beefeater*, but after an exchange of letters with John Hare, *The Yeomen of the Guard* was Gilbert's final choice of title for the new work. The Queen's Body Guard of Yeomen of the Guard, founded in 1485 after the Battle of Bosworth Field to protect the king's person in battle, is the oldest surviving military corps in the world. The last occasion on which it carried out its proper duties in the field was at Dettingen in 1743, when the English monarch led his troops into battle. Since then the duties of the Yeomen of the Guard have been of a purely ceremonial nature, attending the monarch at Maundy and at Garter services, or at investitures, state visits, garden parties and the like. It is they who search the cellars of the Palace of Westminster in November of each year ever since Guy Fawkes tried to blow up Parliament in 1605. Membership is restricted to ex-warrant officers who have served in any of the armed forces, and have a good conduct record of at least 22 years standing.

Oddly enough, the Tower of London plays no part in ceremonial duties or responsibilities discharged by the Yeomen of the Guard. These are carried out by a separate body known as the Corps of Yeomen Warders of the Tower, whose uniform is similar to that worn by the Yeomen of the Guard. And neither, contrary to popular belief, are the Beefeaters who were originally yeomen retainers who served the buffet at St. James's Palace and so became known as Buffetiers.

On the face of things it looks as though Gilbert followed the popular fallacies and failed to distinguish between the two Corps. But a close examination of dates suggests otherwise. The Corps of Yeomen Warders did not come into being until 1548 four years after the death of Sir Richard Cholmondley – who, incidentally, is the only real historical character to appear anywhere in the Savoy operas. He was Lieutenant of the Tower from 1513 to 1534 serving under two Constables, Sir Thomas Lovel and Sir William Kingston. It is true that by then King Henry VIII no longer used the Tower of London as a permanent residence, but he did leave a small detachment of twelve Yeomen of the Guard to show that it was still a royal palace. So from a strictly historical point of view most of the facts fit if the action takes place before 1548. Most, but not all – for Leonard Meryll would certainly not have qualified for inclusion. But perhaps he represents the limit of Gilbert's poetic licence?

Although the garrison chapel contains the tomb of Sir Richard and Lady Cholmondley, bearing their recumbent full-length effigies in alabaster, his actual burial place is something of a mystery. The sarcophagus was made in 1522, more than 20 years before his death, while he was still Lieutenant of the Tower. Excavation work in 1856 revealed that the tomb itself was empty. The dedication of the garrison chapel is to St. Peter ad Vincula, doubtless with the Apostle's own sufferings much in mind. The names of the occupants of many of the graves make awesome reading – Anne Boleyn, Katherine Howard, Lady Jane Grey, Sir Thomas More (whose head rests at Canterbury), Thomas Cromwell, the Dukes of Monmouth, Somerset, Suffolk, Norfolk and Northumberland, the Earl of Essex and the Earl of Arundel, Viscount Strafford and the Countess of Salisbury – all of whom met their end on the executioner's block. At the end of Act 1 of *The Yeomen of the Guard* Gilbert sets the execution scene on Tower Green. However, this picturesque spot was only used for such purposes on six occasions – a mere trifle by Tower of London standards. The place was, in fact, reserved for those whose noble birth or whose rank gave them the right to be executed in private. That, at least, was the theory. In practice, the actual choice of killing ground almost certainly rested more on political expediency than on an observance of finer feelings. Tower Hill was too public a place for the execution of such popular figures as Anne Boleyn, the Countess of Salisbury, Katherine Howard and her companion Jane, Viscountess Rochford, not to mention Lady Jane Grey and the Earl of Essex. Their public deaths would have provoked riots in the streets of the capital: far better that they should be done away with quietly, without fuss and out of sight.

The dramatic effect of using a single bell to accompany the executioner's procession is well-founded on historical fact, for the bell of St. Peter's always tolled for executions both on Tower Hill and on Tower Green. Whether the headsman always entered on the eleventh stroke as he does in *Yeomen of the Guard* is more of a matter for conjecture, but the use of the real bell in four productions staged in the moat of the Tower in 1962, 1964, 1966 and 1978 added a chilling touch of authenticity. These performances were given as part of the Festival of London, and in the last of them the part of Jack Point was played by Tommy Steele. In Gilbert's day, the effect was created by a 2 cwt. bell provided by the stage manager, J.M.Gordon, which had to be carefully positioned so that the percussionist could see the conductor at all times: a wrong entry would have been quite unthinkable. After the first production of the opera, the bell found its way into the billiard room of Gilbert's house, Grim's Dyke.

Tower Hill

116

Scenes from 'The Yeoman of the Guard' featured on the front page of 'The Graphic', 13 October 1888

The royal chapel, dedicated to St. John the Evangelist, is to be found in the oldest part of the fortress built in Norman times, the White Tower. To the west of the scaffold site by Tower Green stands the Beauchamp Tower, which dates from about 1300. Curiously, this tower remained unnamed for many years and it was not until Thomas Beauchamp, Earl of Warwick, was incarcerated here in 1397 that his name came to be used. From that time on it became a place of confinement for those of high rank. Edward Seymour, Lord Protector Somerset, was held prisoner here, and fell victim to the axe in 1552. So was Lord Protector Somerset, who fell victim to the axe in 1552. Within a year the man who had plotted his death, John Dudley, Duke of Northumberland, occupied the same cell and met the same fate. Such were the hazards of political rivalry in those turbulent times. There are more than 90 inscriptions on the walls of Beauchamp Tower, carved by its prisoners down the centuries. To these have been added facsimiles and, in some cases, actual stones bearing similar inscriptions found in other parts of the Tower of London, to form a permanent display. From the Dudleys to Rudolf Hess, who was held in the Tower for three days in May 1941, these carvings bear mute testimony to the sufferings of those held within its dank and cheerless cells. As we know from a reference made by Phoebe in the opera, the only exercise space for the prisoners was the turret roof.

The Coldharbour Tower, which was demolished in about 1670, consisted of two turrets linked by a portcullis gateway. Built by Henry III it, too, contained a number of small cells which were used to house longer-term prisoners. A point of interest is that from the copy of *The Yeomen of the Guard* which Gilbert filed with the Lord Chamberlain's office to obtain the necessary performing licence, it is clear that he had originally intended that the existing reference to the Coldharbour should relate to the White Tower under whose dungeons can be found the cell of Little Ease. This is so called because of its cruel dimensions (4ft square by 9ft high), giving the prisoner just enough room to sit or crouch, but not enough to lie down. And as Guy Fawkes, to name one among many others, found to his added discomfort there is virtually no light or ventilation in this notorious place.

Until the early part of the 13th century the only access to the Tower of London by river was at high tide by means of a water gate in St.Thomas's Tower, which later became known as 'The Traitors' Gate'. Once Tower Wharf was built, this access was used not only for landing men and supplies but also as a platform for heavy cannon, which can still be seen to this day. Those at the western end are used to fire gun salutes on royal birthdays and other state occasions. Members of the Honourable Artillery Company perform this ceremonial duty which dates back to the reign of George I. After Tower Wharf was first opened to the public in August 1893 it soon became a popular place for a Sunday afternoon stroll.

The original set for *The Yeomen of the Guard* showed the White Tower and Coldharbour Tower, with the Lieutenant's house stage right. The foreground action was therefore assumed to take place on Tower Green. Gilbert wanted the backcloth to Act 2 to show the Tower from the river wharf but he did not achieve this until a revival in 1897 when Hawes Craven was commissioned to prepare the designs, and the two men visited Tower Wharf together. A much later set by Peter Goffin in 1940 for the D'Oyly Carte Company made no visual reference whatever to the Tower of London, and provoked much controversy as a result.

Follow the perimeter wall past Tower Hill station to traffic lights by Towergate. Turn left along the Minories and left again into Aldgate.

Bear right into Leadenhall Street. 2nd turning right is St.Mary Axe

The street which runs between Leadenhall and Houndsditch near the eastern boundary of the City is most curiously named – St.Mary Axe. This derives from a church which stood on this site for a short time during the 16th century dedicated to St.Mary the Virgin. It was believed that among the treasures in this church was the axe by which St. Ursula was martyred in 1514. No.70 St.Mary Axe, to which reference is made in *The Sorcerer* did not exist in Gilbert's day although, quite by chance, the number 70 briefly appeared in the early 1940s over a blue doorway leading to a flat above shop premises actually in Houndsditch, and not in St. Mary Axe proper. This building was demolished in 1974 to make way for an extension to the Houndsditch Warehouse which, in its turn, has now also closed down.

From Leadenhall Street turn right: at the lights cross over to Cornhill and to the Bank Underground station

The main focal point of the City of London is without doubt the great junction in front of the Mansion House and the Bank of England, where Poultry joins Threadneedle Street, Lombard Street, Princes Street, Queen Victoria Street and King William Street. The Royal Exchange is now the home of the London International Financial Futures Market. Not far up Threadneedle Street is the impressive new Stock Exchange building. Admission to the Visitors' Gallery is free of charge, but there is not much activity to be seen on the Stock Exchange floor since new technology was introduced.

From Farringdon Underground station turn left and left again into Turnmill Street. At the end cross Clerkenwell Road and bear right into Clerkenwell Green

The old Sessions House, built in 1779-80 but very substantially altered in 1876, dominated Clerkenwell Green until its demolition after the Second World War. Tradition has it that Gilbert modelled his set for *Trial by Jury* on this particular courtroom, and certainly he would have come here during his pupillage to the London Quarter Sessions (now the Crown Court). Later in Gilbert's lifetime the building was also used for the Middlesex Quarter Sessions. In 1913 these were moved to the gothic-styled Guildhall in Parliament Square, and in 1921 the London Sessions moved across the river to a new Sessions House at Newington Causeway, which is still in use.

Bear left and right into St. James's Walk at the end of which cross diagonally into Rosoman Street. Take the 4th turning right, Rosebery Avenue. 300 yds north is Sadler's Wells

Although Sadler's Wells occupies a comparatively new building opened in January 1931, it is in fact one of London's oldest theatres outside the the West End. It was in 1683 that Thomas Sadler discovered a spring on the site and enclosed it with a garden to make a pleasure resort. He opened a 'Musick House' which was later considerably extended and re-built between 1746 and 1753. In the late 1820s Sadler's Wells was the home of the famous clown Joseph Grimaldi.

When the Theatres Act of 1843 came into force and broke the monopoly of the Royal Patent theatres, a new era dawned for minor theatres like Sadler's Wells, for they were now free to perform Shakespeare and other important works from the classical repertoire. A century later, Lilian Bayliss formed the Sadler's Wells Opera and Sadler's Wells Ballet companies in the 1930s. These have both flourished, gaining international stature as the English National Opera and the Royal Ballet. Not long before assuming its new name Sadler's Wells Opera presented *Iolanthe* on 24 January 1962. Earlier, in March 1951, Sadler's Wells Ballet staged the premiere of *Pineapple Poll* with music by Sullivan brilliantly arranged by Sir Charles Mackerras, choreography by John Cranko and set designs by Osbert Lancaster. This fine piece, based on *The Bumboat Woman* and *The Yarn of the Nancy Bell* from Gilbert's *Bab Ballads*, has secured a permanent place in the repertoire of most modern ballet companies.

In June 1935 Sadler's Wells played host to the D'Oyly Carte Opera Company for a season lasting four weeks. The experiment was repeated a year later, after which the theatre building was closed for extensive alterations. The Scala Theatre was used instead, but the D'Oyly Carte returned to Sadler's Wells in 1939 and, after the war, in 1947 and again in 1948. The stores of the opera company suffered a direct hit during the London air raids which resulted in the loss, among other things, of all the sets and costumes for *H.M.S.Pinafore*. So an entirely new production was prepared for the 1947 season: no easy task in the austere postwar period. From June to August 1953 a special Coronation season of Savoy operas was mounted at Sadler's Wells, but it was not until the 1970s that the theatre became the London base for the D'Oyly Carte. A series of hugely successful Christmas seasons followed which became a feature of the decade, and in more recent years Sadlers Wells Opera has put several of the Savoy operas into its own repertoire, including a centenary production of *Ruddigore*.

At the end of Rosebery Avenue turn left into St.John Street and to the Angel Underground station

Although this extended tour of the City of London comes to an end at the Angel underground station, devotees may wish to make separate journeys to see two other buildings closely associated with Gilbert and Sullivan. The first is the formidable Pentonville Prison which Gilbert visited in January 1911. He was allowed to see the condemned cell, the execution room and the gibbet from which Dr. Crippen had recently been hanged. The last play from Gilbert's pen was a short one-act piece *The Hooligan*, which dealt with the last hours spent by a man in the condemned cell.

Not much can now be seen of the second place of interest to Savoyards, the old Standard Theatre at 204 Bishopsgate Street, now called Shoreditch High Street. The building was gutted long ago and converted into shops and offices. But some of the exterior plasterwork remains and can best be seen from across the road. It was here that the rival *H.M.S.Pinafore* production came to die after failing at the Olympic Theatre. And here, too, as early as 1879, that the D'Oyly Carte Company performed in a suburban theatre tour which also took in Kennington and Camden Town. The Standard survived as a popular venue for Variety until the First World War, during which time it was affectionately referred to as the People's Theatre.

'Belgravia out of Doors'
by Richard Doyle, 1864

Chapter 13

BELGRAVIA

Hyde Park Corner to Victoria Underground stations: allow 2 hours

Some of the finest Victorian and Georgian houses in the whole of London are still to be found in Belgravia, an exclusive and prestigious residential district between Sloane Street, Hyde Park Corner and Grosvenor Place. It is no mere flight of fancy to suggest that the architecture itself reflects the social order of the day: upstairs, the imposing facades with their very handsomely-proportioned windows and impressive doors with pompous porticos, and downstairs the basement areas and the tradesmen's entrances where the postmen flirted with kitchen-maids and milkmen made eyes at the cooks. It was a world in which everyone knew without question their proper place in the social pecking order. A world in which you might well expect to find Gilbert wintering in London, and in which you might well expect Sullivan to keep a mistress. And on both counts you would be absolutely right.

From Hyde Park Corner the former St.George's Hospital can be seen. Opposite stands Apsley House

The immensely valuable Grosvenor family estates of Mayfair, Belgravia and Pimlico were created by Hugh Audley, 1577-1662, who with great foresight purchased manors other men considered worthless. One of these was a rural holding called Ebury, regularly flooded by the Thames. It was inhabited by a few farmers, and its lanes were infested by vagabonds and thieves. It is now the most valuable single estate in the whole of Great Britain. Audley died without heir and his property was divided between a number of distant relatives, one of whom was a great-nephew, Alexander Davies. His daughter, Mary, was married at the age of 12 to Sir Thomas Grosvenor, descendant of a knight called the Great Hunter (or Gros Veneur) who came to England with William at the time of the Norman Conquest. In this way did the riverside estate of Ebury become attached to the valuable Grosvenor lands in Cheshire and in Lancashire, with their major country seats at Eaton Hall and Halkin Castle. On these estates were to be found the villages of Belgrave, Minera, Eccleston, Beeston and many others.

Sir Thomas and Lady Mary Grosvenor had three sons, each of whom succeeded to the baronetcy in turn, and made his own distinctive contribution to the Mayfair part of the Ebury estate during the early part of the 18th century. But another hundred years were to pass before the great-grandson, Robert, Earl Grosvenor and First Marquess of Westminster, embarked on the difficult task of draining and of laying out the remainder of the manor grounds. He started with what we now know as Belgrave Square and the streets radiating from it; Halkin Street, West Halkin Street, Kinnerton Street, Wilton Place, Wilton Terrace and Wilton Crescent, all of which he named after his wife who was daughter of the Earl of Wilton. Then, working southwards, he drew up plans for Eaton Square and Eaton Place, Eccleston Street, Eccleston Place, Beeston Place and Minera Mews. The last area to be turned over to urban development was Pimlico, and this is the only part of the huge Westminster estate ever to have been sold, being auctioned off in 1950 to meet death duties. All the rest of the property remains in the ownership of the Grosvenor family, Britain's wealthiest private landlords, who enjoy such resplendent titles as barons Grosvenor of Eaton.

Leave Hyde Park Corner by way of Grosvenor Crescent

Grosvenor plans began to take shape in the 1820s when a bill was placed before Parliament setting out a scheme to build 'a new and healthy town' on 'fields of no mean health' between Westminster and Chelsea. The bill went through and received the royal assent from George IV. In 1826 Thomas Cubitt started work on the focal point of the project which eventually gave its name to the district as a whole – Belgrave Square.

One of the houses which the Gilberts took on lease for the London social season from January to March each year was 4 Grosvenor Crescent. This was their winter address for four years in succession, 1904 to 1907, to which they came after spending the earlier part of the cold weather travelling abroad in warmer climates. Another winter base for the Gilberts was nearby in Chesham Place, which takes its name from one of the villages owned by the Lowndes family. Here at No. 18 Gilbert spent his first London season after moving to Grim's Dyke, as is

Cross Belgrave Square to Chesham Place

Bear right to Pont Street and Cadogan Place

shown by the address on the notepaper used for the correspondence generated by the Great Carpet Quarrel during the months of January and February 1891. Some eight years later, after the spell at Grosvenor Crescent, the Gilberts chose 52 Pont Street as their winter quarters, within easy reach of Harrods and other fashionable shops.

For nearly thirty years one of the most celebrated music salons was to be found at 7 Cadogan Place, where the Carlton Tower Hotel now stands. This was the home of Mrs Pierre Lorillard Ronalds, born Mary Frances Carter. She was known as Fanny Ronalds to her intimate friends among whom was Arthur Sullivan, whose mistress she was for 23 years. This remarkable woman, by birth an American, came to London from Paris after an agreed separation from her husband in 1867. She set up home first at 84, then at 104, Sloane Street, before moving to Cadogan Place which then, as now, was very much in vogue. The Queen Anne style houses with their high gables and red brick facades replaced many small, mean properties which previously occupied the Earl of Cadogan's estate. They and their indigent occupants had all been swept aside.

4 Grosvenor Crescent

Her social skills were such that Fanny Ronalds soon made her mark on the London scene. She included among her many friends Napoleon III and the Empress Eugénie, and the Prince and Princess of Wales with whom she stayed on close terms after his accession to the throne. She was treated almost as a permanent United States ambassadress to the Court of St. James, and her apartments became virtually an annexe of the Court to which royalty could make regular and informal visits. With these social assets came a highly-developed musical gift. She had a beautiful singing voice and made the very first phonograph recording in England, in which she sang Sullivan's *The Lost Chord*. The reputation she established for her regular Sunday musical entertainments was such that many leading singers and musicians gave their services without fee. There was no better introduction to the musical life of the capital than by way of Mrs Ronalds salon in Cadogan Place. One of the many young musicians she encouraged and supported was Henry Wood. She persuaded another friend, Lillie Langtry, to make the stage her career.

Sullivan first met Fanny Ronalds in about 1871, and their relationship remained very close until his death. She acted as hostess at the parties he gave at his Queen's Mansions flat and elsewhere, and he often sought her views on musical matters including casting. The couple were seen frequently in each other's company, and in 1889 she brought about a reconciliation between Sullivan and Gilbert after they had quarrelled during the run of *The Yeomen of the Guard*. Her considerable influence on the London social scene survived the deaths of both Sullivan and King Edward VII. She herself died on 28 July 1916 and was buried at Brompton, not far from the Sullivan family plot.

122

52 Pont Street

It is a commonplace these days, but in Victorian times not many churches or chapels were converted into theatres. But in 1870, a chapel on the south side of Sloane Square became the New Chelsea Theatre. Later that same year it came into the hands of Walter Emden, who completely transformed the building and created a brilliantly-lit bijou theatre capable of seating nearly 1,100 people. The Court Theatre, as it had now become, opened on 25 January 1871 with Mary Lytton in a production of Gilbert's comic drama *Randall's Thumb*, a notable start to his long association with that theatre. In its issue dated 4 February 1871 *The Illustrated London News* described the brilliant setting of the opening night in these terms:

> … it is gorgeous in gilding, profuse in ornamentation, and its hangings and box curtains are of a pinkish mauve satin, which has a novel and very gratifying effect. Two huge griffons flank the proscenium and frescoes by Dalziel depict the life of St. George.

This opening production was followed by another drama by Gilbert, *Creatures of Impulse*, which ran from 15 April 1871 for a rather less successful run of six weeks. This was immediately followed on 29 May by his adaptation of *Great Expectations*, which was warmly received by the critics. Gilbert's boundless admiration and enthusiasm for the works of Charles Dickens was well known. The piece ran for five months and was followed in its turn by a Gilbertian comedy *On Guard*, which opened on 28 October. 1871 was indeed an extremely busy year for Gilbert at the new Court theatre.

More successes were to follow. The night of 3 May 1873 saw the opening of his burlesque *The Happy Land*, which he wrote under the strange pseudonym of F.Latour Tomline. This highly controversial romp was to prove Gilbert's biggest hit during the 1870s and contained a satirical attack on Gladstone and two of his ministers, Ayrton and Lowe. The Lord Chamberlain threatened to close the play unless the characters were disguised. Gilbert obliged by having them wear their hats with brims pulled well down and coat collars turned up, making them look more conspiratorial than before. Needless to say, the box office did tremendous business.

After two more comedies, *The Wedding March* on 15 November 1873 and *The Blue-Legged Lady* on 4 March 1874, Gilbert brought to the Court Theatre one of his blank verse dramas, *Broken Hearts*. This ran for 85 nights from 9 December 1875. The great success of this extremely sentimental piece did not prevent

Gilbert's burlesque 'The Happy Land' at the Court Theatre in 1873 was censored by the Lord Chamberlain

Gilbert from arguing furiously with the Kendals, stars of the production, nor with John Hare who had by this time taken over the management of the theatre.

In January 1884 May Fortescue, after leaving the D'Oyly Carte Company at the end of the *Iolanthe* run, made her debut at the Court in a revival of Gilbert's *Dan'l Druce*. In the event, it turned out to be the last of his works to be seen at the Court, which closed in July 1887 and was later demolished in the redevelopment of Sloane Square. However, a year later, on 24 September 1888, the Royal Court Theatre opened more or less as we know it today. It was here on 27 April 1892 that the first professional performance was given of Gilbert's *Rosencrantz and Guildenstern,* which many people regard as Gilbert's finest theatrical work. Those taking part included Weedon Grossmith, Gertrude Kingston and Brandon Thomas, author of *Charley's Aunt.*

From Sloane Square make for King's Road towards Victoria via Cliveden Place and Eaton Gate. Eaton Square is set on either side of King's Road

The last of the many houses in this area rented by the Gilberts for their winter seasons in town was 90 Eaton Square. The rental was £315 and it is clear from correspondence that Gilbert had a fierce row with the owner of the property, Lord Normanby, about bringing dogs with him from Grim's Dyke. Other surviving letters from this address to Helen D'Oyly Carte deal with such matters as the Fushimi incident and revival seasons for the Savoy operas. Near at hand in Chester Square stands the church of St.Michael. In the summer of 1861, not long after his success with incidental music for *The Tempest*, Sullivan was invited to audition for the post of organist at this large and very fashionable church. The annual stipend offered was £80 – a magnificent sum compared with most. Even Barnby at the Chapel Royal earned only £35 a year. The church was built in the 1840s to an undistinguished design by Thomas Cundy the Younger (1790-1867). It soon attracted a congregation drawn from the ranks of the military, the aristocracy, Members of Parliament, surgeons and the Bar. St.Michael's also seems to have served as a kind of garrison chapel for the local police station in Gerald Road. Church parades were held for their benefit every Wednesday morning.

From Eaton Square walk down Eccleston Street to Chester Square

18 Chesham Place

Sullivan was chosen from five candidates for the post, and as soon as he took up his appointment in October 1861 he set about the task of making the choir of St.Michael's one of the finest in London. He recruited boys from the local National School, and overcame the usual problem of shortages among the tenors and basses by calling upon the local constabulary for assistance. The Chief Superintendent's response was quite overwhelming: six tenors, six basses and a reserve team of six more voices to cover vacancies arising from sickness or leave. That Sir Richard Mayne, Commissioner of Metropolitan Police, was himself a member of the congregation may have had something to do with this uncharacteristic enthusiasm for choral music on the part of a local police force. Be that as it may, Sullivan composed a great deal of music for his choir, and in later years said that he often had his policemen in mind when composing music for *The Pirates of Penzance*.

Near the southern end of Eccleston Street is Ebury Street, leading to Grosvenor Gardens. Cross into Beeston Place. 2nd turning right is Victoria Square. Take unmarked turning which leads into Lower Grosvenor Place. Follow the one-way system to reach Victoria B.R. and Underground stations

In 1869 Sullivan took on a further commitment when he became organist of St.Peter's Church in Cranley Gardens, and as a result he started to cut back on his work at St.Michael's. Within three years an ever-increasing workload and travelling schedule forced him to give up the post altogether. He was paying the penalties as well as reaping the rewards of success: not an easy lesson for any young man to learn.

Chapter 14

CHELSEA AND PIMLICO

Pimlico to Sloane Square Underground stations: allow 3 hrs

The derivation of the word Pimlico has often puzzled London historians, and two very different theories exist as to its origin. The first suggests that in the 1590s there was a famous ale-house known as Ben Pimlico's in the well-known pleasure ground at Hoxton, near Shoreditch, and that its name was transferred to a 17th century tavern, Jenny Whim's, at Ebury Bridge on a site long since covered by railway lines. Apparently the two taverns were very similar, which explains why the name was carried forward from one to the other in popular imagination.

Not very likely, perhaps, but the second theory is no less implausible. This holds that in the 18th century there was a wharf nearby on the Thames which was called Pimlico because it handled timber, especially mahogany, imported into England from Pimlicay in Honduras. What is beyond question is that a map dated 1628 shows a small field, not far from the present site of Buckingham Palace, which was called Pimplico. Another undisputed fact is that until the dawn of the present century this area of London was over-shadowed by the massive bulk of the largest prison in Britain, the Millbank Penitentiary. It was situated immediately north of Ponsonby Terrace and was built between 1813-1816. Later, in 1870, it was converted into a military prison. After it was demolished in 1903, part of the site was used for the Tate Gallery, and what was Crescent Road became Millbank.

From Pimlico Underground station turn south and cross Bessborough Gardens to Millbank, turning left to the the foot of Ponsonby Terrace

The approach road to Vauxhall Bridge was called Ponsonby Street in those days, a name which survives in Ponsonby Terrace, off Millbank. It was John Ponsonby, First Baron Duncannon of Bessborough, who started developing the area in 1841 and was responsible for the choice of name – Pimlico Square. He was the brother-in-law of Lord Melbourne, the Prime Minister to whom the young Queen Victoria was so devoted during the early years of her reign. With a display of nepotism remarkable even by the standards of those times Melbourne appointed Ponsonby First Commissioner of Woods and Forests, which gave him not only a lucrative post but also provided the land he needed for his development plans. These substantial favours, however, failed to secure Ponsonby's support when it became clear that Melbourne's marriage to the notorious Lady Caroline was heading for disaster. He wrote saying that he could not allow his sister to be trampled upon, and that Melbourne owed her a great deal for 'deigning to marry someone of such inferior social position'. It is to be hoped that Melbourne derived some wry satisfaction from the report brought to him by his sister Emily that Ponsonby was held 'to be an ass and a jackanapes by everybody.'[1]

Ass and a jackanapes he may have been, but we owe Pimlico to his cupidity if nothing else. And somewhere in this district, then also known as South Belgravia, the young Education Office clerk took rooms in a boarding house from about 1858 to 1863 to escape the parental home which, comfortable as it was, had

[1] Cecil, Lord David *Melbourne* London: Constable/Reprint Society, 1955

North along Vauxhall Bridge Road: the 5th turning on the left is Tachbrook Street, at the end of which turn right. Cross Belgrave Road into Moreton Street, leading to Lupus Street. Turn right and then left into Claverton Street

129 Tachbrook Street

Turn right at the foot of Claverton Street into Grosvenor Road alongside the Thames. Beyond Chelsea Bridge, on the right hand side, are the gardens of the Royal Hospital

an atmosphere poisoned by frequent rows. Gilbert soon became known to his fellow-lodgers not only for the practical jokes he played on them but also for the long hours he spent writing and drawing cartoons.

It was at about this time that the Sullivan family decided to return to London to enable young Arthur to develop his career. By an odd coincidence their choice also fell upon Pimlico. It was neither fashionable nor prosperous as suited their limited means, but at least it stands north of the river and was therefore regarded as socially more acceptable than areas south of the Thames. As Sullivan's career prospered so did the fortunes of the family as a whole, and their progress can be traced by various moves of house within a very small area. They settled first in Ponsonby Street early in 1860 when young Arthur was abroad at the Leipzig Conservatory. From here they moved for a short period into a house in Lupus Street, but returned to Ponsonby Street in time to welcome the budding young composer home from his studies. He decided to take lodgings not far away, but rejoined the family soon after they moved into a larger house at 47 Claverton Terrace (renamed Claverton Street) which forms the western side of St. George's Square. It was while living at Claverton Terrace that Sullivan composed his early songs and took up his posts as organist at Covent Garden under Costa and at one, then two, fashionable churches in Belgravia. He invited his friends to regular Saturday night gatherings at the house; in 1867 he formed a string quartet, and during the following year Tennyson made several visits to the family home as his friendship with Sullivan burgeoned. It was from this address that the young composer carried on his correspondence with Rachel Scott Russell during their unresolved affair.

In 1870 Sullivan decided that the time had come to set up on his own, but he was careful to take nearby lodgings at 129 Tachbrook Street, which has changed little in character although it is now a good deal more dilapidated than it was in his day. It is was a purely temporary move, for Sullivan had already set his sights considerably higher: within 12 months his finances were such that he was able to take his first apartment in Victoria Street, at 8 Albert Mansions.

The lad from Lambeth had arrived.

The Royal Hospital, or Chelsea Hospital as it is known by many people, is a home for some 600 military pensioners, founded by Charles II in 1682. The creation of a standing army under the Commonwealth meant that provision had to be made for loyal soldiers in their declining years no longer capable of earning a living by other means. Charles II took the idea from the Hôtel des Invalides in Paris which Louis XIV established in 1670, and not from his mistress Nell Gwynn as popular legend would have us suppose. The King, who was always short of cash, reputedly funded the project by transferring £6,787 from secret service monies and by levying one day's pay from every serving soldier, backdating the order to 1676. The buildings, mainly of brick, enclose three sides of a large quadrangle with the open side facing the river, and have further wings to the east and west. They were designed by Sir Christopher Wren.

Within three years the estimated cost of the project had increased to a staggering £150,000, and Charles II did not live to see its completion. It was during the reign of William and Mary, who had the gardens laid out in formal Dutch style, that the Royal Hospital opened its doors for the first time, in 1694. Since then some 20,000 old soldiers of exemplary character and blameless record have lived out their lives in the comfort and security of a quasi-military environment, and out-pensions paid to many hundreds of thousands of their dependants. Sullivan's paternal grandfather, Thomas, was a Chelsea Pensioner, and died in the Royal Hospital on 6 February 1838.

The Annual Parade and Inspection takes place every year on Oak Apple Day, 29 May, the anniversary of King Charles's birthday and which commemorates his narrow escape after the Battle of Worcester when he hid in an oak tree near Boscobel, in Shropshire, to avoid capture by Cromwell's Roundheads. Among the guests at this important annual ceremony in 1911 was W.S.Gilbert, invited by his good friend Major-General Sir Charles Crutchley, Lieutenant Governor of the Royal Hospital since November 1908. Both he and his wife, Lady Sybil, were regular guests at Grim's Dyke, so doubtless this was an agreeable and appropriate way of returning some of Gilbert's hospitality. He watched the parade and the inspection, but left to take luncheon at the Junior Carlton Club before visiting May Fortescue in hospital. He returned home to an appointment of a very different kind, for later that afternoon, from the bathing lake in the grounds of Grim's Dyke, gardeners fished out his lifeless body.

Continue along Chelsea Embankment to Cheyne Walk

A short distance westwards along the Chelsea Embankment is Cheyne Walk, one of the most historically significant stretches of river bank on either side of the Thames. For here are memories of Catherine Parr, Thomas More, Lady Jane Grey and, in more recent times, Rossetti, Swinburne, Carlyle, Attwood and many others. In the 1850s the Rev. Thomas Helmore and his family lived at 6 Cheyne Walk (Cheyne derives from the title of the Lord of the Manor of Chelsea). Helmore was, among other things, a highly gifted choir-master who had run the Church of England's first national training college at St.Mark's, Chelsea, where daily choral worship was open to the public, and had gone on to become Master of the Children of the Chapel Royal. In 1849 he edited a book of psalms which was widely used in Anglican churches for many years.

Cheyne Walk, Chelsea

Thomas Helmore's house

There were ten choristers whose homes were outside London and who therefore lived in the Cheyne Walk house with the Rev.Helmore and his family. Of these, Sullivan was by far the eldest. His exceptional treble voice and outstanding musical talent, first recognised by Plees, had so impressed Sir George Smart that he immediately passed him on to Thomas Helmore for an audition. This was on 8 April 1854. Sullivan was nearly twelve years old, three years beyond the normal age of entry, and a further difficulty was that he lived too far away in Camberley to allow regular visits from London during normal school holidays. So obvious were his gifts, however, that Helmore persuaded the Bishop of London to make an exception on both counts after giving an assurance that he would happily accommodate Sullivan in his own house throughout the year, and not just during the school terms. Four days later Sullivan found himself in the scarlet and gold robes of the Choir of the Chapel Royal and a member of the crocodile that walked to St. James's Palace every day, twice on Sundays and Saints' Days, to the ribald accompaniment of jeers and worse from street urchins on the way, in order that they might sing to members of the royal family and their guests.

Sullivan became First Boy of the Choir in October 1856, by which time he had already started to write music of his own. Some of his earliest student work dates from 1855. However, his remarkable musical talent in no way prevented him from being beaten for deficiencies in other studies, notably in Latin and Greek. But Helmore exercised a wise and, on the whole, a benevolent discipline, and it was under his guidance that Sullivan gained the coveted Mendelssohn scholarship at the Royal Academy of Music. Indeed, he did much more: he passed on to his young pupil a love of church music which remained with Sullivan for the rest of his life. When his voice broke he was, of course, obliged to leave the Choir, but his scholarship award meant that he was able to carry on with his music studies despite limited means.

Retrace a few steps, turn left up Flood Street and then turn right into King's Road

There is yet another link with the Sullivan family not far away in King's Road, Chelsea, where the headquarters of the Duke of York's Regiment are to be found. This building, which occupies a former 12-acre market garden, was originally the Royal Military Asylum for the Children of the Soldiers of Regular Army, established in 1801 by the then Duke of York with money from the Earl of Cadogan. This solid construction of red brick faced with Portland stone, with its immense porticos, housed no fewer than 700 boys. 300 girls were transferred to another home in 1823. Dependants and orphans of serving soldiers were admitted between the ages of 9 and 11, and stayed until they were 14 or 15. Their red and blue uniforms became a distinctive feature of the neighbourhood, in which this vast institution was known as the Duke of York's School. It had its own military band, and the training given to the children was very much on Army lines. From 1814 to 1820 it numbered among its pupils the junior Thomas Sullivan, who left at the age of 15 to become a bandsman at the Royal Military College at Sandhurst.

Northumberland House

Further west along the King's Road is Fulham which, in the 1860s, was separated from Westminster by green fields. Here, in the area known as Parsons Green, just by the railway bridge that crosses New King's Road, is a Georgian building called Northumberland House. After the composer's elder brother, Fred, died at the early age of 39, Sullivan moved his mother into Northumberland House and called on her every Sunday, as far as his busy schedule allowed, until her own death on 27 May 1882. Hers had been a very closely-knit and intensely loyal family, and she had the satisfaction of living long enough to see her son, Arthur, winning the fame and fortune his talents – and her upbringing – so richly deserved.

Continue along King's Road to Sloane Square Underground station

Chapter 15

KNIGHTSBRIDGE

Knightsbridge to South Kensington Underground stations: allow 2 hrs plus time for museum visits

The shopping street between Hyde Park Corner and Rutland Gate with a reputation for luxury goods known all over the world, has given its name to one of the wealthiest and most fashionable parts of London. The derivation of the word Knightsbridge is not the obvious one: it comes from the ancient manor of Neyt which had within its boundaries a bridge crossing one of the lost rivers of London, the Westbourne, which still feeds the Serpentine in Hyde Park. The area expanded rapidly during the 1860s, when important new exhibition centres were built between Queen's Road and Exhibition Road. Rapid residential development followed, and soon Knightsbridge was regarded as an even more desirable area in which to live than its slightly Bohemian neighbour, Kensington.

The following advertisement appeared in *The Times* on 10 January 1885:

Take the Sloane Street exit from Knightsbridge Underground. Cross over and carry on through the block on the northern side to Carriage Road at Albert Gate

A Japanese village erected and peopled exclusively by Natives of Japan under the distinguished patronage of H.R.H. Princess Christian and H.R.H. Princess Louise, Marchioness of Lorne, will be opened this day at 2 o'clock by Sir Rutherford Alcock, K.C.B., late Envoy and Minister Plenipotentiary in Japan, at Albert Gate, Hyde Park (top of Sloane Street). Admission half-a-crown, (the entire receipts of the day to be devoted to some charitable institution).

Promotor and Managing Director: T.Buhicrosen

Open daily from 11am – 10pm   Admission 1/-, Wednesdays 2/6d.

This most unusual attraction was presented at Humphrey's Hall in Carriage Road. The village consisted of dwellings, shops, tea-houses and a temple of Japanese design 'carried out with thoroughness and good taste' as *The Times* reported, all erected under the cover of the hall and brought to life by about 100 Japanese, of whom 26 were women and children. To quote *The Times* report once more:

On entering the hall the visitor finds himself in a broad street of shops and houses from which rows of smaller shops forming narrow lanes are laid out to the right. These are not merely painted fronts but well-built apartments of multi-coloured bamboo with single or thatched roof painted by native artists.

A prominent feature was a demonstration of lacquering and of wood-carving, with samples of ivory, copperwork, ceramics, fans and textiles on display and available for sale. There were demonstrations of fencing, dancing and wrestling given throughout the day, and the whole exhibition captured the imagination of the London public to a remarkable degree. Textiles, wall-coverings and bric-a-brac in Japanese style became all the rage, and the influence of Japanese design was to endure for almost forty years.

It is much more likely that Gilbert drew his inspiration for *The Mikado* from all this excitement than from a Japanese sword suddenly falling down from the wall of his study, as he later claimed. The original productions put Nanki-Poo's address at Knightsbridge and nowhere else, although from the 1908 revival

*Afternoon tea at the
Japanese Village in
Knightsbridge, as
illustrated in 'The
Graphic', 13 March 1886*

onwards he was allowed other addresses as topicality or the place of performance seemed to suggest. Gilbert wrote to Helen D'Oyly Carte granting permission on this fine point of detail, since when it has been estimated that Nanki-Poo has resided in more than 70 different places in various parts of the world. The Savoy Theatre announced in advance that its well-known writers intended to produce a Japanese opera, and Gilbert enlisted the help of Buhicrosen in providing a male dancer, and a tea waitress to teach the company proper Japanese deportment, posture and carriage. They were shown how to use fans and to apply Japanese make-up, and how to make the curious hissing sound which passes for laughter among high-born Japanese ladies of medieval times. The supervision of costumes and of incidental dances was undertaken by Arthur Doisy of the Japanese Legation in London.

**Turn west along Carriage
Road.
Hyde Park is on your right**

Hyde Park and the neighbouring Kensington Gardens occupy between them an area of well over 600 acres, by far the largest open space in the whole of central London. For 200 years or more it has provided natural sanctuaries for birds of many different varieties with its fine, mature trees and large shrubberies. It has been a source of recreation and leisure for Londoners of many generations, from the fashionable riders in Rotten Row to the loud-mouthed hecklers who still gather at Speakers' Corner, near Marble Arch. One of the many attractive features is the Serpentine, an artifical lake of some 40 acres, which lies across the boundary between the two parks.

**At the end of Carriage Road
turn right
along Kensington Road**

For the 'Great Exhibition of the Works of All Nations', sponsored by the Prince Consort and opened on 1 May 1851, 87 acres were set aside between Albert Gate and Rutland Gate. Sir Joseph Paxton's vast steel and glass exhibition hall, which soon became known as the Crystal Palace, was built in just five months. Nothing on the huge scale of the Great Exhibition had been attempted

130

before in any country, and well over six million visitors came to Hyde Park to see the remarkable range and variety of exhibits drawn from all over the world.

After 114 days it was all over. The structure was dismantled and taken to Sydenham Hill, but the site remained in the hands of the Royal Commission which had been set up to mastermind the whole grand design from start to finish. And with the vision and foresight characteristic of that confident age plans were drawn up for the impressive public buildings that we see today: the Victoria and Albert Museum, Imperial College, the Royal College of Art, the Royal College of Music and many others.

Travelling westwards along Kensington Road, the keen-eyed traveller will see that for a short stretch of about 300 yards it becomes Kensington Gore. The name comes from a large Georgian house which once stood here, and derives from an area of very muddy ground on which it was built. From 1808 to 1821 the house was occupied by the great protagonist for the abolition of slavery, William Wilberforce. He was a popular figure who received many visitors, but from Hyde Park Corner onwards they travelled in groups for their mutual protection, so great was the danger from footpads, rogues and vagabonds on the open road. Gore House was considered in those days to be in the country, well outside London. It was purchased in 1836 by Lady Blessington, who created a literary *salon* with Bulwer Lytton, Benjamin Disraeli and Walter Savage Landor in regular attendance. The house also became the first London refuge for the émigré Louis Napoleon. In 1851 it was acquired by the Commissioners and converted into a restaurant for visitors to the Great Exhibition. When that came to an end Gore House was demolished, the 3½-acre site cleared, and in due time the huge rotunda of the Albert Hall rose in its place. Once again, it was Prince Albert who proposed that a large public hall should be built in this part of London to provide a proper setting for musical performances of all kinds, especially oratorios. By the time the project got under way the Commissioners widened the terms of reference to include exhibitions of arts and the sciences. The greater part of the building costs came from public subscription: in a very real sense the Royal Albert Hall became the nation's true memorial to the Prince, who did not live to see his dream realised. The form of the building is a huge ellipse 220ft wide and 250ft long, covered by a dome which rises to 130ft. It was originally designed to seat an audience of 6,000 with standing room for another 1,000 people. The superb Willis organ contains no fewer than 9,000 pipes and is one of the largest in the world.

Since it was opened by Queen Victoria on 29 March 1871 the Royal Albert Hall has been used for all manner of purposes, some of which could hardly have been envisaged by the Commissioners, such as boxing matches, political rallies, business conferences (complete with packed lunches), evangelical missions,

27 Prince's Gardens, where Gilbert spent the winter of 1898, is now the temporary home of the Iranian embassy in London

The Royal Albert Hall, c.1900

trade fairs and, for many years, the Chelsea Arts Ball. Within five weeks the widowed Queen carried out her first official engagement in the Albert Hall by attending the musical celebrations marking the opening of the International Exhibition on 1 May 1871, for which occasion Arthur Sullivan conducted the first public performance of his dramatic cantata *On Shore and Sea*. The first orchestral concert in the new hall took place one month later, and was conducted by the French composer Charles Gounod.

Although Sullivan was by no means a regular conductor at the Royal Albert Hall his appearances included a performance of *The Martyr of Antioch* given before the Prince of Wales early in April 1881, a royal command performance of his *Golden Legend* on 8 May 1888, at which Queen Victoria told him once again that he really ought to write a grand opera, and lastly on 20 January 1900 when he conducted an arrangement for massed bands of his song *The Absent-Minded Beggar*, originally written to words by Rudyard Kipling to raise fund for victims of the Boer War.

The Royal Albert Hall remained the main concert venue in London for more than 80 years. Indeed, after the loss of the Queen's Hall in 1941 it was the only concert hall in London until the development of the South Bank. Although selections from the Savoy operas feature in the Proms season each year, the first full costume production at the Albert Hall was *The Mikado*, presented by Norman Meadmore's London Savoyards on 2 December 1978, with a chorus of 232 singers drawn from local amateur societies. More recently, a performance from scratch of *H.M.S.Pinafore* took place: with his meticulous attention to production detail one wonders what Gilbert would have made of that particular enterprise.

The interior of the Royal Albert Hall

The Albert Memorial

Not even the Albert Hall was enough to satisfy the Victorian appetite for monumental masonry: another and more personal tribute was erected on the opposite side of Kensington Gore to commemorate the Prince Consort. This extraordinary structure has come in for a good deal of criticism, not to say ridicule, since it first appeared on the London scene. Below a canopy on which a spire rises to a height of 180ft stands an effigy in gunmetal of Prince Albert. In his hands is not a copy of the Bible as Victorian piety might well have decreed, but the catalogue of the Great Exhibition of 1851. It is, perhaps, as good a passport to the hereafter as any other. The departed Prince is by no means alone: he is attended by 24 other statues, not to mention 169 worthies drawn from the worlds of poetry, architecture, music and the arts, depicted on a freize around the base. The entire confection stands on a rising staircase in marble which is 200ft long on each of its four sides. In recent years as the taste for Victoriana has grown so criticism of the Albert Memorial has become muted, and it is increasingly accepted as a rich and unique example of its kind. Recent alarming reports of a threatened collapse as a result of corrosion may well give rise to a strong public demand for restoration work to be carried out: it will be interesting to see if this comes about.

133

*Arthur Sullivan
in his late forties*

**At the rear of the Royal
Albert Hall is the Royal
College of Music**

*The Royal College of
Organists, formerly
the National Training
School for Music*

When Gilbert was taken to task for his choice of title for *Ruddigore*, he countered by suggesting that piece might be called *Kensington Gore*, or *Robin and Richard Were Two Pretty Men*. Not surprisingly little more was then heard of the proposal to amend the title or of Gilbert's reaction to it.

Immediately to the west of the Albert Hall is another remarkable building with mock Jacobean graffito panelling, built in 1875 to house the National Training School for Music, all part of Sir Henry Cole's grand design to use the Exhibition site and adjacent areas for a huge complex devoted to the arts. To set up a new college for musical education was another of Prince Albert's ideas, which he first mooted in 1854. The intention was to give free tuition to promising young musicians by means of scholarships funded by town and county local authorities.

A campaign to raise money for 300 such scholarships was launched in 1875 but by the time the College opened in May of the following year only 82 places were endowed. Sullivan, then aged 34, was invited to accept the post of Principal, an honour he sensibly declined as he disliked teaching. But he had reckoned without his powerful patrons the Duke of Edinburgh and the Prince of Wales, both of whom brought pressure to bear with the result that he felt obliged to accept the post in 1876. He also found himself occupying the chair of Composition at an annual salary of £400. In his reminiscences to Arthur Lawrence, Sullivan later recalled:[1]

> The Royal Academy of Music had fallen into very low water at that time and Sir Henry Cole thought it was a favourable opportunity to establish an institu-

[1]Lawrence, Arthur *Sir Arthur Sullivan – Life Story, Letters and Reminiscences* London: James Bowden, 1899

tion for musical education. It was his desire to get everything central at South Kensington so as to bring all the arts schools together. I very unwillingly accepted the post of Principal and held the position for six years ... the Royal College of Music was founded on the basis of the Training School which I had conducted. It was to all intents and purposes the same institution. They took over our building, our library and our teaching staff. Sir George Grove was appointed Director and carried on the institution on the lines which I had already laid down. So you see that the National Training School of Music was really the forerunner and parent of the Royal College of Music.

During his time as Principal, Arthur Sullivan frequently complained to Sir Henry Cole about lack of funds, and on one occasion in April 1881, when the great Russian pianist Anton Rubenstein visited the National Training School of Music, it was said that Sullivan dipped into his own pocket to keep the finances afloat. He resigned at Easter 1881, and the post was then filled by John Stainer.

Left along Prince Consort Road to Exhibition Road. Cross over the Prince's Gardens

The Royal College of Organists, mainly an examining body, took over the building previously occupied by the Royal College of Music when, in May 1904, it moved to its own premises in Prince Consort Road, facing the steps at the back of the Royal Albert Hall. Today, it is a very much larger institution than when it was established by royal charter just over a century ago. In its first year there were 92 students altogether, of whom 50 were scholars and the rest fee-payers. Now the Royal College of Music has 700 full-time students and a library which has

Victoria and Albert Museum

135

*The Imperial Institute
c.1900*

among its many treasures the autograph score of *The Yeomen of the Guard* which was bequeathed by the composer. Before the College came formally into being concerts were held in the building to raise money for the whole project. One of the more outstanding occasions was on 13 May 1882 when Sullivan accompanied the Duke of Edinburgh, no less, playing the violin. Madame Albani, the well-known soprano, also appeared in the same programme.

On his retirement Grove was succeeded by Sir Hubert Parry, who held the office of Principal until 1918. He presented an organ for the new concert hall, the first of a number of major extensions to the College which have helped it to keep pace with the growing demand for places.

Return to Exhibition Road and turn left. First right is Imperial Institute Road

Before we leave this part of London it should be noted that Gilbert spent two of his winter seasons nearby in Prince's Gardens. In 1894 he took a lease on No.36 for three months and in 1898, for a similar term, he rented No.27.

Another building in the area with which Sullivan is closely associated is the Imperial Institute, which was built to mark the golden jubilee of Queen Victoria. The original plan had been to create a prestigious show-case for the raw materials and finished products of the British Empire, and to provide the headquarters of a new imperial club. This latter idea failed despite, or perhaps because of, the very modest subscriptions it was proposed to charge to members. Nowadays, the building is used by the University of London for administrative purposes, and by the faculties of the Imperial College of Science and Technology.

When the foundation stone was laid on 4 July 1887 Sullivan conducted pupils from the Royal College of Music in the first performance of his *Ode*, to words by Lewis Morris, which was specially written for the occasion at the request of the Prince of Wales. In formal levée dress, and accompanied both by Fanny Ronalds and the Duchess of Marlborough, he attended the opening ceremony performed by the Queen on 10 March 1893. For this he composed an *Imperial March* which he conducted at a Philharmonic Society concert five days later.

Return to Exhibition Road. Turn right towards South Kensington Underground

No visitor to London should miss the great museums of South Kensington on Exhibition Road. The Science Museum, where one can still see the 15ft model of *H.M.S.Queen* that took pride of place in the Gilbert households at Harrington Gardens and at Grim's Dyke, the Geological Museum, the Natural History Museum and, of course, the Victoria and Albert Museum. No other part of the capital expresses more eloquently the dignity and the grandeur of Britain's imperial past. In no other part of the capital do we find the confidence of the Victorian age at its zenith expressed with such overwhelming confidence and optimism.

Chapter 16

SOUTH KENSINGTON AND BROMPTON

Walk from South Kensington to West Brompton Underground stations: allow 4 hrs including Brompton Cemetery

The grandiose schemes of Sir Henry Cole had a profound effect on the South Kensington area as a whole. Alongside the main colleges there grew up private academies promoting new trends in design, art, fashion and literature. All this sudden burgeoning of educational opportunity soon created a large student population, which almost certainly accounts for the somewhat raffish and Bohemian reputation South Kensington still has. Students in Victorian times were not teenagers, but mostly young men in their early 20s. And women students, even in the arts faculties, were few in number mostly because the doors of the recognised professions were still firmly shut against them. Nevertheless, enough youthful high spirits remained to make it a much livelier place than its rather stuffy neighbour Knightsbridge.

For a time the area attracted quite a large number of creative people from various fields. Gilbert lived here for most of his working life; Millais had a large house here; Burnand lived in South Kensington during his editorship of *Punch*; Beatrix Potter lived in Bolton Gardens; both Jenny Lind and Adelina Patti made their homes here, as did politicians such as Joseph Chamberlain and Sir Charles Dilke. But fashions change, and by 1900 South Kensington was no longer so desirable a residential area. The land was low-lying, and thought to be unhealthy as a result. The heavy clay on which the houses of the well-to-do were built caused dampness in the autumn, and humidity in the summer, which damaged the fabric of the buildings – or so it was thought. Consequently, the descendants of the wealthy families who flocked here from such places as Regent's Park and Bloomsbury in the late 1840s and early 1850s, returned whence they came at the close of the century.

From South Kensington Underground station walk south to Onslow Square. Turn right into Onslow Gardens, at the end of which turn left into Cranley Gardens

At the time of the Crystal Palace concerts Sullivan, through a mutual organist friend, met the Hon. Francis Byng, an Anglican curate who made a speciality of breaking-in new churches. In June 1867, shortly after he took up his appointment at St.Peter's in Cranley Gardens, built by Sir Charles Freake, he asked Sullivan to design an organ for the church and to find him a resident organist. The post was even more fashionable than Sullivan's own, although probably not so well paid. Unable to find the right man for the job he offered to deputise on a temporary basis. They agreed that Byng would send a telegram to Sullivan on Saturday evening if his services were required so that he, in turn, could get Cellier to stand in for him at St.Michael's the following day. Sullivan also set to work preparing the consecration service for the new church, which was conducted by the Bishop of London on 29 June 1867. Two years later he handed over his responsibilities at St.Michael's to Franklin Taylor and became the permanent organist at St.Peter's until February 1872. Growing pressure of work forced him to give up this post also and he handed over to James Hamilton Clarke who, interestingly enough, later conducted for Henry Irving at the Lyceum and wrote incidental music for the theatre. The Hon. Francis Byng rose in the world by becoming chaplain to the Speaker of the House of Commons, before succeeding to the family title of Earl Strafford.

From St.Peter's take next turning right, Evelyn Gardens. Turn right and then left to Roland Gardens and then into Drayton Gardens. Cross over to Priory Walk, at the end of which turn right into The Boltons

24 The Boltons

In the summer of 1876 Gilbert acquired the lease of 24 The Boltons, where he lived for seven years, during which time he wrote *Engaged*, *The Sorcerer*, *H.M.S.Pinafore*, *Gretchen*, *The Pirates of Penzance*, *Iolanthe*, *Patience* and *Foggerty's Fairy*. The land on which the Boltons estate stands was once part of the manor of Brompton, which had stayed largely undeveloped until about 1800. Then, in the middle of the 19th century Robert Gunter purchased 93 acres from the Bolton family, hence the name, and together with George Godwin sent comprehensive development plans in March 1850 to the Commissioners of Sewers, the appropriate authority in in those days. Over the next 25 years, some 1,100 houses were built, 90 mews properties, two churches and five pubs.

The Boltons is the centrepiece of the development and consists of 28 very substantial properties, of which all but two had been completed by 1871. An official census carried out that year reveals that owners and their families accounted for 87 of the residents, but that they were outnumbered by their 97 servants. Among the heads of households there was an industrialist, a house-property owner, two landowners, a ship owner, a broker, a magistrate, an artist and a retired servant of the Honourable East India Company. When the Gilberts took up residence their immediate neighbour was the singer Jenny Lind, renowned as 'The Swedish Nightingale' and an early patroness of Arthur Sullivan. Frank Burnand also lived in The Boltons at that time, as did Madame Albani.

39 Harrington Gardens

The entrance hall, with an imposing oak staircase and inglenook

138

*The drawing room with
its ornate embossed
ceiling*

**At the northern end of The
Boltons cross Brompton
Road into Bolton Gardens.
Straight on to Collingham
Road. First right is
Harrington Gardens**

Although little is known of the Gilberts' domestic life at this time, it is quite certain that the famous children's parties started while 'Bab' lived here, and that Gilbert began collecting carved ivories, old masters and antique furniture. In his library could be found most of the classics of English literature, with pride of place given to the works of Charles Dickens. It was also during his time at 24 The Boltons that Gilbert created his scale model theatre and the coloured blocks he used to work out his quite revolutionary concepts of stage direction. For the production of *H.M.S. Pinafore* there was a half-inch scale model of the quarter deck of a ship-of-the-line, accurate to the last detail. He had his first telephone installed at a cost of £20 per annum, and while they were working on *Iolanthe*, in February 1882, he urged Sullivan to follow his example, presumably so that they could keep in touch more easily as their joint labours progressed. By 1883 Gilbert had prospered to such an extent that he felt able to build a mansion to his own specifications on a site just half-a-mile away. So in October of that year 24 The Boltons was put on the market: now in a conservation area, it stands today with its exterior more or less unchanged.

His choice fell on Harrington Gardens and it was here, at No.39, he spent the next seven years, the most productive of his highly productive career. *Princess Ida, Comedy and Tragedy, The Mikado, Ruddigore, The Yeomen of Guard, Brantinghame Hall, The Brigands* and *The Gondoliers* were among the many works of this period.

It was the revenue from *Patience* that enabled Gilbert, Sullivan and D'Oyly Carte to change their life styles considerably. Gilbert entered into an agreement with Henry Coke to acquire the Harrington Gardens plot and to share it between them, thus Coke became his immediate neighbour at No.41, although Gilbert's house carried the number 19 when he moved into it. Ernest George and Peto were engaged to design the new house and Stephens and Bastow were appointed building contractors, with a typical warning from Gilbert that he would move in on 1st October 1883 whether the work was finished or not, and that he would charge demurrage for each day thereafter. This threat was in all probability carried out, for Sir Theodore and Lady Martin recalled that workmen were still on the site as late as November 1883, 18 months after the starting date.[1]

The flamboyant exterior of the house is topped by a huge stepped gable of nineteen stages which in turn is surmounted by a weathervane model of *H.M.S.Squirrel*, the ship in which Sir Humphrey Gilbert was lost. Red brick and stone facings are used for the facade; leaded windows feature various insignia relating to Gilbert, and drainpipes bear his initials. The chimneys are massive: that to the west is shared with the house next door. The rear elevation is quite symmetrical, with two-storey tile-hung bay windows beneath a large gable which has at its centre an ornamental sundial. The interior of the house is no less spectacular. The hallway is oak-panelled and dominated by one of a number of chimneypieces made of carved stone from floor to ceiling, with a blue-tiled inglenook in which Gilbert is said to have hung hams. The hall also features glass panels painted in a style reminiscent of Holbein, and originally had on its walls leather stamped paper which has since been replaced. The handsome oak staircase has a window opening on to the stairwell from a room at half-landing level which Lady Gilbert used as her boudoir. It was from this window that Gilbert lowered presents for the children at parties often attended by as many as two hundred guests.

Some of the doors on the ground floor are inscribed with whimsical mottoes. That to the dining room, which has a beam and gilt-edged panel ceiling, reads 'All hope abandon, ye who enter here.' And at the rear of the house there is a magnificent drawing room, now used as a boardroom, with rosewood panelling and a richly sculptured alabaster chimneypiece and fireplace, which has this inscription on the door: 'And those things do best please me, that befall preposterously.' A very Gilbertian sentiment, one suspects. His study was on the first floor and it was here in the window niche that he did most of his writing. The room is partly oak-panelled and partly finished in leather red and gold wallpaper which is original, although somewhat faded. Also on the first floor was the billiard room. The remaining three floors consisted of guest rooms and bedrooms, while in the basement there were self-contained quarters for the servants.

Like D'Oyly Carte, Gilbert believed in keeping up with the times. He had no fewer than 77 electric light fittings installed, with a generator in the basement to provide the necessary power. In addition, he had oil-fired central heating put in, and it says much for the system and for the heating engineer that it still works to this day, after more than 100 years. There was a bathroom on each of the upper floors, an unheard-of luxury, and in a small cupboard next to the fireplace in his study there was, needless to say, a telephone.

In *The Era* of 17 January 1885 we find that 'few more artistic and elegant residences are to be seen in the metropolis than the abode of this distinguished author.' The report appeared after a performance of the second act of *Patience* given in the house as an after-supper entertainment. Both Grossmith and Barrington took part, with a cast of society amateurs; accompaniment was provided by Arthur Sullivan on the harmonium, and by Cellier at the piano.

The stamp of Gilbert's personality is to be seen throughout the house, but it has to be remembered that he spent only seven winters within its walls. By the summer of 1890 we find the Gilberts already at Breakspears waiting for the decorators to finish work on their house Grim's Dyke, at Harrow Weald. The sale of 39 Harrington Gardens was entrusted to George and Peto. For many years is was the national headquarters of the Board of Midwives, and in 1929, following

[1]Sheppard *General Survey of London* London: Athlone Press, 1983

Gilbert's library, where he wrote 'The Mikado'

representations made by the Gilbert & Sullivan Society, the L.C.C. put one of its familiar blue plaques on the house: 'Sir W.S.Gilbert (1836-1911) Dramatist, Lived Here.' Today it is a Grade II listed building of historical interest which means that no alterations can be made either to the structure or to the decorations. However, consent for office use has been granted, and when the property last came on to the market in 1983 the asking price was in excess of £400,000. Today it would probably fetch well over £1 million.

Return to Collingham Road. Turn left to Brompton Road. Turn right and continue across Earls Court Road and Warwick Road until you reach the northern entrance to Brompton Cemetery

There is a final postscript which throws further light on Gilbert's quirky sense of humour. He insisted that while working in his study a Japanese sword fell from the wall and that this incident first inspired him to write the libretto of *The Mikado*. How likely this story is, when the whole of London was agog with the Japanese village exhibition in Knightsbridge, within very easy reach of Harrington Gardens, is best left to the reader to judge.

Brompton and Bromptonville were areas of marshland used for market gardening from the 16th century to the mid-19th century, as London's population steadily increased. Then, private hospitals and clinics were set up to enable people 'to take the genial air', and this in turn led to residential development. The huge Brompton Cemetery (the West London and Westminster Cemetery, to use the correct title), covering an area of 139 acres, started as a private venture in 1840, but got into financial difficulties and was compulsorily purchased by the Board of Health in 1855. From that time on it became the chosen burial place for Victorian London and by 1889 it contained no fewer than 155,000 graves. With the Royal Hospital at Chelsea close at hand it is not surprising that many soldiers are buried here. In addition, Brompton Cemetery is the resting place for many famous names connected with literature and the arts.

Among the friends of Gilbert and of Sullivan buried here are Frederick Clay (1889), Augustus Harris (1896), Lionel Monckton (1924), Henry J. Byron (1884), Brandon Thomas (1914) and the actors Benjamin Webster (1882) and William Terriss (1897). In the plain and unpretentious grave of the Sullivan family lie the composer's parents Thomas (1866) and Mary Clementina (1882), and his elder brother Frederick (1877). There are two empty spaces: one for him and one for his wife, had he married. On the bare flank of the gravestone next to his mother's name, there is space for his own. The tomb was opened in November 1900 to receive him, but it was the Queen's wish that Sir Arthur Sullivan should be laid to rest in the chilly splendour of St.Paul's Cathedral, and not in the comfortable, reassuringly middle-class setting of Brompton Cemetery

And royal wishes are not be ignored, even in death.

Brompton Cemetery

With so large a number of graves it is not surprising that Brompton Cemetery has many examples of Victorian monumental architecture at its exuberant best. The grounds are full of historical interest and a visit is strongly recommended. They are open from 9am to 1pm and 2pm to 4pm, Mondays to Saturdays. The Clerk of the Works can be available to give directions provided he is given reasonable notice: he can be contacted on 01-352-1201.

The Cemetery is no longer used for burials and is under the care of the Department of the Environment, who employ a team of ten gardeners to look after the grounds.

The Sullivan family grave (No.111588) is not easy to find. It lies in compartment 'M', at a point 226ft from north to south and 37ft east to west. Alternatively, it can be identified as the grave some 15ft to the north-east of the mausoleum which stands by a junction on the east side of the central pathway, nearly midway between the main entrance and the chapel.

Immediately beyond the Cemetery, to the left, on Old Brompton Road, is West Brompton Underground

Some distance away lies the grave of Mary Frances Ronalds, who died on 28 July 1916. She is buried in compartment 'E4' at a point 80ft from north to south and 20ft from east to west. The grave number is 173742.

142

Chapter 17

FROM KENSINGTON TO MARYLEBONE

Gloucester Road to Notting Hill Gate underground stations: allow 2 hrs

From Gloucester Road station cross Cromwell Road, go up Grenville Place to its junction with Kynance Mews. Turn left, right and left into Eldon Road

At the end of Eldon Road turn right into Stanford Road and pass into Kensington Court Place. Bear left to the High Street and turn left. Pass Church Street on the right. The 4th turning on the right is Argyll Road

28 Eldon Road

From the 12th century to 1539 most of Kensington and the parish of St. Mary Abbotts, for which the first church was built before 1100, belonged to the Abbey of Abingdon. Kensington Palace, to the west of Kensington Gardens, was used by the sovereign as a private residence from 1689. When William III came to live here, after major alterations to the building had been made by Sir Christopher Wren, Kensington became a fashionable area where many famous people chose to live. Further additions to the Palace were made by William Kent for George I, and Queen Victoria was born here. In the late 1860s, when the Metropolitan District Railway linked High Street Kensington with the line to Victoria and Westminster, the district became a major shopping centre specialising in fashions and antiques, as well as a much-favoured residential area.

After their marriage in August 1867 William and Lucy Gilbert chose the top floor flat at 28 Eldon Road for their first home, where they lived for just over eight months. Not long after they moved in Gilbert secured commissions from three different theatres to write new pieces for their forthcoming Christmas seasons. In a characteristically creative burst he wrote *Allow Me To Explain* for the Prince of Wales Theatre, *Highly Improbable* for the Royalty, and *Harlequin, Cock Robin and Jenny Wren* for the Lyceum Theatre. The fees he earned for his pieces were not large by any manner of means, but added to his income from other work, which continued to increase, they did enable him early in his married career to consider moving into a larger property.

Not long after the wedding, the old church of St. Mary Abbots, on the corner of Church Road, was rebuilt in the Decorated style and is one of the best examples of the work of Sir Gilbert Scott. The original pulpit and some of the old monuments have been kept. Near the west end of the church James Mill, father of John Stuart Mill, was buried in 1836. The move to 8 Essex Villas, off Argyll Road to the north of Kensington High Street, represented a step up the social ladder for the Gilberts. It was a large and spacious house with its own library in which he spent many productive hours. They could now afford to employ domestic servants for the first time, a prequisite for those about to assume the mantle of Victorian middle-class respectability. During his eight years in this part of Kensington Gilbert wrote 33 plays, including *The Princess, The Palace of Truth, Pygmalion and Galatea, Thespis* and *Trial by Jury.* It was his usual practice to work in the early hours of the morning, and then go to bed. In February 1876 there began a long-running dispute with his neighbour, a man called Furlonger, who lived at 6 Essex Villas and whose servants were so noisy in the morning that, according to Gilbert, he was quite unable to sleep. In reply, Furlonger complained about the late-night Sunday parties thrown by the Gilberts earlier in the year. On at least two of these occasions Sullivan was among the numerous guests.

This was not the only dispute Gilbert conducted from 8 Essex Villas, for it was from here that he dealt with much of the correspondence which was generated by

Return to Argyll Road, turn left up the hill and right at the end into Upper Phillimore Gardens. At junction with Campden Hill turn left and left again to Campden Hill

his bitter quarrel with Henrietta Hodson. On a rather happier note, not long after his parents had separated, Gilbert managed to persuade his father to visit the house, in late June 1876. Soon after that Gilbert decided to move once more, possibly on account of the row with Furlonger, but more likely because of the large income he was now earning from two important successes *Trial by Jury* and *Pygmalion and Galatea*.

The top of Campden Hill commands a view of Holland Park and of the Orangery, in which a number of notable productions of the Savoy operas have been staged. To the right stands Holland Park School, built on the site of Moray Lodge which was demolished in 1955. It was built by John Tasker in 1817 and originally called West Lodge. When John Malcomson, a true Scot, became the occupant in 1844 he decided to change the name to Moray Lodge, by which it continued to be known. By any standards it was a very large town house, with 20 bedrooms, five bathrooms and four main reception rooms. In the wooded

Moray Lodge, Kensington

8 Essex Villas

A COUNTRY HOUSE IN THE HEART OF LONDON

ON THE SUMMIT OF CAMPDEN HILL
KENSINGTON
STANDING IN COMPLETELY WOODED GROUNDS OF 4½ ACRES

AMIDST ENTIRELY COUNTRY-LIKE SURROUNDINGS COMMANDING EXTENSIVE PICTURESQUE VIEWS, AND WELL REMOVED FROM ALL TRAFFIC, THUS ENSURING PERFECT PEACE AND QUIETUDE.

A MODERNISED RESIDENCE

APPROACHED BY LONG AVENUE, WITH SPACIOUS ENTRANCE HALL.

FOUR HANDSOME RECEPTION ROOMS—ALL PANELLED WINTER GARDEN.

20 BED AND DRESSING ROOMS (INCLUDING BEST BEDROOM SUITE, CONSISTING OF BEDROOM, DRESSING ROOMS WITH FITTED WARDROBES AND CUPBOARDS, BOUDOIR AND BATHROOM, ETC.

FIVE BATHROOMS.

AMPLE AND COMPLETE DOMESTIC OFFICES

SERVICE LIFT.

DETACHED GARAGES FOR SIX LARGE CARS WITH SEVEN ROOMS OVER FOR CHAUFFEURS.

TWO ENTRANCE LODGES, ONE WITH BATHROOM.

TENNIS LAWNS AND EN-TOUT-CAS COURT.

FLOWER AND KITCHEN GARDENS, PEACH HOUSE, VINERY, ETC., AND OUTBUILDINGS.

THE 23 YEARS' LEASE OF THIS UNIQUE PROPERTY FOR SALE.

FOR APPOINTMENT TO VIEW APPLY TO THE AGENTS:

CHESTERTON & SONS,
116, KENSINGTON HIGH STREET, W. 8
Telephone: WESTERN 1231

J. D. WOOD & CO.,
23, BERKELEY SQUARE, W. 1
Telephone: MAYFAIR 6341

A VIEW OVER PART OF THE GROUNDS FROM THE HOUSE

14 Pembridge Gardens

Return to Campden Hill Road and turn left. At Notting Hill Gate turn right. First turning left is Pembridge Gardens

Ignatius Paul Pollaky, forerunner to Sherlock Holmes?

gardens, which commanded splendid views over London, there were two tennis courts. From 1861 to 1893 Moray Lodge was the home of Arthur Lewis, of Lewis and Allenby, the well-known firm of silk mercers. Arthur Lewis and his wife Kate Terry, grandparents of Sir John Gielgud, turned Moray Lodge into a Bohemian centre for artists, writers and musicians. Their dinner parties and evening entertainments attracted a remarkable array of Victorian talent and enterprise. Their guests included members of the royal family, and such famous figures as Charles Dickens, Wilkie Collins, Anthony Trollope, Sir John Millais, Sir John Tenniel, Dante Gabriel Rossetti, George du Maurier, Canon Harford, Holman Hunt, Gustave Doré, Felix Moscheles, Tom Taylor, Val Princep, Tattersall, the horse dealer, Poole, the tailor, Burnand and Sullivan.

From January to April each year, on the last Saturday of each month, Arthur Lewis threw enormous stag parties, which cut across class and social barriers as well as professions and academic disciplines. From these parties emerged a group of singers, calling themselves the Moray Minstrels, who regularly met together to perform glees, madrigals and part-songs. And it was at Moray Lodge on 26 May 1866 that they gave the the first private performance of a work written by two of their number, Burnand and Sullivan. This was *Cox and Box*, an adaptation of Maddison Morton's play, and the only non-Gilbertian libretto to Sullivan's music in the permanent repertoire of the D'Oyly Carte Company.

The ownership of Moray Lodge changed hands in 1910 and again in 1931. At the outbreak of the Second World War the house was requisitioned for the duration, but remained in official hands until its demolition. Not far away in Notting Hill Gate is 14 Pembridge Gardens where Gilbert spent his boyhood, when his parents were in London, and when he was away from his boarding school at Ealing. His father was a retired naval surgeon who wrote several plays, poems, biographies and novels, and who seems to have taken a quite remarkable interest in insanity. In May 1876 he walked out of the house and went to live in Salisbury, where the Gilbert family is said to have come from. Today, more than 100 years later, the houses in Pembridge Gardens have changed very little in their external appearance.

To the west and north of Kensington are situated Paddington, Bayswater and Marylebone, where links with our two heroes can be found. They are of marginal interest, however, and too far apart to make a structured or planned tour worthwhile. For example, at 139 Westbourne Terrace Sullivan rented his first private rooms after leaving the home of his parents in Ponsonby Street. He later returned to Pimlico to be nearer his family. From the age of 9½ he had boarded at a private school or academy, as its owner William Gordon Plees preferred it to be known, in Porchester Road at 20 Albert Terrace. By the end of his first year he had set his heart on joining the choir of the Chapel Royal and letters to his parents, who had returned to live at Sandhurst, were full of entreaties seeking their permission. His father countered with suggestions that he should follow up his interest in chemistry, but finally relented in the face of young Arthur's determination to follow his musical star. Just before his 12th birthday he was taken by Plees to see the Chapel Royal's organist and composer, Sir George Smart, who was greatly impressed. In later years he said that he had been particularly struck by Sullivan's knowledge of music as a whole, but Hesketh Pearson[1] rather sourly suggests that this was almost certainly a case of wisdom after the event. At that crucial audition all that would have concerned Sir George would have been the quality of Sullivan's voice, and that it was this alone that won him a place in the choir well over the normal age of entry.

[1]Pearson, Hesketh *Gilbert and Sullivan*, London: Hamish Hamilton, 1935

Paddington Green was the home of Paddington Pollaky, or Ignatius Paul Pollaky to give him his full name. He was a remarkable character, of Austrian nationality, whose brilliant work as a detective was recognised not only in this country, but also in many places abroad. He was almost a prototype of that other internationally-known sleuth, Sherlock Holmes. Many people thought that Pollaky was a member of the Metropolitan Police on the strength of Paddington Green police station, but he remained a private enquiry agent throughout his career, with his own office at 13 Paddington Green. Eventually he retired to Brighton, where he became an habitué of the chess room in the Royal Pavilion. He died in 1918 at the age of 90.

Near Baker Street station is Melcombe Street which leads into Dorset Square where, at 26-28, lived the famous actor and author George Grossmith (1847-1912): his substantial town house is now used as offices. A much more familiar landmark in this part of London is Madame Tussaud's, although in Arthur Sullivan's time it was in Baker Street and not in the Marylebone Road, as now. It was here that the young composer spent his 21st birthday, in the company of the Lehmanns, and a rueful entry in his diary describes the waxworks museum as a place of 'delirious dullness'.

*George Grossmith's
house in Dorset Square*

At York Gate in Marylebone Road is the Royal Academy of Music, now regarded as the principal music teaching establishment in Britain, with some 700 full-time students of composition and the performing arts, and its own graduate school. The Academy's premises have been enlarged and extended twice in the 1960s and 1970s. Regular concerts and recitals are given in the Duke's Hall, while opera is performed in the Sir Jack Lyons Theatre. In October 1987, following the donation of research material from his recent book, Dr.Arthur Jacobs opened a Sullivan archive at the Academy. A far cry indeed from those early, formative years under Sir Arthur Sullivan, whose bust, by Goscombe John and presented to the Academy by the Sullivan Memorial Committee in 1902, gazes benevolently on the music students of today as they hurry back and forth through the entrance hall. How many of them, one wonders, will write compositions as memorable and as tuneful as their illustrious predecessor?

Chapter 18

THE TWO PALACES

Two tours from central London by car

For the first tour to Crystal Palace cross the river to Elephant and Castle. Follow the Walworth Road to Camberwell Green: 2 miles

By far the most important port of call in the whole of south London is the site of the Crystal Palace, where Sullivan's career as a composer was so brilliantly launched. By following a slightly roundabout route, for which a car is certainly recommended, it is possible to include other places of marginal interest on the way. The first of these is Camberwell, which was listed as Cabrewell in the Domesday Book. The first parish church was built four centuries earlier in 670 A.D., while the present church standing on the site in Camberwell Church Street, by Gilbert Scott, dates from 1844. One of London's most undistinguished suburbs, Camberwell was in Gilbert's time a predominantly middle-class area.

Of rather more interest is the inner suburb of Clapham, an ancient village which developed on high ground between Lavender Hill and St. John's Hill overlooking the Thames. The name means 'homestead on the hill' and, unlike Camberwell, Clapham has kept its medieval open ground immediately south of the village. Clapham Common is one of the large open spaces which do much to relieve the drab uniformity of many south London boroughs and provide much-needed recreational space for their inhabitants.

From Camberwell Green to Denmark Hill. Turn right to Coldharbour Lane: follow the road to Brixton, cross Brixton Hill and turn into Acre Lane at the town hall. Follow the signpost to Clapham. Cross over into Clapham Park Road. Turn left and bear left past Clapham Common underground to Clapham Common South Side

Among Clapham's many famous residents were Lord Macaulay, J.F.Bentley, architect of Westminster Cathedral, Sir Charles Barry, Samuel Pepys and Henry Cavendish. In the late 18th and early 19th centuries the 'Clapham Sect', or The Society for the Increase of National Righteousness and the Conversion of the Heathen, later to be known as the Abolition Society, held sway. The main object of the Society was to achieve the abolition of slavery throughout the Empire. William Wilberforce and other leading members such as Zachary Macaulay, the Thorntons and the Venns are commemorated in a memorial tablet at Holy Trinity Church, built in 1776. In recent years Clapham has become a well-to-do area once more and there are a number of fine Georgian and Victorian houses which overlook the Common that have been thoroughly modernised internally, with exteriors carefully and sensitively renovated and restored. Gilbert would have no difficulty in recognising the area were he alive today.

From Clapham Common turn into Cavendish Road (A205). Cross Brixton Hill into Christchurch Road and on towards Tulse Hill

To the south-east of Clapham is one of the more agreeable of London's inner suburbs, Streatham, whose most famous resident is probably Doctor Samuel Johnson's close companion, Mrs Thrale. It was in her house that he wrote part of his *Lives of the Poets*. After his death, Mrs Thrale gave a vivid account of the Doctor in her *Anecdotes of the late Samuel Johnson* published in 1786, and in her correspondence with him which was published some years later.

Streatham derives its name from the Saxon, meaning 'settlement by the road', but as a place it is of much more recent origin than Camberwell, for example. The parish church of St.Leonards dates back only as far as 1230 and it was not until the 17th century, when water said to be of medicinal quality was found, that a fashionable spa developed around the area which we now know as Streatham Vale. Substantial country houses were built facing the Common, while for

At the end of Christchurch Road turn right into Norwood Road and bear left on to the one-way system past the church at West Norwood. Carry along Norwood High Street and Elder Road, at the end of which turn left along Central Hill, which becomes Westow Hill. Pass through the roundabout at Crystal Palace Parade. Turn left along the parade to car park. Walk round the site to the new Museum on the left at the top of Anerley Hill

visitors taking the waters a well-house was built in a park called the Rookery, which exists to this day. Following the discovery of more wells in 1792 a pump house was built in Valley Road.

Near the crest of Tulse Hill to the north-east can be seen the expanse of Brockwell Park, where one of the most remarkable of all the D'Oyly Carte Company seasons was staged in the summer of 1943. This was part of a London County Council campaign launched by Ernest Bevin to promote 'Holidays At Home' as a wartime economy measure.

When the Great Exhibition ended in October 1851 the huge steel and glass structure was carefully dismantled and transported to a 349-acre site on top of Sydenham Hill. A company was formed by the directors of the London, Brighton and South Coast Railway to acquire the materials and the site to establish a huge and permanent exhibition centre which they proposed to call the Crystal Palace, so formally adopting the name that the public had already given to the 1851 Exhibition Hall. A former head gardener to the 6th Duke of Devonshire at Chatsworth, Sir Joseph Paxton, was appointed chief engineer. He re-designed the whole structure which soon rose to dominate the south London skyline, from land 360ft above sea level. The new building measured 1,600ft in length and 300ft at its highest point. Part of the site was sold off to help finance the project, but the remaining 200 acres were planted out as a magnificent park with no fewer than 11,788 fountains, some of which rose to a height of 250ft. Over six million gallons of water, recycled at the rate of 120,000 gallons a minute, were needed to feed the system. There were three reservoirs and two huge water towers, 280ft high, were built in 1880 to create the necessary pressure in the water supply. These were not destroyed in the disastrous fire of 1936, but were pulled down in May 1940 to prevent their being used as navigation points by German bombers over London. In 1958, the BBC erected a 708ft television mast on the site.

Work was still being done to the fountains and to the park when Queen Victoria opened the Crystal Palace on 10 June 1854. Nearly 2,000 singers and other musicians took part in the inaugural celebrations, among them master Arthur Sullivan, chorister of the Chapel Royal. Two years later, in June 1856, the Queen returned to Sydenham for the 'Grand Waterworks': with a single turn of a switch she brought the 11,788 fountains to life simultaneously. Such occasions must be rated among the compensations of monarchy.

The vast auditorium in the Crystal Palace held 20,000 seats, with room for up to 4,000 performers. In addition, there was a small concert hall, a theatre, art and sculpture galleries, exhibition areas, tropical and botanical gardens and a venue for a wide range of sporting events. There was a cricket ground with its own independent club, whose secretary was none other than the redoubtable W.G.Grace. In 1894 the great basins of the larger fountains were filled in and a football pitch laid down upon which were played all the F.A. Cup Finals from 1895 to 1914. The Crystal Palace Football Club was established in 1905, and in later years a motor racing circuit was built in the park.

The enterprise of the LBSCR directors was well rewarded, for by 1862 two million people travelled by train every year in order to visit the Crystal Palace. From central London the combined rail fare and entrance charge was 2/6d at weekends, and 1/- only on weekdays. A new direct line was laid alongside the existing Croydon track to a station built inside the grounds, Anerley Park. This was a remarkably ornate affair, with a 720ft glass canopy leading directly to the Palace. Business was so brisk that the rival London, Chatham and Dover Railway Company built their own new station opposite the Palace on the main road at the top of Sydenham Hill, which was served by a branch line running from Peckham.

The Crystal Palace. In the foreground is a small, square building where Sullivan taught at the School of Art

Anerley Park station, now known simply as Crystal Palace, still keeps some of its former glory. It provides an access to the extensive grounds which, in their heyday, were filled with statuary and *wasserspielen* to rival Versailles itself, and exhibits of 'an educational and improving nature'. Some of these, life-size prehistoric animals to illustrate the various ages of the earth, can be seen today on an island in one of the smaller reservoirs, while all around are the remains of the magnificent formal gardens, English and Italian, complete with maze and rosary.

In 1979 the Crystal Palace Foundation was set up to promote interest in the Palace and its history, and to protect and restore the site and the park. An important outcome of this initiative has been the creation of a museum at Anerley Hill where, among other things, details are to be found of the guided tour which lasts two hours. The Foundation is also responsible for other activities and events, including joint productions featuring the work of Arthur Sullivan.

For despite all the many other attractions on offer, it was music that dominated the part played by the Crystal Palace in the life of Victorian England. The huge auditorium, the immense organ and the great festivals, including the triennial Handel festival from 1857 to 1926, brought to the Crystal Palace thousands upon thousands of visitors from all over the world. The early appointment of George Grove as secretary to the Company had a profound effect on the musical life of the country as a whole, as did the appointment of two German conductors, Henry Schellehn – who later became the first director of Kneller Hall – and August Manns who acted as his assistant.

Nor was this all. Part of its success as a concert venue rested on the simple fact that with so large a seating potential, promoters were able to keep admission prices to an absolute minimum and so undercut most of the other concert halls in London and elsewhere. Furthermore, Grove and Manns, who took over as

149

A Handel Festival in the Crystal Palace concert hall in the main transept, c.1907

principal conductor in 1855, were determined to follow a policy of popularization, with the result that many works by Liszt, Schubert, Schumann, Brahms and Smetana were performed at Crystal Palace before they reached the central London halls. There was an equal determination to promote contemporary home-grown talent as represented by Stanford and Parry, which fostered a revival of interest in English music generally. Under the direction of Manns, regular concerts every Saturday afternoon were given from 1855 to 1901 – nearly fifty years of music-making that provided the firmest of foundations for all the other musical events that took place at Crystal Palace. Small wonder that it was here, rather than in central London, that the focal point of British musical life was to be found.

Sullivan first met Grove shortly after his return from Leipzig, and despite an age discrepancy of twenty-two years between the two men, they became the firmest of friends. Although it was the policy to perform the works only of recognized composers at Crystal Palace, Grove decided to include Sullivan's incidental music to *The Tempest* in one of the Manns concerts. Some revisions to the original score had to be made, but the young composer eagerly dealt with these, and the work was performed on 5 April 1862. It was an immediate and overwhelming success, and Sullivan awoke the next morning to find himself famous. By public demand the piece was repeated a week later. Charles Dickens went backstage after the performance, seized the nineteen-years-old composer by the hand and said, 'I don't pretend to know much about music but I do know

I've been listening to a very great work.' The admiration was mutual, although Sullivan appears to have been impressed more by Dickens the man than by Dickens the writer. As an established figure, he was able to make some valuable introductions on Sullivan's behalf which furthered very considerably his social career. Grove, meanwhile, secured for Sullivan the professorship of 'Pianoforte and Ballad Singing at the Crystal Palace School of Art, Science and Literature (Ladies Division)', a post he held until 1873. In his Saturday afternoon concert programme on 10 March 1863 Manns included an orchestrated version of the wedding march Sullivan had written to celebrate the marriage of the Prince of Wales. Other first performances of his works conducted by Manns included the symphony *In Ireland*, on 10 March 1866 before an audience of 3,000 people; the *Cello Concerto in D* on 24 November of the same year; the overture *The Sapphire Necklace* together with two of his songs, on 13 April 1867, and a revised version of *Marmion* on 7 December 1867.

Sullivan's star was so much in the ascendant that many of his larger-scale works, mostly forgotten today, were also performed at the Crystal Palace. His oratorio *The Prodigal Son*, for example, was presented on 11 December 1869, and three years later he conducted his very successful *Festival Te Deum* with 2,000 performers in front of an audience of 26,000. This piece, first performed in St. Paul's Cathedral, was composed for the national day of thanksgiving declared after the Prince of Wales had recovered from a typhoid fever attack. Following the Crystal Palace performance, popular demand was so great that it was repeated on 18 July and again on 1 March of the following year.

His next great success was the dramatic cantata *The Golden Legend* which was first performed at the Leeds Festival in October 1886, and given its second airing, one of many, at Crystal Palace on 4 December of that same year. The concert, at which Sullivan deputised for Manns, also included the overture to *The Sapphire Necklace* and his incidental music to *The Merry Wives of Windsor*. On 8 May 1887 *The Golden Legend* was given once again, with a choir of 3,500 voices, this time in the presence of Queen Victoria. Near the end of his life Sullivan conducted a revival of his *Irish Symphony* on 29 April 1899, and made his final appearance on the Crystal Palace platform on 21 July 1900. By then he was a director of the Crystal Palace Company, but it was as the country's leading composer that he had been invited to be guest of honour at the National Brass Band Festival and to award prizes to the successful contestants.

On 8 December 1900, shortly after Sullivan's death, Manns conducted a memorial concert which included the overture from *The Tempest*, a setting of Tennyson's *In Memoriam* and selections from the *Festival Te Deum*, *The Martyr of Antioch*, *The Golden Legend* and *The Merchant of Venice*.

Although his connection with Crystal Palace was a very close one, and his commitments there were numerous, at no time does he appear to have considered taking rooms nearby. It is true that early in 1867 he stayed with Thomas Franklyn, a local resident, in an unsuccessful attempt to complete his operetta *The Sapphire Necklace*, and he was frequently a guest of George Grove, who first lived at an address which is now known as 1 Church Meadow, Sydenham, before moving to 'a quaint wooden house' in the same area, the precise location of which is unknown. It was Grove who introduced Sullivan to John Scott Russell, who also served on the board of the Crystal Palace Company, but was better known for his work as an engineer especially in shipbuilding. He collaborated with Brunel in *The Great Eastern* steamship project. Scott Russell was a wealthy man who maintained a lavish household at Westwood Lodge, near the Crystal Palace, where the elite gathered after the Saturday concerts. Among his regular guests

The site of Westwood Lodge can be reached either by car or on foot. At the end of Crystal Palace Parade bear right into Westwood Hill. Turn right into Crystal Palace Park Road. Westwood Lodge stood on the left between Chulsa Road and Border Grove

Turn back up Crystal Palace Park Road and turn right into Westwood Hill once more. Carry on along this road (A212) for less than ½ mile and then turn sharp left up Kirkdale. Follow this A2216 up Dartmouth Road, turning left into London Road which soon becomes Lordship Lane. Continue along the A2216 to Camberwell for the City or the West End

were Grove, Frank Burnand and John Millais, who were soon to be joined by Arthur Sullivan. He often found himself accompanying singers of such renown as Adelina Patti, persuaded by Scott Russell to entertain his guests with impromptu recitals.

It was here at Westwood Lodge that Sullivan first met, and fell in love with, Rachel, the youngest of the Scott Russells' three daughters. Their affair lasted some six years, and is well documented by Rachel's letters to Sullivan, which he kept most carefully. Their relationship developed into a secret engagement but when, on 29 June 1867, Rachel's mother discovered what had been going on she banned Arthur Sullivan from the house and told him in no uncertain terms that on no account was he to make any further attempt to see, or get in touch with, her daughter again. Despite this ban, the lovers continued to meet clandestinely in Grove's office at the Crystal Palace.

It is little to Sullivan's credit that he allowed the affair to drag on. His intentions were uncertain, but he made no attempt to clear his substantial debts, to give up smoking, to abandon his bohemian ways, to stop flirting with other women or to start saving for married life. Eventually these truths dawned even upon Rachel herself, and she went off to Switzerland with her father for six months. Whereupon, her elder sister Louise stepped in and started writing to Sullivan on her own account, but that little adventure came to an end on Rachel's return.

From central London make for Twickenham Bridge and the Chertsey Road. Turn right up Whitton Road and follow this round past the Rugby Union ground into Kneller Road. Kneller Hall is on the right

Like quite a number of our time-honoured traditions, the excellence of British military music is of more recent origin than is often supposed. As late as the 1850s the standard of regimental bands in the whole of the British army was a disgrace, and a number of prominent men urged the Duke of Cambridge to do something about it. Their entreaties did not fall on deaf ears, for the Duke had himself suffered the unforgettable experience in 1854 of hearing British massed bands playing 'God Save the Queen' simultaneously in different arrangements and in different keys. Matters came to a head during the Crimean War of 1854-6, when even some members of our own Imperial General Staff noticed that matters were not as they should be. The military bands of our gallant French allies were vastly superior to ours, a situation which clearly could not be allowed to persist. And so it was decided that at the end of the war, or as soon as possible thereafter, a school of military music should be established to train band masters, bugle majors, trumpet majors and bandsmen in an endeavour to raise musical standards throughout the army as a whole.

An interior view of the Crystal Palace

152

*Kneller Hall, Twickenham,
the Royal Military
School of Music*

**Return to Chertsey Road,
turn left at the junction with
A310. Continue up
Twickenham Road which
joins the London Road
(A315). This in turn becomes
Brentford High Street, at the
end of which turn left up the
A 3001 (Ealing Road) and
continue to St.Mary's Road**

The Military Music Class, as it was then called, came into being in March 1857 in government premises once owned by Sir Godfrey Kneller, at Twickenham. After a hesitant start the institution found its feet and was restyled the Royal Military School of Music. At this point Henry Schellehn, previously of the Crystal Palace but now bandmaster to the 17th Lancers, was appointed Director. One of the three instructors, each of professorial rank, who assisted him was Sullivan's father, who had won his appointment on the strength of his own considerable musical abilities. His salary of £115 p.a. enabled him to move house to Pimlico, whence he travelled to Twickenham each day. Thomas Sullivan remained at Kneller Hall until his death in September 1866.

Not far to the north of Twickenham lies the suburb of South Ealing, in which Gilbert's *alma mater*, Great Ealing School, was to be found. Between 1698 and 1846 it was housed in the Old Rectory, a moated 17th century building which stood where Ranelagh Road now joins St.Mary's Road. It was one of the first private boarding schools in the country and at the peak of its fame in the 1820s, under the headmastership of the Rev.Dr.David Nicholas, it had about 300 scholars and a reputation second only to those of Eton or of Harrow. In 1846 it was found that the Old Rectory was damaged beyond repair by dry rot, and the school moved to newer premises further along St.Mary's Road. Gilbert was sent to the school the following year, at the age of 13, and soon got a bad name for bullying and frequent fighting. His masters regarded him as clever, but lazy. His leisure time was devoted mostly to writing and taking part in sketches put on by the school dramatic society. Despite his unpopularity he was head boy by the time he left the school in 1851.

*The first faculty at
Kneller Hall. Sullivan's
father, Thomas, is seated
second from right*

Continue along the A3001 to Ealing Broadway. Turn right along The Mall and then left up Hangar Lane (A406), part of the North Circular Road. Keep on until you reach the junction with the A504. Turn right towards East Finchley and carry on to Muswell Hill. Follow the signs to Alexandra Palace

Alexandra Palace

Although Great Ealing School and all its records have disappeared, the list of those known to have been pupils makes impressive reading. Apart from Gilbert himself, we find in the literary field the names of Charles Knight, Captain Marryat and William Thackeray. Clergymen included John Henry Newman, Zacchary Pearce and a number of bishops, among whom was Bishop Selwyn, in whose memory Selwyn College, Cambridge, was founded. The great biologist and philosopher Thomas Huxley, whose father taught at the school, was a pupil, as were many renowned soldiers and rulers of Empire such as Sir William Rawlinson and William 'Hicks Pasha'. Among the staff was the future citizen-king of France, Louis-Phillipe, who in the early 1800s taught mathematics and geography. He returned in exile to Twickenham after the 1848 revolution without, it would seem, resuming his teaching duties.

Prompted by the success of the Crystal Palace a new company was formed in 1859 to provide matching facilities for Londoners north of the river, and an estate of 480 acres on Muswell Hill including the eastern summit, was acquired. Following the example of the Crystal Palace entrepreneurs the directors sold off more than half the land to finance the project, and by 24 May 1873 the spectacular new Alexandra Palace standing in its own 220-acre park, was ready for its formal opening. Sixteen days later it burned to the ground.

With true Victorian resolve, reconstruction work using the existing foundations was immediately put in hand, and two years later, on 1 May 1875, the doors were opened to the public once more. One contemporary account described the new building in these terms:[1]

The new Alexandra Palace is a substantial structure of brick, iron and glass, unncessarily ugly externally from whatever point it be viewed, but of vast extent and capacity, its dimensions being 900' x 430' and the area included 7½ acres. Of the interior, the chief feature is the great Central Hall, 368ft long, 184ft wide and 85ft to the centre of the semi-cylindrical roof. It has a great organ and an orchestra for 2,000 performers. West of the hall is an enclosed garden, 240ft by 140ft. Theatres, concert rooms, picture and sculpture galleries, reading and billiard rooms, corridors, banqueting halls and a conservatory ... leave ample room for ethnological models and exhibitions, collections of arms and armour, stalls for objects of ornamental art, and other articles ...

[1]Thorne, James *Handbook to the Environs of London* London: Geoffery Cave, 1876, repr.1983

The grounds are pleasant, in part well-timbered, and afford fine views across the valley of the Lea and over more or less of Middlesex, Essex, Kent, Surrey and Hertfordshire. In one part of the grounds is a Japanese village, in another a lake with pile-dwellings. A race-course of over a mile, with grandstand, has been provided for visitors needing excitement, as well as cricket, croquet, archery and trotting grounds, a circus etc.

On Whit Monday, 1875, no fewer than 94,125 persons visited the Palace.

The opening attractions included a revival of Gilbert's *Creatures of Impulse*, with music by Alberto Randegger, which was first seen at the Court Theatre in 1871. In May 1876, two performances of *Trial by Jury* were presented with the original cast.

Unlike its Sydenham Hill rival, the Alexandra Palace is still in use, although in 1983 a serious fire destroyed the Great Hall and its superb organ. Restoration work is well in hand, and the remaining facilities and the park still represent an entertainment centre of considerable importance to north London. The magnificent views remain more or less unchanged, and continue to draw many thousands of visitors each year.

In these days of changing tastes and techniques it is difficult to say what the future may hold for Alexandra Palace, but its place in entertainment history is permanently assured. From a small studio on an upper floor in 1936 the BBC started to transmit the first regular television service anywhere in the world. The picture was small, the image blurred and the range extremely limited. For once, all those tired old clichés of show business can be used without embarrassment. It was the dawn of a new era. The world would never be the same place again. The age of television had arrived.

And it all began at Ally Pally.

Return to Muswell Hill (A504), turn left and follow the main road to Seven Sisters. Turn right on to the A10 and follow the road signs to the City or the West End

155

Chapter 19

ONE TREE HILL AND ROSHERVILLE

To reach One Tree Hill travel by car or by boat to Greenwich, or by British Rail to Maze Hill: allow 40 minutes

From central London cross the Thames by Tower Bridge. At the Bricklayers Arms intersection keep east along the Old Kent Road and follow road signs to Greenwich. Follow the one-way system into the town centre, and make for Maze Hill by way of Trafalgar Road.

References in *The Sorcerer* to One Tree Hill and to Rosherville have long intrigued Gilbert and Sullivan enthusiasts, and over the years there has been a lot of speculation about their significance and whereabouts. Both sites certainly exist. The first is very little changed, but the second can only now be recognized by the topography of the Northfleet area, an hour and a half from central London. Controversy about the location of One Tree Hill has been fuelled by the fact that there are, according to Harry Benford[1], at least seven contenders for the honour in and around Greater London, ranging from the Laindon Hills in Essex to Sevenoaks in Kent, and taking in on the way Hornsey Rise, Blackheath, New Cross, Honour Oak and Greenwich.

The enjoyment of pointless argument is a very English foible, and a lot of fun can be had with these suggestions, most of which are purely fanciful and can be safely disregarded. Only two need to be considered seriously, Greenwich and Honour Oak, with the balance of probability leaning heavily towards Greenwich. The answer to the question 'what happened at One Tree Hill?' is rather trivial, to

[1]Benford, Harry *The Gilbert and Sullivan Lexicon, etc.* New York: Richards Rosen, 1978, Theater Students Edition

*The café chantant
at Rosherville Gardens*

**By boat, take the William
Walk from the pier, through
Greenwich Park.**

**From Maze Hill station turn
up the hill. After 300 yds,
opposite Vanbrugh Castle a
gateway leads into Greenwich
Park. The path which bears
right along the ridge leads to
One Tree Hill**

say the least. It seems that some Victorians took to rolling down hills on their afternoons-off as a form of relaxation. Whether this was done to impress lady-friends, or whether for the simple pleasure of finishing in a dishevelled heap at the foot of the hill, helpless with laughter, is not known nor does it matter. In those innocent days before the coming of the cinema, the wireless and the television, people took their pleasures where they could find them, and if rolling down hills on a sunny afternoon seemed to our great-grandfathers an agreeable way of passing the time, who are we to deny them? Hill-rolling on an organised basis was certainly a regular attraction at the annual Greenwich Fair until 1871, which is the last recorded date as such. Doubtless the practice persisted thereafter to make the references in *The Sorcerer* still reasonably topical. A visit to One Tree Hill today is unlikely to reveal any hill-rollers, but what remain are the views of London and over Greenwich itself which have attracted generations of amateur artists and photographers. The Observatory is no longer at Greenwich, but the Meridian remains, as do the *Cutty Sark*, the National Maritime Museum, Wren's superb Greenwich Hospital, now the Royal Naval College, and Greenwich Park, one of the most beautiful in the whole of the Greater London area. On a fine day a trip down the river to Greenwich is an unforgettable experience for Londoners and for visitors alike: a day's outing not to be missed.

And what, you may ask, about Honor Oak? It still has its adherents, including Leslie Ayre, who even goes so far as to suggest that One Tree Hill at Greenwich is too flat. But a careful examination of Stanford's *Library Map 1862-1884*, reveals that the park at Honour Oak, now known as One Tree Hill, did not exist when *The Sorcerer* was written.

The defence rests.

Rosherville Gardens, which are mentioned in *Cox and Box* as well as in *The Sorcerer*, were one of the most popular and successful of all the mid-Victorian leisure resorts. The enterprise started in 1837 when the Chairman of the Kent Zoological and Botanical Institute, George Jones, bought the lease of Crete Hall from one Jeremiah Rosher. In the grounds of the house at Northfleet, just west of Gravesend, were disused chalk quarries. The whole area, bounded to the north by the Thames and to the south by a cliff face rising to a height of between 50ft

[2] Ayre, Leslie *The Gilbert and Sullivan Companion* London: Pan, 1972

and 100ft, was very sheltered and humid, making it an ideal place for the many flowers, shrubs and trees Jones proposed to grow there in order to establish the Kent Zoological and Botanical Gardens. The plan fructified, in every sense of the word, and the Gardens were opened. The original intention had been to keep them purely educational to appeal to a small, select public. But George Jones soon had to abandon this policy because there were many rival establishments competing for the same kind of business. He reluctantly decided to move down-market, as we would say today, and add popular features designed more for amusement than instruction. By 1840 the place had become a pleasure garden with a maze, an aviary, a bear-pit, monkey cages and other side-shows. In addition, an enormous banqueting hall was erected, together with a bijou theatre and an open-air theatre capable of seating an audience of 1,000. A four-storied tower was built on top of the cliff, from which Blondin once walked a tightrope to the terrace below. Leading music-hall artists were engaged for the theatre, and during the season the gardens were illuminated every night. Having decided to turn his high-minded enterprise into a place of popular entertainment, George Jones certainly did the job properly. No holds were barred: no expense spared.

By the early 1840s the place had become known as the Terpsichorean Gardens or the Rosherville Gardens. In the immediate area houses, shops and hotels were rapidly constructed to cater for the growing number of visitors, who could travel

Blondin walking the tightrope at Rosherville in 1884

from London for 6d, including admission. A popular way of visiting the Gardens was by paddle steamer along the Thames from London Bridge or Greenwich. Quick to realise the potential of this traffic Jones had a pier built to provide safe anchorage and landing facilities. It was not until 1870 that an entrance was created on the upper London Road to cater for road users. By that time no fewer than 37 stage coach lines passed through Gravesend, and road travel had become sufficiently comfortable and inexpensive to be considered as an alternative to travelling either by rail or by steamer.

Rosherville Gardens were open all the year round, with the main season extending from Whitsun to October. They offered spectacle, gaiety and entertainment at a price most people could easily afford. Within a few years they had become London's most popular resort. The whole enterprise had blossomed in a most extraordinary way. For a contemporary account, one need look no further than in the *London Journal* of 13 May 1848:

> The variety and nature of the amusements, the pleasant accommodations, the salubrity of the air, the beauty of the surrounding scenery, and the short distance from the metropolis, have, within the last few years made Rosherville Gardens a favourite place of resort... Mondays, Wednesdays and Saturdays, throughout the season, are gala-nights, when the gardens are decorated with small variegated lamps suspended in festoons from tree to tree, and all the entertainments close with a display of fireworks equalling the famed pyrotechnic exhibition of Vauxhall. Occasionally there is a balloon ascent; and last year Mr. Gale, with his new improved balloon, ascended several times. This popular place of recreation is provided with many delightful accommodations all of which are of the most varied and extensive character. The Banqueting Hall alone is capable of seating 1,000 persons. It is a room of immense dimensions, fitted up in antique style, and, with its mullioned windows, its ornamental rafters, and its tall pillars, affords a very picturesque appearance. Banners and standards with various devices upon them are suspended from the ceiling. And on each side of the hall are spacious tables, groaning under the weight of the rarest delicacies and wines of the choicest qualities.

After George Jones died in 1872, Rosherville Gardens were sold by his executors for a total of £24,000. They remained highly profitable for some time, but towards the close of the century trade rapidly fell away, and in 1900 the business was put up for sale. No bidders came forward to buy it as a going concern, and between 1903 and 1914 attempts were made to re-open the Gardens as a fun fair. All these failed, and in 1914 a film production company, Magnet Films, acquired the property and used it for location work and as a permanent set. In 1936 the Gardens were opened to the public for the last time for a local pageant and fete, but by the outbreak of the Second World War the site had been cleared and all the land sold off.

Today those 20 acres house heavy industry and the Northfleet power station. Rosherville still survives as a drab, rather forlorn, district of Gravesham, which can be reached from the A226, the road that runs between Dartford and Gravesend and which was once the main London road. Now the atmosphere of decline is reinforced by the fact that even this is now a quiet backwater, having been by-passed by the M2 motorway. Few signs of the past remain. A small grocery bears the name 'Rosherville Stores'. From the road weaving its way through the industrial site the cliffline can be clearly seen, but there is no trace of the tower, the entrance or of the gardens. Far more rewarding than this exercise in nostalgia is a visit to the Central Library in Gravesend which has a fascinating local history collection, including many photographs taken in and around Rosherville Gardens at the peak of their popularity.

And that is how they are best remembered.

Chapter 20

GRIM'S DYKE AND BEYOND

From central London take
the A5 Edgware Road for
about 12 miles through
Edgware to Stonegrove. At
Canons Corner roundabout
turn left on to London Road,
signpost Stanmore. Pass
Stanmore Underground
station on the left, and at the
2nd light-controlled junction
bear left into Church Rd.
About 400 yds on the left,
where Old Church Lane joins
Uxbridge Road stands the
church of St. John the
Evangelist. Continue along
Uxbridge Road for about a
mile. At the small
roundabout, turn right up
Clamp Hill for Grim's Dyke.
Or, at this point, you can go
straight on to the church of
All Saints, Harrow Weald,
where there is a memorial to
Gilbert (see page 171) The
church is about 500 yds on
the right, beyond the
roundabout

At the top of Clamp Hill
cross over into Old Redding.
The entrance to Grim's Dyke
is at the gate lodge about
800yds on the right

If you are travelling by
Underground take the Jubilee
Line to Stanmore
and then hire a taxi

The name Grim's Dyke belongs to the ancient defensive earthwork running for just over three miles from Pinner Hill to Bentley Priory. It formed part of the boundary of the territory belonging to the Catuvellauni, a tribe that came into conflict with Rome. Today, remains of the earthwork can probably best be seen at Wealdstone Common. The dimensions are most impressive: the base of the mound, or *vallum*, measured up to 63ft in width, was 5ft high and no less than 15ft wide at the top. The ditch, or fosse, on the other side was as much as 12ft deep. Nothing on this scale survives within the grounds of the house bearing the name Grim's Dyke, but the outlines and main contours can still be very clearly seen.

For reasons which are unknown but which probably have more to do with the vagaries of English spelling than anything else, the earthwork was known as Grim*e*'s Dyke in medieval times. This is how it appeared on local maps and, as late as 1911, in the Victoria County History. The first owner of the house, Frederick Goodall R.A., the eminent Victorian painter of biblical scenes, used to explain that his architect Norman Shaw begged him not to use that form of spelling because it would give an unfortunate impression that the house itself was grimy and dirty. And so the more genteel, but totally misleading, Graeme's Dyke was adopted. Gilbert would have none of this, and not long after he took possession he robustly changed the name back to its original and proper form.

Frederick Goodall was the son of one of Turner's favourite engravers – a sentimental artist who belonged to a clique that in the 1840s met at Redleaf, near Penshurst, in Kent. He made his fortune with Egyptian and Levantine panoramas, then very much in vogue. In 1856 he purchased 100 acres of land at Harrow Weald, subject to the remaining 12 years of a lease held by the jam and pickle magnate Charles Blackwell, who lived on the neighbouring estate. Goodall, unable to build for that time, had to be content with landscaping the area and planting conifers. Within the grounds he set aside 30 acres running parallel to the ancient earthwork for the house he had in his mind. In Norman Shaw, then aged 39, Goodall found a kindred spirit, for the architect was at that time perfecting his own particular style of romantic, mellow-brick Old English house.

Shaw's ideas came at the end of a long period of Gothic revivalism. He took the best of that tradition and married it to the late-Elizabethan style, with its high red-tiled gables, clustered high moulded chimneys, leaded lights and great oriels mullioned with stone, vaulted arches, timber framing, brick-nogging and tile-hanging. Yet for all this mixture of oddities, they were put together in such a masterful fashion that the beautiful house looked as though it had been there for a very long time which, of course, was exactly the effect Shaw wanted to create. It was also designed to match the mature grounds, especially the thickly-wooded areas nearby and the ancient moat, overgrown with aquatic plants.

Grim's Dyke, Gilbert's country home 1890–1911

Building work started in 1870, at which time Goodall left on a tour of the Near East, lasting for two years. Shaw followed the approved plans with only one or two minor variations of detail, and the house was ready in 1872. From the higher parts of the estate, about 460 feet above sea level, there are views over four counties, but the house itself is in a hollow and masked from the outside world. A gabled, red-brick, timbered lodge stands at Old Redding, and from here a carriageway ½ a mile long, leads through copses of pine and silver birch, bordered by rhododendra planted by Gilbert. The house suddenly appears in a clearing set on two sides by small, well-tended lawns.

Goodall intended the studio to be the main feature of the house and to ensure north-south light, this vast and grandiose room was turned on its axis and set against the rest of the building. He did most of his work, it is believed, at the northern end, where he sat in a bay specially angled to catch the sunset. Under a wagon roof there is a minstrels' gallery, which suggests that the studio was also to be used for entertaining on a scale to be expected from a successful society painter. The interior of the rest of the house was quite modest by comparison, certainly while it remained in Goodall's hands. From a low-ceilinged hall there was a small breakfast room and a stone-faced dining room with an ingle nook, on the ground floor. The graceful oak staircase remains an outstanding feature to this day, giving access to the studio and then, doubling back on itself, to some unpretentious bedrooms on the upper floor. Even the main bedroom, above the

162

library, was a simple room positioned to catch the morning sun, taking advantage of the slightly concave frontage facing west and south.

To the south, Shaw built a small lodge, a walled garden, outhouses and stables, and over the moated dyke were two bridges in which flints and old stones from Harrow Church, were mixed with the brickwork. The gardens were terraced, and to the east of the lawns a tennis court was laid out.

In 1880 Goodall sold the house, letting it be known that he needed to be nearer town. A more likely reason for his move to St. John's Wood is that he found the upkeep of Grim's Dyke beyond his means. It was bought by Robert Heriot, a partner in Hambros Bank, who added a billiard room next to, and partly below, the studio. This room also featured an ingle nook, but it was designed in a coarse Gothic style quite out of keeping with Shaw's original scheme. Ten years later Heriot put the house on the market, retaining Shaw's services as an agent. By now the grounds were showing signs of neglect, but this did not deter the Gilberts: no sooner had they viewed the property than they set about organising the purchase, almost regardless of cost.

From September 1890 until the end of the year Gilbert supervised the various alterations he wanted, calling up from Kensington the architects George and Peto who had designed his house in Harrington Gardens. A new suite of bedrooms was put over the billiard room, and the exteriors of both floors were matched to the main structure. The dairy was converted to a small hall for servants, the kitchen was completely rearranged and the original drawing room became Gilbert's library. The studio was made into a new drawing room to which was added a vast Cornish alabaster chimneypiece, almost certainly based on a sketch prepared by Gilbert and then worked up by a French sculptor. It is the only feature in Grim's Dyke which is at all reminiscent of the many neo-Flemish flourishes in Harrington Gardens. When they were satisfied with all these alterations, the Gilberts moved in bringing with them all the memorabilia of his plays, writing and foreign travels, not to mention a growing collection of *objets d'art*, porcelain and many other curios.

The model of H.M.S. Queen, now in the Science Museum

In the entrance hall was placed a model of a great three-deck man-of-war *H.M.S.Queen*, which saw active service during the Crimean War. It was 16ft long and accurate to the finest detail in its spars and rigging, overhauled each year by John Smith who was rigging expert of the United Services Museum in Whitehall. At the foot of the staircase stood a full suit of armour, while the three niches above the hall fireplace housed 14th century alabaster carvings. Oak furniture in the dining room dated back to Charles I. Particularly impressive was a massive sideboard made in 1631 for Sir Thomas Holt, a cavalier who gained a certain notoriety by murdering his own cook. The dining table sat 24, and Lady Gilbert's only published work, *Kitty's Cookery Book*, contains recipes for that number of guests. On the dining room walls hung oil paintings by Van Everdingen, Giorgione, Van Der Kapelle, Maes, Tintoretto and others.

Gilbert worked at Grim's Dyke from an armchair in his library, looking out through the French windows on to the croquet lawn. It was here that he wrote his last ten plays, including *Rosencrantz and Guildenstern*, *Utopia Limited*, *The Mountebanks*, *His Excellency*, *The Grand Duke* and *Fallen Fairies*. The fireplace, now a bar, still has the copper surround that Gilbert had fitted, and the white shelves, said to have carried 4,000 volumes, are still a feature of the room. The library was mainly devoted to literature and the classics: on display were 70 *papier maché* heads brought back from India, as well as drawings by Caracci, Watteau, Lancret, Salvator Rosa, Del Sarto and Rubens.

163

A gentle caricature of Gilbert from 'The Ludgate Magazine'

The drawing room, or music room, contained a number of valuable works by Boughton, Perugini, Stokes, Tenniel, and the only known oil painting by Duncan, although some of his watercolours were also in the collection. One painting which dominated the rest was Gilbert's own portrait by Frank Holl. Nearby stood a 150-years-old musical clock, and elsewhere in the room there were Italian and Japanese inlaid and tortoiseshell cabinets from the 14th century containing Japanese weaponry, lacquerwork and elaborate porcelain.

Immediately outside the drawing room was a winding staircase, hidden from view, leading to Gilbert's 'Flirtorium', just to the east of the minstrel gallery, where he trained his protégé actresses. The stairs also led down to the billiard room, the walls of which were decked with hundreds of photographs and drawings of Victorian actors, Henry Irving, Compton, Hare and many others. All the artistes as they first appeared in his works were here, together with the 50 original drawings made by Gilbert for the 1898 edition of *Bab Ballads*. Nearby, from the original production of *The Yeomen of the Guard*, stood the gong which had been specially cast, together with the headsman's axe and block. And on the mantelpiece stood statuettes of Thackeray and Tom Robertson.

During Gilbert's 21 years at Grim's Dyke there were many changes made to the grounds surrounding the house. The estate included a model, or home, farm which he was very keen to develop and which gave him plenty of scope to indulge his great fondness for animals. He grazed a small herd of thoroughbred Jerseys, and kept pigs as well as fowl. There was a staff of 20 including gardeners, and many of them gave the Gilberts long and devoted service. Their butler stayed with them for 26 years, and three of their gardeners worked on the estate for 14, 12 and 11 years respectively. Lady Gilbert became a keen gardener, and the flower beds were her special domain. A sunken rose garden was built on the terrace above the moat, reached by a staircase flanked by bronzes of birds from Japan. In the centre of the lawn there stood a sundial from the Army & Navy Stores to which Gilbert later had added Lady Vavir's words from *Broken Hearts*:

> It is a holy thing that bears a warrant,
> Sent from the source of Life,
> To tell the Earth
> That even Time is hastening to its end!

Beyond the moat and over the Dyke a series of substantial greenhouses were built. These provided in their due seasons peaches, grapes, melons, nectarines and bananas, and an abundant supply of less hardy annuals to decorate the house. Behind the lodge there was a well-stocked kitchen garden with orchard and

One of Gilbert's favourite cars was a Darracq

Gilbert's music room, formerly Frederick Goodall's studio

vineries, all of which made the estate virtually self-sufficient in food. Gilbert had the tennis court extended beyond regulation length to keep his prodigious forehand drives in court. He had adopted a similar ploy earlier at Breakspear House: what his opponents thought about such tactics is not known, which is, perhaps, just as well.

Outside the library he had a lawn specially prepared for croquet, a game he took up with a great deal of passion. Indeed, there is much evidence of Gilbert's many enthusiasms to be found at Grim's Dyke. He made one of the outhouses into an observatory and, at the turn of the century, he had the stables converted to house his growing collection of motor cars which included a Darracq, a Rolls-Royce and, later, a Cadillac which he had specially imported from the United States. He was so keen on driving that he often took the wheel himself, regardless of the fact that two-full time chauffeurs were on the domestic staff.

But undoubtedly his pride and joy was the large lake he had built to the east of the house, beyond the formal gardens. Work began in the summer of 1900 and such was his commitment that Gilbert actually helped with the digging out of a large area of ground, about 1½ acres in all. Designed to a tapering shape, the lake had an island in the middle, and a boathouse and changing hut were built on the

165

shore. To give the whole scheme a well-established look to match the rest of the property, large numbers of bulrushes and forget-me-knots were planted with pink, white and yellow water lilies. The lake was drained and refilled each year to keep it in good condition, and was well stocked with Californian trout. In 1905 it was extended to a roughly rectangular shape measuring 170 yds by 50 yds. For Gilbert it was a favourite place: every day during his summers at Grim's Dyke, from about March to September, he came here to bathe. It became one of the fixed pleasures of his daily routine: one which was to cost him his life.

As the proud owner of a substantial property Gilbert decided to throw himself wholeheartedly into playing the part of a country squire. He became a benefactor to the local community; he served on the local bench for 18 years; he established the Conservators of Harrow Weald with the help of his neighbour, Blackwell; he was also President of the Grim's Dyke Golf Club, which he helped to set up in 1906. He lived in great contentment surrounded by his pets and his animals. His concern for wildlife soon became widely known, if not always fully understood, in the area. He gave strict orders that no hunting of any kind was to take place on his land, which consequently became a refuge for local foxes as well as for birds and other forms of wildlife. Two dovecotes were placed on the east lawn, occupied by over 50 fan-tailed pigeons. There were beehives in the kitchen garden, turkeys were reared on the home farm, and two cranes were encouraged to settle on the shores of the lake. The great number and variety of domestic pets at Grim's Dyke aroused much interest and curiosity, so much so that Nancy McIntosh wrote an article about them published in *Country Life* in June 1911. All the dogs and cats lived as part of the family, with stools and baskets provided for them in the garden and their own bowls, placed on cloths, in the dining room, where they were served at family mealtimes. There were two fine Persian cats, William and Mary: Mary it was who ruled over all the other pets in the house. The dogs included a collie, a Scotch terrier, a pekingese, a spaniel, a French poodle and a pug. There was even a garden donkey trained to pull the lawn mower. Because of her extremely high-pitched bray she was rather unkindly called Adelina, after the soprano Adelina Patti. Her great friend (the donkey's not the soprano's) was a fallow deer fawn given to Gilbert as a present. The two animals escaped from the grounds at regular intervals, and were sometimes found together wandering through fields up to three miles away, before they were caught and brought home. The fawn was eventually put with the herd at Bentley Priory, but she would still come to Gilbert when he called her, on his subsequent visits there.

All these animals were allowed to wander freely about the house. They especially enjoyed the sunny library where Gilbert worked, and whose papers were often put at risk by their presence. In addition, there were caged birds everywhere, of which the most celebrated was a parrot in the entrance hall that lived for 20 years and had an extraordinarily large vocabulary. Gilbert was very fond it, and of some piping bullfinches in a gilded cage, which he gave to his wife as a birthday present. But his greatest favourites were his Madagascar lemurs and monkeys. He brought his first pair of monkeys back from India and these bred successfully, creating at one time a colony of significant size. One called Paul loved to perch on Gilbert's shoulder, even when he was in his dressing room or at the dining table. A special grave was dug for him near the croquet lawn. Another monkey, Babs, used to go into the library regularly to beg for fruit.

So visitors to Grim's Dyke would find the Gilberts surrounded by a great menagerie. This was certainly the very clear impression made on Nancy McIntosh, when she came to live with them in 1892. She was a young American actress, who was adopted by the Gilberts as their daughter. Entries in Gilbert's

Gilbert's cats and dogs had places laid for them on the dining room floor

later diaries indicate that there was a lot of domestic activity of various kinds: church parties, bathing parties and vistis to Harrow School and to Bushey Heath Cottage Hospital. There were detailed notes about his photographic and astronomical activities, his games of tennis, croquet and cribbage in the evenings, and about the season's crop of mushrooms, strawberries and asparagus. Then, of course, there were lists of guests to the dinner parties and large-scale garden parties on the lawns during the summer, to which were invited actors, writers, statesmen, churchmen and lawyers, but never members of the high society in which Sullivan moved with such apparent ease. Gilbert had only a few real friends of his own sex, men like Henry Rowland Brown, Robert Marshall and Cyril Maude. He much preferred the company of young actresses, with or without their husbands. Seymour Hicks and Ellaline Terris were frequent visitors.

Arthur Sullivan went to Grim's Dyke on only one occasion, after his reconciliation with Gilbert in January 1893. Accompanied by his nephew, Herbert, the composer was a house guest for three days at the end of May during which time the two men settled down to discuss details of *Utopia Limited*. There is a sad corollary to this brief appearance by Sullivan in the Grim's Dyke narrative. As a result of his strenuous digging when the lake was being built, Gilbert contracted rheumatic fever, and it was decided that he should go to Egypt in order to convalesce. So it came about that he was out of the country when Sullivan died,

The lake, where Gilbert met his death, as it appears today

and was thus prevented from attending the funeral. Although their relationship was neither as cordial nor as close as it had been, Gilbert felt the loss keenly and the fact that he was unable to be among the mourners was a matter of the deepest regret to him for the rest of his life.

The story of his own heroic end is well-known. On 29 May 1911 Gilbert invited two local girls, Ruby Preece and Isobel Emery, to swim in the lake. They met at about 4 p.m. and there is no more graphic account of what happened than the evidence given by Ruby Preece, a schoolgirl, at the coroner's inquest which was held in the billiard room at Grim's Dyke on the following Wednesday:

> 'I found I could not stand and called out and Sir William swam to me. I put my hand on his shoulder and I felt him suddenly sink. I thought he would come up again. My feet were on the mud then. Miss Emery called for help and the gardeners came with the boat.'[1]

The family doctor, Dr.W.W. Shackleton of Bushey, and Dr. Daniel Wilson of Bushey Heath Cottage Hospital, certified that Gilbert died at 4.20 p.m. that afternoon and that the cause of death was syncope as a result of excessive exertion. At the direction of the coroner, Dr.Gordon Hogg, the jury of local people returned a verdict of accidental death. Gilbert was 74.

Shortly after his death the bathing lake was closed off and, for the most part, drained. A copy of Frampton's memorial plaque was placed in the main entrance porch of the house. Lady Gilbert stayed on with Nancy McIntosh, tending her gardens and working for local charities until her own death in 1936. With both foster parents gone, Nancy decided to move into town and took a flat at 59 Wynnstay Gardens, Kensington. In her will, Lady Gilbert left the statue of King Charles II to Soho Square and made a number of other personal bequests. The rest of her estate, worth £84,463 all told, went to various theatrical charities.

Apart from certain items removed by Miss McIntosh, the contents of the house were publicly auctioned on 17/18 March 1937, realising a total of £4,600. Although Savoy opera treasures were not included in the sale, all Gilbert's curios, artwork and furniture went under the hammer. His antique cabinets, Italian carvings, brassware, Nanking china, Chinese bronzes, Persian rugs and the suit

[1]*Harrow and Middlesex Observer*, Friday, 9 June 1911

of armour were sold, together with rare plants from the conservatory. All his old masters went as well.

The house was acquired jointly by the Middlesex County Council and the London County Council, who leased it to the North West Regional Hospital Board from 1937 to 1963 as a rehabilitation centre for women suffering from tuberculosis. It was fitted out to take 50 patients. The studio, or drawing room as it became, was turned first into a large dormitory. When both men and women were admitted to the centre, after the Second World War, it was turned into a games room. Lady Gilbert's own sitting room on the ground floor became the Matron's office, and the dining room was used as a men's dormitory. The gardens and the grounds were well-looked after during this period.

In 1963 the unit was closed down and from that point on the property went into rapid decline. It was used short-term as a film and television location by Hammer Films and by Robert Stigwood Productions. Among the TV series filmed here were *The Champions* (1967), *Jason King* (1971) *Department 'S'* (1970) and *Spyder's Web* (1971). In February 1968 Boris Karloff's last film *The Curse of the Crimson Altar* was made on location here, and in October 1969 Vincent Price made his 100th film *The Cry of the Banshee* at Grim's Dyke. The house and grounds were also used as the setting for a Ronnie Barker comedy in 1969, and as recently as 1982 it was the location for the TV film *Colour Him Dead*.

In February 1969 the Greater London Council granted Harrow Council a 999-year lease on the property on the stipulation that if, as seemed possible, the house could be converted into a private hotel, steps must be taken to preserve links with its Gilbertian past. Tenders for hotel use were invited, and for clinic or training centre use as well. On 27 May 1970 the Ministry of Housing and Local Government designated Grim's Dyke a building of special architectural and historical interest, thus safeguarding its future as far as possible.

On 5 April the Grim's Dyke Hotel and Country Club opened under the management of Mr. and Mrs. Alberto Della Valle, who did much to restore the Victorian atmosphere. Gilbert's library became a bar, and both the drawing room and the billiard room were converted into restaurants. There have been several managements since that time, but the memory of Sir William Schwenck Gilbert has been respected and retained. Weekly performances given by the English Heritage Singers have become a regular feature, and a summer season of the Savoy Operas has been introduced in recent years. These activities and, of course, the house itself, attract many thousands of Gilbert & Sullivan enthusiasts from all over the world every year.

In the late summer of 1883 Gilbert rented a 17th century hunting lodge between Watford and Bushey, the ruins of which stand in Oxhey Woods. It was called Eastbury, now the name of the residential district near the site, and it was here that he worked on the libretto of *Princess Ida* taking most of it from his earlier blank verse burlesque *The Princess*, produced at the Olympic Theatre in 1870.

Half a mile south of the village of Harefield is Breakspear House, a large Georgian mansion set in extensive grounds. Some believe that the name provides a direct link with the only English family to have produced a Pope: others go further and suggest that Nicholas Breakspear, otherwise Pope Adrian IV (1154-59), actually lived in an earlier house on the site, but there is no evidence to support this.

What is certain is that Gilbert took the house as a summer retreat from February to October each year, from 1883 to 1890, at an annual rent of £800. He

Turn right out of Grim's Dyke to the end of Old Redding, turn right on to A4008 Oxhey Lane and left on to B4542 Little Oxhey Lane. Turn left into Prestwick Road and carry on to The Woods at Oxhey. The area beyond the woodland is Eastbury

Turn left into A4125 Watford Road and right into B469 Green Lane. Under the railway bridge at Northwood Station to the A404 Rickmansworth Road. Turn right up Batchworth Heath Hill and left down White Hill. On to Northwood Road and then into Harefield. Turn left into Breakspear Road North

Vine Street station,
Uxbridge

spent spring weekends and the whole of the summer here when he was not travelling abroad. Work on *Princess Ida* was started in this house, and much of the libretto of *The Gondoliers* was written here. In his leisure hours, Gilbert played tennis on a court which, as at Grim's Dyke, he had specially extended.

For his frequent journeys to London, Gilbert usually travelled by rail from Vine Street, Uxbridge. One one occasion ...

> I was on my way from Uxbridge to Paddington and, having missed my train at Uxbridge, I had an hour to wait, and so it came to pass that I had plenty of time to study the advertisements on the walls. The Beefeater on the placard suggested to me an effective libretto might be constructed, the scenes in which should represent two views of the Tower of London, with a body of Beefeaters as the male chorus ... a picture of a jester in a magazine which I had bought to read while I was waiting suggested to me the advisability of putting the piece back into the Tudor age.[2]

Gilbert's placard was an advertisement for the Tower Furnishing Company, long since gone, as, indeed, has the station. And although Gilbert is a notoriously unreliable source when it comes to details of his own life, there seems no reason to doubt the veracity of this particular anecdote. In any case, it is such a good story that the least we can do is to give him the benefit of the doubt.

Continue to Breakspear Road South. At the A40 turn left for London

The village of Stanmore Magna, or Great Stanmore, is mentioned in the Domesday Book and owes its name to the Saxon word for boundary stone, stan-meare. It lies on the borders of Hertfordshire and Middlesex, and its parish church, just to the west of the present village is dedicated to St.John the Evangelist. Behind it, in picturesque ruin, is the Old Church. This red-brick tower, embowered in ivy, was built in 1632 by Sir John Wolstenholme and consecrated by the then Bishop Laud. Picturesque it may be, but thanks to poor workmanship it was also extremely unsafe. For that reason it was condemned in the early 1840s.

The foundation stone of the new church was laid in November 1849 by Queen Adelaide, who, since the death of her husband William IV in 1837, had lived at Bentley Priory nearby. It was her last public engagement, for she joined her husband on 2 December, a few days after the ceremony. Five yards or so from the south door of the church an angel keeps watch over the flat tomb of Sir W.S.Gilbert. Here his ashes were laid to rest on 2 June 1911, to be followed in

[2]Bell's ed. *The Savoy Operas* Introduction by W.S.Gilbert

170

Gilbert's tombstone in Stanmore churchyard

time by those of his wife and of Nancy McIntosh. The ashes were carried to the churchyard by his friend Rowland Brown and by Herbert Sullivan, after cremation at Hoop Lane Crematorium in Golders Green. The funeral itself was very simple, but was attended by a huge number of distinguished mourners from the worlds of theatre, literature, the arts and the law. These included, *inter alia*, Rupert D'Oyly Carte, the Burnands, the Trees, Hares, Bancrofts, Cyril Maude, Arthur Bouchier, Pinero, Arthur Collins, Herkomer, Alma-Tadema, Sir Charles Matthews and Anstruther Gray, K.C. Over 300 wreaths covered the graveyard including one from the American ambassador, Whitelaw Reid.

The grave and the memorial were the work of Frederick Pomery A.R.A. who, four years earlier, had created the 'Lady of Justice' above the Old Bailey. The plain inscription sets out names and dates: around the edge of the tombstone a further inscription was added after the death of their adopted daughter.

The 125th anniversary celebrations of the Church of Saint John the Evangelist were held in 1975. At evensong on 13 July the chairman of the D'Oyly Carte Trust, Bishop Stopford, preached a sermon, and members of the company sang quartets from *Princess Ida*, *The Yeomen of the Guard*, and *Iolanthe*. The grave had been restored for the occasion with the help of a grant from the Royal General Theatrical Fund, one of the principal beneficiaries of the Gilberts' estate.

In the tiny Normanesque transept of the parish church of All Saints, Harrow Weald, built in 1845, there is a memorial to Gilbert placed there by his wife. It is a bas-relief portrait showing his left profile, by Sir Bertram Mackennal R.A. On each side are marble statuettes, Justice to the left, and Comedy to the right. Above are the symbolic masks of Tragedy and Comedy. The inscription reads:

William Schwenck Gilbert KT
Poet and Dramatist
1836-1911

Below is the following quotation from Proverbs, chosen by Rowland Brown:

The tongue of the just is as choice silver

Outside the church, in the cemetery on the other side of the road may also be found the grave of Gilbert's mother-in-law, Herbertina Turner. It is the fifth grave on the right along the path from the road itself. Mrs. Turner, who survived her son-in-law by two years, is described on her tombstone as the widow of Capt. Thomas Medcalf Blois Turner, Bombay Engineers, and daughter of the late Sir Herbert Compton, Chief Justice of Bombay.

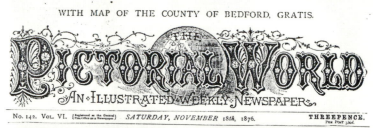

No. 142. Vol. VI. [Registered at the General Post Office as a Newspaper] SATURDAY, NOVEMBER 18th, 1876. THREEPENCE. Per Post 3½d.

ARTHUR SULLIVAN.

[From a Photograph by Elliott and Fry, Baker Street.]

Arthur Sullivan in 1876

Chapter 21

HERTS, HANTS, BUCKS AND BERKS

For the excursion to Stagenhoe Park take the A1 and A1(M) from central London to the north. Just beyond Hatfield, take the A6129 to Wheathampstead. Turn right on to the B651 to Kimpton and then (across the B652) on to Whitwell

Return to London using the same route

For the Windsor round trip take the M4 from central London, then M25 (south) to reach M3. Turn off at junction 4 to Frimley, North Farnborough and, by the B3014, Fleet. Down the narrow main street, 100 yds beyond the traffic light, is a police station on the left. Almost directly opposite, on a bank above the roadway, is Booth Lodge, now called Stanton Lodge, North and South

From Fleet take the B3013 to Hartney Wintney. Turn right on to the A30 and carry on to York Town. Pass the A321 junction: 400 yds on the right, set back from the road, is Albany Place

Go back on the A30 and turn right along the A321 to Little Sandhurst

Ugly abbreviations for Hertfordshire, Hampshire, Buckinghamshire and Berkshire, four beautiful counties within easy reach of London, where many of Sullivan's summer retreats can still be found. Indeed, in following his footsteps away from the busy metropolis it is possible to plan a couple of very pleasant one-day excursions to be kept in reserve for fine days. The first of these takes the visitor to Stagenhoe Park, somewhat apart from Sullivan's other summer haunts. But the journey is well worth the effort, through some pleasant English countryside to an area with strong literary associations, Ayot St. Lawrence and George Bernard Shaw.

Stagenhoe Park lies just outside the village of Whitwell. The earliest reference, in the 11th century, is to a hunting chase of that name. But by medieval times a substantial house serving as the manor of Whitwell occupied the site. This in its turn disappeared long ago, and the house there today, which Arthur Sullivan rented for a month in 1884, is now a residential home belonging to the Sue Ryder Foundation. His lease ran from mid-August to mid-September, but we know from his diary that he extended his stay. An entry for 9 October tells us that he had the midnight train from King's Cross to Hatfield run the 14 extra miles to Hitchin so he and his guests could safely return home for the night. The cost of this concession was a mere 14/-: a shilling a mile. Two years later, in September 1886, on his way back from a rehearsal in Leeds, he arranged for the London-bound express to make a non-scheduled stop at Hitchin to enable him to complete his journey to Stagenhoe Park with minimum inconvenience. Expansive days indeed.

The summer of the intervening year, 1885, he spent in the U.S.A. His main task the following summer was the completion of 'Jo' Bennet's *The Golden Legend* for the Leeds Festival. On 23 July 1886 he brought the unfinished drafts of the work to Stagenhoe Park, where he stayed until September of that year. He actually started work on the cantata in his old boyhood home in Sandhurst, where he had spent his early formative years before being sent off to the Plees boarding school in Bayswater before he was ten years of age. He persuaded a certain Mr. Harris, one of his father's old bandsmen who now occupied the house, to give him lodgings. Clearly, it was a place that had happy memories for him, for he stayed for two months from 23 April to 18 June 1886.

Sandhurst plays an important part in Sullivan's boyhood for he was not yet three years of age when his parents moved from Lambeth to live here. The family home was, in fact, a very small two-up, two-down cottage just off the grounds of the Royal Military College and south of its main entrance. 4 Albany Place, as it was then, bears a plaque to mark the connection, but sadly the property is now under threat of redevelopment. The growing family lived in extremely cramped conditions but there was, inevitably, a piano in the parlour. As an Army family they lived on an 'all found' basis, and to augment his father's basic pay of 3/-a day

both of young Arthur's parents gave music lessons in their spare time. That the tiny house was alive with so much music-making could not have failed to have made its mark on the boy, young as he was.

The Sullivans remained at 4 Albany Place (later redesignated 171 York-town Road) until Thomas Sullivan was offered his position at the Kneller Hall School of Music at Twickenham. But Arthur saw very little of the family home after he was sent off to boarding school. So that it is all the more remarkable that he should have chosen to make a sentimental journey here in the full flight of his career. During his stay he went to the old church of St.Michael and All Angels where, it is said, he played the organ on more than one occasion in his very tender years and where, seated in the high-backed pews, he would certainly have heard a a great deal of music on Sunday afternoons. The congregation was often accompanied in their hymn-singing by an unusual combination of cello, clarinet and bassoon playing from a musicians' gallery at the far end of the church which, since Sullivan's time, has been replaced by a later building bearing the same dedication. While Sullivan was still making his way socially and professionally he had to rely on the hospitality of his rich friends during Ascot week. But from the mid-1880s onwards his growing income enabled him to lease his own summer accommodation and to make arrangements to suit his own tastes and requirements. He was, as we have seen, a man well-versed in the social arts and he repaid past favours on a lavish scale. By this time he was also rich enough to have horses of his own, and this meant that he could indulge his passion for racing and for gambling to the full. In May 1887 he spent an enjoyable summer at Meadowbank, a house which still stands near the village of Winkfield, not far from Windsor, with Epsom, Kempton Park and Ascot all within easy reach. Eight years later he rented the house for a second time, and took refuge there while his London flat was being redecorated and partly refurnished.

In 1888 his choice fell on a large cottage called Booth Lodge at Fleet in Hampshire, which was a good deal further away from central London than most of his summer retreats. Sullivan's commitments at this time were even heavier than usual, so perhaps he decided to put himself more out of reach of casual callers who he was always very pleased to see (they gave him a good excuse for not getting on with his work, after all), but who took up far too much of his time. Another possible explanation for his choice of Fleet is that not far away, only five miles or so, is Farnborough, where lived the Empress Eugénie, with whom both Sullivan and his mistress were on terms of close friendship.

Albany Place, 171 Yorktown Road, the boyhood home of Arthur Sullivan

174

Ashridgewood House at Wokingham, where Sullivan worked on 'The Rose of Persia'

Continue on the A321 through Wokingham and then turn on to the B3034. Ashridgewood Manor is on the right

Make for Windsor via Ascot and Windsor Great Park

At all events he took out a six-weeks lease on the cottage and settled down to work on the score of *The Yeomen of the Guard*. Not surprisingly, perhaps, Booth Lodge is sometimes referred to by local people and by visiting Savoyards as 'Yeomen Cottage', which is as nice a tribute as any which can be paid to the demanding Muse. Although Arthur Sullivan had to spend a great deal of time at his desk, he did manage to attend a few race meetings at Sandown Park, near Esher, and spent other leisure hours rowing along the eight-mile stretch of canal to the quiet and pleasant town of Odiham. And a few visitors did call on him, among them Fanny Ronalds and her mother, and his devoted nephew Herbert.

Just outside Wokingham is Ashridgewood House, now Ashridgewood Manor, which Sullivan leased for six weeks towards the end of his life, in the summer of 1899. Here he finished the last complete opera he was to write for the Savoy, *The Rose of Persia*. The house, which cannot easily be seen from the road, is still privately-owned and stands on open, windswept ground above the downland which falls gently away in the direction of Reading. Gilbert makes a very brief appearance in this part of the narrative, for in 1885 he stayed as a guest in a country house called Ramslade, at Harmans Water, not far from Bracknell. It is used today as an R.A.F. staff college.

By this somewhat circuitous and far from chronological route we reach the very heart of royal England, Windsor Castle, the oldest of all the royal palaces in the country, and the largest in the whole of Europe. It has been the residence of the British sovereign for more than 800 years, and its familiar outline against a dappled summer sky is as powerful a symbol to the Englishman in exile as the Palace of Westminster, Saint Paul's Cathedral or the Tower of London. Among the many magnificent and richly-furnished rooms and apartments is the

Command performance of 'The Gondoliers' at Windsor Castle, from the 'Daily Graphic' of 9 March 1891

175

Windsor Castle, 1851,
after the painting by
C.J. Greenwood

Waterloo Chamber, which takes its name not directly from the battle, but from the gallery of 38 portraits of monarchs, soldiers and statesmen who played a crucial role in the Napoleonic wars. Over the years it has been very occasionally been used for theatrical performances. One such, a production of *The Gondoliers* was given on 6 March 1891, thirty years after the death of the Prince Consort. It was the first time the widowed Queen had allowed drama in any form to be given within the castle precincts since she went into mourning. In attendance with her was her eldest daughter, Victoria, the Empress of Germany, who had herself been recently widowed. Francois Cellier conducted the performance, and afterwards the entire company was presented to their majesties by Richard D'Oyly Carte, in an adjoining drawing room.

Much has been made of the fact that only the name of Arthur Sullivan appeared on the printed programme as author of the piece, but the Queen's own diary shows that she was well aware of, and appreciated, Gilbert's libretto. The occasion seems to have been a great success, for a touring company in Aberdeen was asked to present *The Mikado* at Balmoral, in September later in that same year.

Tennyson's *Becket*, which starred Henry Irving and the Lyceum Company, was performed by royal command in the Waterloo Chamber towards the end of Victoria's reign. Edward VII and Queen Alexandra entertained the King and Queen of Portugal here during a state visit with a production of Barrie's *Quality Street*, in which Ellaline Terriss and Seymour Hicks played the leading rôles. Some 70 years later, a Gilbert and Sullivan opera was heard once more in this

176

splendid setting. As part of the celebrations to mark the Silver Jubilee of Queen Elizabeth II, a command performance of *H.M.S. Pinafore* was given by the D'Oyly Carte Opera Opera Company on 16 June 1977.

Arthur Sullivan was no stranger to Windsor Castle. His first visit, on 22 May 1883, was made in great style. Together with George Grove and George Macfarren he was taken by special train to Windsor station where carriages of the royal household were waiting to convey them through the town to the Castle. In accordance with strict ceremonial they were then ushered into the Queen's audience chamber, and each received a knighthood for their services to music.

Sir Arthur Sullivan, as he now was, collected the nobility and the crowned heads of Europe as other men collect antique furniture. He moved in all the right circles, and already counted among his many friends and admirers the Prince of Wales, the Duke of Edinburgh, the exiled Emperor Napoleon III and Empress Eugénie, the Kaiser and Prince Henry of Prussia and many others. His works were known and admired in court circles, and he possessed an undeniable boyish almost feminine charm of manner which the widow of Windsor, like so many others, found irresistible. To have won the favour of his own dear Queen was a glittering prize indeed.

On one occasion the Queen asked him for a complete set of his works, and on another she even suggested to Sullivan that he might care to go through and to correct the amateur scores written by her beloved Prince Consort. She frequently encouraged him to write a grand opera, and when he eventually responded with *Ivanhoe*, she readily allowed the composer to dedicate the work to her.

Sullivan was asked to conduct a concert at Windsor Castle on the eve of the wedding of Princess Marie Louise, 5 July 1891. And a few years later, in the late autumn of 1897, he recorded in his diary that he had spent 'much time' at Windsor and that he had three private conversations with the Queen. What, one wonders, did the aged monarch and her gifted courtier-composer find to say to each other? And while he waited in an antechamber for those private and informal audiences to begin, what were the thoughts that passed through Sullivan's mind as he gazed out beyond the courtyards and the terraces, the turrets and the battlements, to the sweet Thames beyond, the river along which so much of England's history has unfolded?

For the return journey from Windsor follow the signs to the M4, and so back to central London

The upper reaches of the Thames, where both Sullivan and D'Oyly Carte spent their summers

Chapter 22

THE UPPER THAMES

From central London take the A4 Great West Road to Hounslow. Bear left at the Cranford roundabout on to the A30 or Staines Road. Follow the one-way signs and cross the Thames by Staines Bridge. Turn left at once into Farmers Road which becomes the A320 Chertsey Road. After 1½ miles, some 200 yds past the Norlands Road junction, set back from the road on the left, is Penton Hook Island

Follow the A320 into Chertsey and then take the A317 into Weybridge. At the top of the High Street turn left into Thames Street. Park near the Lincoln Arms and turn right past the Weybridge Tennis and Sailing Club, and carry on until Eyot Island comes into view

A remarkable party gathered on Sunday, 9 August 1878, at Paddington Station, the London terminus of the Great Western Railway, and boarded a train for our last destination, Windsor. Among those present were Richard D'Oyly Carte, Arthur Sullivan and the entire D'Oyly Carte Opera Company. They were met at Windsor Station by Gilbert who, with military precision, shepherded the party down to a jetty on the Thames where two steam launches were puffing and pulling at their moorings, as if eager to complete the last stage of the journey to Cliveden. On arrival, the happy throng disembarked to find a sumptuous picnic awaiting them. This was D'Oyly Carte's delightful way of saying thank you to everyone who had contributed to the enormous success of *H.M.S.Pinafore*.

Thus was established a tradition, for this picnic became an annual event to be awaited with eager anticipation. From the summer of 1879 to that of 1888 the isle of Penton Hook remained the chosen spot, but from 1880 onwards the picnics were held at Carte's own property, Eyot Island. Each year the two steamers, one under Gilbert's flag and the other with Sullivan's colours aloft, would carry the company to their designated moorings and after disembarkation, doubtless accompanied by a great deal of laughter and innocent merriment, D'Oyly Carte's lavish hospitality would be revealed. After lunch, for those with sufficient energy, there were games of rounders and kiss-in-the-ring: even impromptu concerts were given, largely for the benefit of those in skiffs, punts and other pleasure craft who gathered round to see the fun.

Eyot Island is at the point where the Thames is joined by the river Wey, with Weybridge on the south bank and Shepperton to the north. While his two sons, Lucas and Rupert, were still quite small, Richard D'Oyly Carte took them on summer camping expeditions along the upper reaches of the river and when, in

Penton Hook island, where the D'Oyly Carte Opera Company took their summer picnics from 1879 to 1888

1887, an opportunity came along to buy the island he did not hesitate. At the same time, he bought a ¾ acre plot on the facing bank on the Weybridge side and had a footbridge built. He also invited Arthur Sullivan, Fanny Ronalds, Whistler and Helen Lenoir to the island and revealed his plans for a luxurious house there.

Some years later, in 1896, Carte decided to use the house as a country annexe to the Savoy Hotel. Extensive additions and alterations were made to develop the property very much as we see it today – a Swiss chalet or villa in the late Victorian style, of which it is a very fine example. But after two years of building work and much expenditure local justices at the brewster sessions refused to grant a liquor licence, and Carte was faced with the choice either of selling the house or of keeping it as his main residence. After a lot of indecision and heart-searching he chose the latter course, much to the satisfaction of his many friends, not least Arthur Sullivan, who spent part of his last summer with the D'Oyly Cartes on Eyot Island.

From the D'Oyly Carte family the house passed into the possession of Lord and Lady May, who sold it to a property development company in 1958. They converted the house into 12 luxurious flats without affecting the main structure, which means that the building can revert to its original form at any time. The river frontage extends for some 1300 ft, with two landing stages and moorings for up to 60 small boats. When the property was last on the market, in 1987, the asking price was in the region of one million pounds.

In the 1880s both Weybridge and Shepperton were quiet, rural villages which had only recently been discovered by wealthy Londoners eager to escape the summer dust and smells of the great city. Less than 20 miles from the West End, and less than half an hour by train from Waterloo, with Kempton, Sandown Park, Windsor, Epsom and Ascot all within very easy reach, the area commended itself to Sullivan just as much as it had done to D'Oyly Carte. In the summer of 1889 the composer moved in to Grove House, not more than half a mile away from Eyot Island.

Continue along the tow-path to a small lane on the right which connects with the roadway, Walton Lane. Carry on until you reach Dorney Close on the left

He discovered the property early in July. On the 5th day of the month he made a tour of inspection with Mrs. Ronalds before hurrying back to town for Queen

Victoria's state concert that evening in the Royal Albert Hall for the Shah of
Persia. Sullivan moved in later that week, and by 12 July he had invited
Alexander Mackenzie to visit him in his new home. When Mackenzie arrived he
found his host hard at work on the score of *The Gondoliers*: the only relaxation
Sullivan allowed himself was by the river's edge, either walking along the
towpath or canoeing to Carte's island. His uncharacteristic single-mindedness on
this occasion paid rich dividends, for by 17 September the greater part of that
delightful score was completed.

When the Great Carpet Quarrel broke out with such ferocity in April of the
following year, Sullivan left London earlier than was his usual practice and took
refuge in Grove House to escape Gilbert's constant protestations. In this he was
only partly successful, for his partner continued to bombard him with letters
dealing with accounting minutiae. At the time, Sullivan was particularly anxious
to get on with scoring *Ivanhoe*, but he found himself distracted and resentful,
unable to complete the task in hand. Work dragged on throughout the summer
and when he found he could do no more, which happened all too frequently, he
would go down to the river and row, or take himself off for long walks in the
surrounding countryside. He even became involved in local events – attending
village fêtes and the like – anything, it seemed, to get away from his desk and the
drudgery of composition. Finally, on the eve of his return to London for the
winter season, he wrote to Gilbert in some desperation seeking a reconciliation. It
was not to come about for almost another twelve months.

Three years were to pass before Sullivan returned to Weybridge for his
summer vacation, by which time the name of the property had been changed to
Dorney House. On 19 June 1893 he set to work on *Utopia Limited*, and found to
his delight that the ghosts of the past had been completely laid to rest. Work
progressed apace, and within a month the first two acts were ready. To his
relaxation repertoire he also made an unusual addition by acquiring a tricycle,
which attracted much attention as he pedalled up and down the towpath think-
ing, no doubt, of some elegant turn of musical phrase or ingenious counterpoint.
On 17 August Gilbert came to visit him, accompanied by Cellier. The local
village and fair were in full swing, with two large musical steam roundabouts

Return to Thames Street and head for Weybridge Green, where the Museum and the column can be seen

plying their trade right outside his house. Despite these distractions *Utopia Limited* was ready eleven days later, much to Gilbert's surprise and his host's satisfaction.

For reasons not entirely clear Sullivan did not lease Dorney House again until 1899. He took up residence in July, after his stay at Ashridgewood near Wokingham, and remained until November, by which time he had completed the score of *The Rose of Persia*. His last visit to Weybridge was in May 1900, but he stayed only for a comparatively short time, leaving for Switzerland in mid-July. By now he had taken the local community very much to his heart, a sentiment warmly reciprocated, and showed much interest in its affairs. Like Richard D'Oyly Carte he was treated with all the respect due to a distinguished resident, as may be judged from the ephemera on display in the Weybridge Museum. It has to be confessed that some of the material is fanciful, but other items on show, including the photographs, are authentic enough.

On the green outside the museum is the great column which once stood at Seven Dials in London. After it was pulled down by the mob in 1773 the stones were taken to Sayes Court, near Weybridge, where they stayed untouched for nearly 50 years. Then in 1822 someone hit upon the bright idea of rebuilding the column on the village green as a memorial to the late Duchess of York, who died in 1820. A pedestal with an inscription no doubt entirely appropriate for the purpose, but now quite illegible, was built and the stones lifted carefully into position. In place of the seven sundials a gilt coronet was mounted on top. The stone originally holding the dials was for many years used as a horse block, but it can now be found opposite the green, facing the column from which it came.

The Seven Dials column at Weybridge Green

These upper reaches of the Thames became a second home for Sir Arthur Sullivan. Although, unlike the D'Oyly Cartes, he never became an owner of

River House,
Walton-on-Thames

Carry on along the A3050, Oatlands Drive, to Walton-on-Thames. At Walton Bridge bear right on to Bridge Street. Turn left at River Mount and right into the unmarked no-through road

property along the river, hardly a year passed without his spending at least a part of each summer somewhere along its banks. When Dorney House was not available he would rent Bridge House (now River House) in nearby Walton-on-Thames. Here, on 11 August 1895, while he was busily engaged on the last of the Savoy operas, *The Grand Duke*, a distinguished member of the Strauss family, Eduard, called to pay his respects. The following year he took Bridge House from mid-July onwards, but by mid-September the lure of Switzerland was to be resisted no longer, and he left a handful of house-guests in the capable hands of Herbert and the maid, Clotilde. In 1897, the most famous musician in the land found himself acting as president of an organising committee for the Walton Amateur Regatta, a key event in the local calendar. Sullivan entered into the spirit of the occasion with great enthusiasm, and held parties for his friends and neighbours on the lawns of River House. These can still be seen sweeping down to the river, although the house itself has since been divided into flats.

Sullivan's love of the river was matched only by his love of racing. Since the early 1880s he had been a very familiar figure on the turf and in April 1886, on the first day of the Spring meeting, he was elected to full membership of the New Club at Epsom Downs. He was often to be seen in the company of his royal patrons, especially the Prince of Wales, with whom he frequently travelled on the royal train. He attended the Prince on at least three Derbys – in 1886, 1889 and again in 1900. It was on that latter occasion that to the great satisfaction of the royal party the long-apparent heir to the throne won the race with a horse called, somewhat belatedly, Diamond Jubilee. 1900. The end of the old century and the dawn of a new and troubled age. Prince Edward of Wales did not have much longer to wait for his inheritance.

Neither did Sir Arthur Sullivan.

Return to central London via Hampton Court, Kingston and Richmond

APPENDIX

References to London in the works of W.S.Gilbert
Original Plays and Bab Ballads (*BB*)

Admiralty	*Utopia Limited*
Alpine Club	*Thespis*
Angel, Islington	*BB: The King of Canoodle Dum*
Army & Navy Stores	*The Sorcerer*
Bailey, Old, Ancient	*Trial by Jury, The Pirates of Penzance*
Ball's Pond	*Foggerty's Fairy*
Barings	*Iolanthe*
Barking	*Thespis*
Barnes	*Foggerty's Fairy*
Battersea	*Foggerty's Fairy*
Bear Street	*BB: Peter the Wag*
Belgrave Square	*Iolanthe*
Belgravian Airies	*Utopia Limited*
Bow	*Foggerty's Fairy*
Brixton	*Foggerty's Fairy*
Brompton	*BBs: The Discontented Sugar Broker, The Baby's Vengeance*
Bromptonville	*BBs: The Discontented Sugar Broker, The Baby's Vengeance*
Burlington Arcade	*Patience*
Camberwell	*Trial by Jury, Foggerty's Fairy, BB: Peter the Wag*
Canonbury Square	*BB: Thomson Green and Harriet Hale*
Chancery Lane	*Iolanthe*
Chelsea	*BB: Babette's Love*
Chiswick	*Foggerty's Fairy*
Clapham	*Foggerty's Fairy, BBs: Brave Alum Bey, The Three Bohemian Ones*
Clapham Rise	*BB: The Three Bohemian Ones*
Coutts	*Utopia Limited, The Gondoliers, BB: The Periwinkle Girl*
Dalston	*Foggerty's Fairy*
Dean Street	*BB: Peter the Wag*
Downing Street	*Thespis*
Drury Lane	*BBs: The Haughty Actor, The Two Ogres*
Ealing	*BBs: The Fairy Curate, The Baby's Vengeance*
Edgware Road	*Foggerty's Fairy*
Fishmongers' Hall	*BB: King of Canoodle Dum*
Frith Street	*BB: Peter the Wag*
Fulham	*BBs: The Discontented Sugar Broker, The Bishop and the Busman*
Gask and Gask	*The Princess, Princess Ida*
Gerrard Street	*BB: Peter the Wag*
Golden Square	*BB: Peter the Wag*
Greek Street	*BB: Peter the Wag*
Grinnidge's Naval Fame	*BB: The King of Canoodle Dum*
Grosvenor Gallery	*Patience*
Gurneys	*Trial by Jury*
Hackney	*Foggerty's Fairy*
Hackney Road	*BB: The Two Ogres*
Harley Street	*Foggerty's Fairy*
Holloway	*Foggerty's Fairy*
Howell and James	*Patience*
Hyde Park	*BB: Sir Macklin*
Kennington	*Foggerty's Fairy*
Kensal Green	*Foggerty's Fairy*
Kensington Gardens	*BB: Sir Macklin*
Kentish Town	*Foggerty's Fairy, BB: Peter the Wag*
Kew	*Foggerty's Fairy, BB: Peter the Wag*
Knightsbridge	*The Mikado*

Lewis and Allenby	*The Princess, Princess Ida*
London Bridge	*Foggerty's Fairy, BB: The Bishop of Rumti-Foo*
Madame Tussauds	*Patience, Mikado*
Maida Hill	*Foggerty's Fairy*
Middlesex Sessions	*Trial by Jury, BB: Middlesex Sessions*
Mortlake	*Foggerty's Fairy*
New Road	*Foggerty's Fairy*
Newport Street	*BB: Peter the Wag*
Old Ford	*Foggerty's Fairy*
Old Kent Road	*Foggerty's Fairy*
Paddington	*Patience*
Pall Mall	*BBs: Disillusioned, Sleep On*
Peckham	*Trial by Jury, Foggerty's Fairy*
Piccadilly	*Patience, Utopia Limited*
Pickfords	*Iolanthe, No Cards*
Poland Street	*BB: Peter the Wag*
Polygon	*BB: The Baby's Vengeance*
Primrose Hill	*Foggerty's Fairy*
Putney	*Foggerty's Fairy, BB: The Bishop and the Busman*
Regent Circus	*Thespis*
Regent Street	*Foggerty's Fairy*
Regent's Park	*Foggerty's Fairy, BB: Thomson Green and Harriet Hale*
Richardson's Show	*Patience*
Richmond Buildings	*BB: Peter the Wag*
Rotherhithe	*BB: Peter the Wag*
Rothschild	*Iolanthe*
Royalty Theatre	*BB: Peter the Wag*
Rupert Street	*BB: Peter the Wag*
St. James's Hall	*Utopia Limited*
St. James's Palace	*Iolanthe, Utopia Limited, BBs: Sir Macklin The King of Canoodle Dum*
St. James's Park	*Iolanthe*
St. John's Wood	*Foggerty's Fairy*
St. Martin's Lane	*An Elixir of Love*
St. Mary Axe	*The Sorcerer*
Sewell and Cross	*The Princess, Princess Ida, Patience*
Shepherd's Bush	*Foggerty's Fairy*
Sloane Square	*Iolanthe*
Soho	*BBs: Peter the Wag, Old Paul and Old Tim*
Somerset House	*Patience*
Somerstown	*BB: The Baby's Vengeance*
South Kensington	*Iolanthe, Patience*
Southwark	*Foggerty's Fairy*
Stock Exchange	*Utopia Limited*
Strand	*Utopia Limited, BB: Tempora Mutantur*
Stratford-le-Bow	*BB: Annie Protheroe*
Swan and Edgar	*The Princess, Princess Ida*
Swears and Wells	*Patience*
Threepenny Bus	*Patience, BB: The Bishop and the Busman*
Tooting	*Thespis*
Tower of London	*The Yeomen of the Guard*
Turnham Green	*Foggerty's Fairy*
Victoria Docks	*Foggerty's Fairy*
Walworth	*Foggerty's Fairy*
Wandsworth	*Foggerty's Fairy*
Wapping Stairs	*BB: Babette's Love*
Waterloo House	*Patience*
Westbourne Park	*Foggerty's Fairy*
Westminster Hall (and Courts)	*Trial by Jury*
Whitechapel	*Foggerty's Fairy*
Whitehall	*BB: Master William*

185

SELECT BIBLIOGRAPHY

Books

ADAIR-FITZGERALD St.J. *The Story of the Savoy Opera* London: Stanley Paul, 1926

ALLEN Reginald *The First Night Gilbert and Sullivan* New York: Heritage, 1958 Limited Editions Club

ALLEN Reginald *The Life and Work of Sir Arthur Sullivan, Composer for Victorian England* New York: Pierpont Morgan Library, 1975

ARUNDELL Dennis *The Story of Sadlers Wells 1683-1977* London: David and Charles, 1978

AYRE Leslie *The Gilbert and Sullivan Companion* London: Pan, 1972

BAILEY Conrad *Guide to Famous London Graves* London: Harrap, 1975

BAILY Leslie *The Gilbert and Sullivan Book* London: Cassell, 2nd ed.1952

BAILY Leslie *Gilbert and Sullivan and Their World* London: Thames and Hudson, 1973, Book Club Associates Edition

BELL Walter *The Tower of London* London: Duckworth, 1935

BENFORD Harry *The Gilbert and Sullivan Lexicon In Which Is Gilded The Philosophic Pill* New York: Richards Rosen, 1978, Theater Student Edition

BESANT Sir Walter ed. *The Fascination of London* London: Adam and Charles Black, 1902

BLOOM Ursula *Curtain Call for the Guv'nor* London: Hutchinson, 1954

BRADLEY Ian *The Annotated Gilbert and Sullivan* (2 vols) London: Penguin, 1982 and 1984

CARKEET-JAMES Col.E.H. *Her Majesty's Tower of London* London: Arco, 1961

CELLIER F. and BRIDGEMAN C. *Gilbert, Sullivan and D'Oyly Carte* London: Isaac Pitman & Sons, 1914

DANIELL Timothy *Inns of Court* London: Wildy's, 1971

DARK S. and GREY R. *W.S.Gilbert -His Life and Letters* London: Methuen, 1923

DUTTON Ralph *London Homes* London: Wingate, 1952, Londoner's Library Series

EDEN David *Gilbert and Sullivan -The Creative Conflict* London: Associated University Presses, 1986

FITZGERALD Percy *The Gilbert and Sullivan Operas* Philadelphia: Lippincott, 1894

FORBES-WINDSOR D. *Daly's -The Biography of a Theatre* London: W.H.Allen, 1944

GILBERT W.S. *The Bab Ballads* London: Macmillan, 6th ed.1908

GILBERT W.S. *More Bab Ballads* London: George Routledge, c.1910

GILBERT W.S. *Original Plays* London: Chatto and Windus First Series, 1903

GILBERT W.S. *Original Plays* London: Chatto and Windus Third Series, 1919

GILBERT W.S. *The Savoy Operas* London: Macmillan Papermac Edition, 1983

GOLDBERG Isaac *The Story of Gilbert and Sullivan* New York: Crown, 1935

GOODMAN Andrew *Gilbert and Sullivan At Law* London: Associated University Presses, 1983

GROVE Sir George *New Grove's Dictionary of Music and Musicians* London: Macmillan, 1980

HARE Augustus *Walks in London* London: Allen and Unwin, 1901

HOLLINGSHEAD John *Good Old Gaiety* London: Constable, 1903

JACKSON Stanley *The Savoy -Romance of a Great Hotel* London: Muller, 1934

JACOBS Arthur *Arthur Sullivan, A Victorian Musician* Oxford: OUP, 1984

KENT William *An Encyclopaedia of London* London: J.M.Dent, 1951

LAWRENCE Arthur *Sir Arthur Sullivan -Life Story, Letters and Reminiscences* London: James Bowden, 1899

MANDER R. and MITCHENSON J. *The Theatres of London* London: New English Library, 1975

PEARSON Hesketh *Gilbert and Sullivan* London: Hamish Hamilton, 1935

PEARSON Hesketh *Gilbert -His Life and Strife* London: Methuen, 1957

SAXE WYNDHAM H *Arthur Sullivan* London: George Bell, 1903

SCOTT Clement *The Wheel of Life, A Few Memories and Recollections* London: Lawrence Greening, 1897

SCOTT Judith *The Story of St.Mary Abbots, Kensington* London SPCS,1942
SERVICE Alastair *London 1900* London: Granada, 1979
SHEPPARD *General Survey of London* London: Athlone Press, 1983
STANFORD Edward *Library Map of London and Its Suburbs 1862* Lympne Castle, Kent: Harry Margary Facsimile Edition, 1980
STEDMAN Dr.Jane W. Ed.*Gilbert Before Sullivan* Chicago: University of Chicago Press, 1967
SULLIVAN H. and FLOWER N. *Sir Arthur Sullivan, His Life, Letters and Diaries* London: Cassell, 2nd ed.1950
TERRISS Ellaline *By Herself and With Others* London: Cassell, 1928
THORNE James *Handbook to the Environs of London* London: Geoffrey Cave, 1876 (reprinted 1983)
TURNBULL Gerard *Traffic and Transport -An Economic History of Pickfords* London: Allen and Unwin, 1979
TWEEDIE Mrs.Alec *Behind the Footlights* London: Hutchinson, 1904
WALBROOK H.M. *Gilbert and Sullivan Opera* London: F.V.White, 1922
WILLIAMSON Audrey *Gilbert and Sullivan Opera -A New Assessment* London: Rockliff, 1953
WILSON A.E. *The Lyceum* London: Yates, 1952 Theatre Book Club Edition
WILSON F.W. *The Gilbert and Sullivan Birthday Book* Dobbs Ferry, New York: Cahill and Co., 1983
WILSON R. and LLOYD F. *Gilbert and Sullivan: The D'Oyly Carte Years: The Official Picture History* New York: Alfred A.Knopf, 1984
YOUNG Percy M. *Sir Arthur Sullivan* London: Dent, 1971

Pamphlets

Central Criminal Court Journalists Association, The. *The Old Bailey* London: Corporation of London, 1976
Crystal Palace Foundation *A Palace for All Seasons: A Pictorial History of the Crystal Palace, Sydenham 1854-1984* Exhibition Catalogue Royal Festival Hall, London 1984
D'Oyly Carte Opera Company *Centenary Programme* 1975
Gilbert and Sullivan Society, The. *An Operatic Glossary from Abudah Chest to Zoffany* London 1975
Kent County Library, Gravesham Division. *Rosherville Gardens.* Local History Pamphlet No.6. February 1982
Laver, James *The Liberty Story* London: Liberty & Co. 1959 (reprinted 1971)
Northeast, Christine H. *The Crystal Palace Park of 1854, A Guided Tour* Cambridge: pub.aut.1979
The Parish of St. Michael and All Angels, Sandhurst: A Short History Booklet June, 1984
Somerville, Robert *The Savoy Chapel: A Guide to the Queen's Chapel of the Savoy* London: Duchy of Lancaster, 1977
Wainwright, E *Army and Navy Stores Centenary Year Brochure* London:1971
Walters, Michael *Gilbertian Gossip* Nos.27 and 28. Private Pamphlet, 1986

Periodicals and Journals

Architecture August 1891
Belgravia Magazine (Vol.2) March 1867
City Press November 1882
Country Life June 1911
The Era October 1882
The Gilbert and Sullivan Journal
    Vol.II nos.4,7 and 12
    Vol.V nos. 7 and 8
    Emergency (War) Issue no.15
    Vol.VI nos.2 and 15
    Vol.VII no.20
    Vol.VIII nos.2,3,4,7,9,10,11,12,13,14,15,16 and 18
    Vol.IX nos.8 and 18
    Vol.X nos.1,2,9 and 11
The W.S.Gilbert Society Journal Vol.I nos.1,2, and 3
The Graphic 13 March 1886

Harrow Advertiser and Gazette 6 November 1936
International Architect 1981. No.6 Vol.I,Iss.6
Middlesex Quarterly Autumn 1955. No.5 N.S.
The Savoyard
  Vol.XI no.1
  Vol.XIII no.1
  Vol.XIV no.1
  Vol.XV no.1
  Vol.XVII no.3
  Vol.XVIII no.1
The Journal of the Sir Arthur Sullivan Society Vols.II and IV
Strand Magazine December 1891
Weekly Telegraph London: 10 May 1930
Your Court: Journal of the Lord Chancellor's Department Vol.I no.4 Apr/May 1986

ILLUSTRATIONS

The author and publishers make due acknowledgement to the following for making available many of the illustrations used in this book, and, where applicable, granting permission for their reproduction.

Army & Navy Stores *p. 94*.
British Tourist Authority *pp. 26, 32, 47, 50 (bottom), 51, 59, 65, 69, 75, 77 (bottom), 78, 83 (top and bottom), 86, 88, 90, 91, 104, 108, 112, 113, 114, 116, 127, 132, 133, 135, 142 and 157*
Crystal Palace Foundation *pp. 149 and 150*
D'Oyly Carte Opera Trust *pp. 36, 37, 61, 74, 105 and 156*
Paul Draper ★*p. 53*
Ede & Ravenscroft Ltd *p. 105 (top)*
Gilbert and Sullivan Society *pp. 97, 126, 138 (top), 143, 144 (left) and 175 (bottom)*
Greater London Photographic Library *p. 154*
Peter Joslin *pp. 44, 54, 56, 60, 77 (top), 95, 96 (top and bottom), 110, 111, 123 (bottom), 134 (top), 145, 153 (bottom), 170 and 175 (top)*
Kensington & Chelsea Library *p. 138 (bottom), 139, 141 and 144 (right)*
Kent County Library (Gravesham Local History Service) *pp. 158 and 159*
Mansion House at Grim's Dyke *pp. 162, 165 and 167*
Prudential Property Services, Riverside Centre, Windsor *pp. 178, 180 and 181*
Savills Ltd *p. 128*
Survey of London *pp. 20, 21 (top), 22, 23, 76, 80, 85 and 142*
Albert Truelove (the late) *p. 28*
Julian Waldon *p. 183*
Weybridge Museum *p. 182*
Wheatland Safty Trust *p. 152*
Illustrations not listed above are either in the public domain or are author's copyright.

★Seven Dials Monument Committee, 1 Shorts Gardens, London WC2H 9AT